FRIENDSHIP AND BENEFACTION IN JAMES

EMORY STUDIES IN EARLY CHRISTIANITY

Editors
Vernon K. Robbins & David B. Gowler

Associate Editor
Robert H. von Thaden Jr.

Editorial Board
Richard S. Ascough
L. Gregory Bloomquist
Peder Borgen
J. J. Bernard Combrink
David A. deSilva
Anders Eriksson
Thomas H. Olbricht
Russell B. Sisson
Duane F. Watson

Number 15

FRIENDSHIP AND BENEFACTION IN JAMES

by

Alicia J. Batten

 **PRESS**

Atlanta

Copyright © 2017 by SBL Press
Originally published by Deo Publishing, 2010

Publication of this volume was made possible by the generous support of the Pierce Program in Religion of Oxford College of Emory University.

All rights reserved. No part of this work may be reproduced or transmitted in any form or by any means, electronic or mechanical, including photocopying and recording, or by means of any information storage or retrieval system, except as may be expressly permitted by the 1976 Copyright Act or in writing from the publisher. Requests for permission should be addressed in writing to the Rights and Permissions Office, SBL Press, 825 Houston Mill Road, Atlanta, GA 30329 USA.

The Odyssea Greek font used in the publication of this work is available from Linguist's Software, Inc., www.linguisticsoftware.com, P.O. Box 580, Edmonds, WA 98020-0580 USA, tel. (425) 775-1130.

Library of Congress Control Number: 2017941594

Cover design is an adaptation by Bernard Madden of Rick A. Robbins, Mixed Media (19" x 24" pen and ink on paper, 1981). Online: http://home.comcast.net/~rick1216/Archive/1981penink.htm. Cover design used by permission of Deo Publishing.

Printed on acid-free paper.

Contents

Acknowledgments vii

Chapter 1
Introduction 1
Structure and Method 4

Chapter 2
Friendship in Antiquity 9
Introduction 9
Virtues of Friends 17
"One Mind/Soul" 42
"All in Common" 44
Friendship and Fictive Kinship Language 47
Friendship with God 48
Conclusion 54

Chapter 3
Friendship, Patronage and Benefaction 56
Introduction 56
Friendship, Politics and Society 59
Benefaction 68
Patronage 75
Patronage, Friendship and Flattery 79
Conclusion 88

Chapter 4
The Exordium: James 1:2-18 90
Introduction 90
James as a Letter 91
James and Rhetoric 93
James 1:2-18
    A. Common Features of the Exordium 99
    B. James 1:2-18 as an Exordium 101
    C. Friendship and Benefaction within the Exordium 107

Conclusion..119

Chapter 5
A Challenge to Patronage..122
Introduction...122
James 2:1-13
    A. Rhetorical Structure..123
    B. Friendship, Patronage and Benefaction in James 2:1-13..................127
James 2:14-26
    A. Rhetorical Structure..135
    B. Friendship and Benefaction in James 2:14-26.................................136
Conclusion..144

Chapter 6
Friendship with God: James 3:13–4:10..145
Introduction...145
James 3:13–4:10
    A. Rhetorical Structure..145
    B. Friendship, Patronage and Benefaction in James 3:13–4:10............169
Conclusion..176

Chapter 7
Conclusion..178
Introduction...178
Patronage as an Exigence...180
Audience...181
Rhetorical Constraints...184
Conclusion..185

Bibliography...186

Index of Modern Authors..210
Index of Biblical and Other References..214

Acknowledgments

This book began as a doctoral dissertation some years ago in Toronto. It is with gratitude that I acknowledge the wisdom and generosity of my supervisor, John Kloppenborg, who sets an excellent example of a scholar/teacher and from whom I continue to learn a great deal. Other readers of the dissertation: Terry Donaldson, Dorcas Gordon, Stephen Patterson and Leif Vaage, provided valuable comments.

The transformation of the dissertation into a book occurred through the help of several people, most notably Vernon Robbins, who provided concrete guidance for revision and reorganization, and accepted the subsequent manuscript for this series. Many thanks go to Todd Penner for suggesting that the *Emory Studies in Early Christianity* series could be a possible venue for publication and to David Orton, editor at Deo Publishing, for his assistance.

Much of the writing of this book occurred during part of a sabbatical from Pacific Lutheran University in Washington State, where I taught from 2000 to 2008. Although I have since returned to Canada, I remain grateful to PLU for the sabbatical and for the general camaraderie of my colleagues in the Religion department there. Particular mention goes to Douglas Oakman for his support. Thanks are also due to the American Council of Learned Societies for a Graves Award which provided supplementary funding.

I appreciate the support for scholarship at my current institution, the University of Sudbury, and the collegiality of people there and at the institutions that comprise its federated partners. Gratitude also goes to members of the Context Group for their encouragement and for the meetings that the group organizes every year.

On a more personal note, thanks to my family for their ongoing interest in my work and overall moral support. Many friends and specific colleagues at a variety of institutions have been helpful in a range of ways. Finally, I am indebted to Terry Rothwell for his continued encouragement, curiosity, and "frank speech." I think that Terry embodies some of the characteristics of a friend that the subsequent pages seek to describe and it is with love and appreciation that I dedicate this book to him.

1

Introduction

After many years of relative neglect, there is a resurgence of interest in the letter of James.[1] Despite the fact that consensus on many historical questions surrounding the letter – such as its date, authorship, and provenance - cannot be found, the array of methods now used to analyze ancient literature, many of which do not seek to answer primarily historical questions, have found plenty in James to explore. Nor is it acceptable to assume that James is somehow theologically marginal because it does not mention the death and resurrection of Jesus; for the question of whether there was some sort of early Christian "core" theology or central "gospel" message is wide open. Indeed, the potential relationship between James and the Pauline corpus does not comprise the chief area of interest; rather, studies of James's literary genre and rhetorical structures, as well as the social, cultural and theological themes it addresses are plentiful, sometimes with no mention of Paul at all. Continual research into the varieties of ancient Judaism, the nature of Hellenism, and the complexity of the origins of Christianity have all contributed to the recognition that James deserves much more attention than it had previously earned, languishing as it did for many years on the edges of biblical studies. James is now studied on its own terms, in its own right.

Scholarship focused upon understanding the literature of early Christianity in the context of Hellenistic moral philosophy has long flourished, however. Texts such as Paul's letters and Luke-Acts have received the most attention here, but others, including James, are not far behind. In recent decades particular interest has been paid to the Hellenistic *topos* of friendship, and how the language and ideas associated with this *topos* were significant to ancient Judaisms, Graeco-

---

[1] See two recent survey articles on scholarship on James, by Todd C. Penner ("The Epistle of James in Current Research," *CurBS* 7 [1999] 257-308), and Mark E. Taylor ("Recent Scholarship on the Structure of James," *CurBS* 3.1 [2004] 86-115) respectively.

Roman culture, and the emergence of early Christianity.[2] The literature on ancient friendship is massive; the use of friendship language is pervasive in a variety of contexts, and thus it is hard to imagine how anyone in the first century Greek-speaking Mediterranean, including the author of James, would be unfamiliar with this often idealized form of relationship.[3]

As this book will argue, James is indeed conversant with traditions of friendship, and uses these traditions within the letter's argumentation.[4]

---

[2] Two very significant volumes are John T. Fitzgerald, ed., *Friendship, Flattery and Frankness of Speech: Studies on Friendship in the New Testament World* (Leiden, New York, Köln: E.J. Brill, 1996), and John T. Fitzgerald, ed., *Greco-Roman Perspectives on Friendship* (SBLRBS; Atlanta: Scholars Press, 1997). In addition to these, a variety of scholars have discussed the function and importance of friendship language in the New Testament. For example, see Hans Dieter Betz, *Galatians* (Hermeneia; Philadelphia: Fortress, 1979); Benjamin Fiore, "Friendship in the Exhortation of Romans 15:14-33," *Proceedings of the EGL and MWBS* 7 (1987) 95-103; F. Hauck, "Die Freundschaft bei den Griechen und im Neuen Testament," in *Festgabe für Theodor Zahn* (Leipzig: A. Deichertsche, 1928) 211-28; Hans-Josef Klauck, "Kirche als Freundesgemeinschaft? Auf Spurensuche im Neuen Testament," *MTZ* 42 (1991) 1-14; Abraham J. Malherbe, *Paul and the Popular Philosophers* (Minneapolis: Fortress, 1989); *Paul and the Thessalonians: The Philosophical Tradition of Pastoral Care* (Philadelphia: Fortress Press, 1987); Peter Marshall, *Enmity at Corinth: Social Conventions in Paul's Relations with the Corinthians* (WUNT 2.23; Tübingen: J.C.B. Mohr [Paul Siebeck], 1987); Alan C. Mitchell, "The Social Function of Friendship in Acts 2:44-47 and 4:32-37," *JBL* 111 (1992) 255-72; Pheme Perkins, "Christology, Friendship and Status: The Rhetoric of Philippians," *Society of Biblical Literature Seminar Papers* (SBLSP 26; ed. Kent Harold Richards; Atlanta: Scholars, 1987) 509-20; Stanley K. Stowers, "Friends and Enemies in the Politics of Heaven: Reading Theology in Philippians," in *Pauline Theology, Volume I* (ed. J.M. Bassler; Minneapolis: Fortress, 1991) 105-21.

[3] Four important and easily accessible histories of friendship in antiquity are L. Dugas, *L'Amitié Antique* (2nd ed., Paris: Librairie Félix Alcan, 1914); Jean-Claude Fraisse, *Philia: La notion d'amitié dans la philosophie antique. Essai sur un problème perdu et retrouvé* (Paris: Librairie Philosophique J. Vrin, 1974); Luigi Pizzolato, *L'idea di amicizia: nel mondo antico classico e cristiano* (Turin: Giulio Einaudi, 1993); David Konstan, *Friendship in the Classical World* (Key Themes in Ancient History; Cambridge: Cambridge University Press, 1997). Franz Dirlmeier's dissertation, φιλός und φιλία im vorhellenistischen Griechentum (Munich, 1931) is also significant. See also the collection of articles edited by Michael Peachin, *Aspects of Friendship in the Graeco-Roman World. Proceedings of a conference held at the Seminar für Alte Geschichte, Heidelberg, on 10-11 June, 2000* (Journal of Roman Archaeology Supplementary Series 43; Portsmouth, RI: Journal of Roman Archaeology, 2001).

[4] I have explored this topic with regard to the figure of God in James: "God in the Letter of James: Patron or Benefactor?" *NTS* 50 (2004) 257-72. Luke Johnson ("Friendship with the World/Friendship with God: A Study of Discipleship in James," in *Discipleship in the New Testament* [ed. F. Segovia; Philadelphia: Fortress, 1985] 166-83) has given some attention to friendship in James but he limits his discussion to Jas 2:23 and 4:4 and focuses more on discipleship than friendship. John S. Kloppenborg Verbin ("Patronage Avoidance in James," *HTS* 55 [1999] 755-94) and Leif E. Vaage ("Ciúdad la boca: la palabra indicada, una subjectividad alternativa y la formación social de los primeros cris-

Although it refers explicitly to a φίλος only twice, language and themes used in Graeco-Roman discussions of friendship appear with an intriguing density. For example, I will argue that God is portrayed as a frank friend and benefactor; and that Abraham proves his friendship with God through testing and the offering of hospitality. James also uses the language and ideas of friendship in his instructions about community life. For example, the readers are exhorted to withstand testing and trials – often a characteristic of a true friend; they are not to be covetous and they should support one another – both aspects of the expected behaviour of friends. James also incorporates some conventions of friendship in the manner in which he communicates with his audience, for example, in his use of affectionate language, references to the audience as brothers, and employment of frank speech, or παρρησία.

This study also joins a number of others in arguing that James urges his audience to resist dependence upon wealthy patrons in favour of reliance upon God as a friend and benefactor, and through assisting others in the community. It is well known that ancient patron-client liaisons masked their relationship with the language of friendship. James, however, will not stand for such a camouflage, and deliberately exposes patronage for what it is: a threat to the community, and a violation of Jewish law.[5] Dimensions of friendship, for James, function importantly in his address to his audience to form a moral paradigm[6] that contributes to an overall resistance to wealth and patronage. I think that James deliberately uses the language of friendship in order to appeal to the audience because he knows that such language is used regularly for patron-client relations. James wants to crack this association of patronage and friendship apart, expose patron-client relations as divisive to community life and contrary to reliance upon God, and ally friendship much more closely with benefaction, which many ancient persons, particularly in eastern parts of the Roman Empire, understood to be distinct from patronage. I assert that the association of friendship with benefaction *in opposition to* patronage emerges in the text, and

---

tianos según Santiago 3,1–4,17," *RIBLA* 31 [1998] 110-21) both discuss the "friendship with the world vs. friendship with God" notion but do not focus upon the language of friendship more broadly throughout James.

[5] This is one of the arguments of Wesley Hiram Wachob in his book, *The Voice of Jesus in the Social Rhetoric of James* (SNTSMS 106; New York: Cambridge University Press, 2000).

[6] For a view of friendship as a moral paradigm in the "Christ Hymn" of Philippians, see L. Michael White, "Morality Between Two Worlds: A Paradigm of Friendship in Philippians," in *Greeks, Romans and Christians* (ed. David L. Balch, Everett Ferguson, & Wayne A. Meeks; Minneapolis: Fortress, 1990) 201-15.

provides grounding for much of the ethical exhortation throughout the letter.

This study will explore how and why James appeals to friendship at three levels: between the author and his audience; among community members; and between the community and God. I am not suggesting that James understands every relationship in the same way nor in identical terms, but that allusions, if not direct references, to friendship at each of these levels serve to strengthen his overall argument. The presence of friendship at each level aids James as he advocates resistance to wealth, and in particular, avoidance of patronage by the rich.

Structure and Method

Before entering into a close study of sections of James, it is important to provide an examination of friendship in a variety of ancient contexts, including early Christian literature. By offering some discussion of friendship in the Jewish and Graeco-Roman world, we can better observe to what extent James borrows from Jewish and Graeco-Roman notions of this *topos*. Chapter 2 thus centres on ancient friendship, with the caveat that the chapter is by no means an exhaustive study of the *topos*, but concentrates instead on those aspects of friendship that emerge in James. The subsequent chapter will focus more closely on the relations between friendship, patronage and benefaction in antiquity, as to my mind James is in the middle of this complicated mix. Scholars have argued that patronage and friendship are very similar, and often for good reason because patrons and clients would, at least in Roman times, refer to one another as "friend" and sometimes pretend that their relationship was one of friendship when it was not. Moreover, as some contemporary authors have concluded that patronage and benefaction are the same in antiquity, it is important to clarify the differences between these latter two concepts. Thus the intricate knot in which patronage, friendship and benefaction were entangled must be untied such that James's strategy of invoking friendship and benefaction to undermine patronage can be understood.

Chapters 4–6 will explore the particulars of James's strategy. Here I join other authors who think that James is a crafted letter displaying familiarity with Hellenistic epistolary and rhetorical techniques.[7] Scholars

---

[7] On epistolary techniques, see F.O. Francis, "The Form and Function of the Opening and Closing Paragraphs of James and 1 John," *ZNW* 61 (1970) 110-26; and John L. White, "New Testament Epistolary Literatures in the Framework of Ancient Epistolography," *ANRW* 2.25.2 (1984) 1755-56. On specific rhetorical and stylistic techniques,

1. Introduction

do not agree with every conclusion made by Fred O. Francis in his groundbreaking article that showed how James and 1 John conform, in many ways, to Hellenistic letters, but his work did open the door to the examination of James *as a letter*, and subsequent studies have compared James to Jewish diaspora letters, in particular.[8] To illustrate this: many, using a range of methods, accept Jas 5:7-20 as a perfectly acceptable closing to the text.[9] In addition, despite the long-held view of James as a loose jumble of teachings lacking overall coherence, scholars are increasingly examining James according to the conventions of ancient rhetoric, either as a whole or in units.[10] Although authors do not agree about the overall rhetorical structure of the letter, or even on whether one can be found,[11] there are sections of James where they have arrived at a certain degree of consensus, such as Jas 2:1-13, which

---

such as diatribe and alliteration, see Ropes, *A Critical and Exegetical Commentary on the Epistle of St. James*, 10-16; Martin Dibelius, *Der Brief des Jakobus* (ed. Heinrich Greeven. Kritisch-exegetischer Kommentar über das Neue Testament [MeyerK]. Göttingen: Vandenhoeck & Ruprecht, 1964); ET: *James: A Commentary on the Epistle of James*, ed. Heinrich Greeven; trans. Michael A. Williams (Hermeneia; Philadelphia: Fortress, 1976) 38; Abraham J. Malherbe, "Hellenistic Moralists and the New Testament," *ANRW* 2.26.7 (1992) 314.

[8] On James as a diaspora letter, see Manabu Tsuji, *Glaube zwischen Vollkommenheit und Verweltlichung: Eine Untersuchung zur literarischen Gestalt und zur inhaltlichen Kohärenz des Jakobusbriefes* (WUNT 2/93; Tübingen: J.C.B. Mohr [Siebeck] 1997) and Karl-Wilhelm Niebuhr, "Der Jakobusbrief im Licht frühjüdischer Diasporabriefe," *NTS* 44 (1998) 420-43.

[9] For example, Hubert Frankenmölle, "Das semantische Netz des Jakobusbriefes. Zur Einheit eines umstrittenen Briefes," *BZ* 34 (1990) 175; Martin Klein, *Ein vollkommenes Werk. Volkommenheit, Gesetz, und Gericht als theologische Themen des Jakobusbriefes* (BWANT 139; Stuttgart: Kohlhammer, 1995); James Reese, "The Exegete as Sage: Hearing the Message of James," *BTB* 12 (1982): 82-85; Robert Wall, *Community of the Wise: The Letter of James* (New Testament in Context; Valley Forge, PA: Trinity Press International, 1998); Wilhelm Wuellner, "Der Jakobusbrief im Licht der Rhetorik und Textpragmatik," *LB* 43 (1978) 36.

[10] For example, see Ernst Baasland, "Literarische Form, Thematik und geschichtliche Einordnung des Jakobusbriefes," *ANRW* 2.25.2 (1988) 3646-84; John H. Elliott, "The Epistle of James in Rhetorical and Social Scientific Perspective: Holiness-Wholeness and Patterns of Replication," *BTB* 23 (1993) 71-81; Lauri Thurén, "Risky Rhetoric in James?" *NovT* 37 (1995) 262-84; Wachob, *The Voice of Jesus*; Duane F. Watson, "The Rhetoric of James 3:1-12 and a Classical Pattern of Argumentation," *NovT* 35 (1993) 48-64; Duane F. Watson, "James 2 in Light of Greco-Roman Schemes of Argumentation," *NTS* 39 (1993) 94-121; Wilhelm H. Wuellner, "Der Jakobusbrief."

[11] See Duane F. Watson, "A Reassessment of the Rhetoric of the Epistle of James and Its Implications for Christian Origins," in *Reading James with New Eyes. Methodological Reassessments of the Letter of James* (ed. Robert L. Webb & John S. Kloppenborg; Library of New Testament Studies 342; London: T & T Clark, 2007), 99-120.

several understand to conform to the elaboration of a theme exercise as outlined in ancient rhetorical handbooks.[12]

Chapter 4 begins the analysis of James's strategy by examining the introduction or exordium, of James, which appears, as will be argued, in 1:2-18. As the study of ancient rhetoric indicates, the exordium is a key component of an argument, as it can often introduce key themes that the writer will develop as well as the ethos or character of the speaker. It sets the tone for the entire text. Therefore, if language and ideas associated with the tradition of friendship emerge in this part of the letter, they must be significant for the letter as a whole. I will explore to what extent friendship and the related concept of benefaction appear in the exordium at the three levels of author to hearers/readers, the desired attributes of community members, and the description of God.

Chapter 5 focuses upon Jas 2:1-26, which several scholars have deemed a discrete unit of the letter that can be divided into 2:1-13 and 2:14-26 respectively. Each sub-section can be understood to be a complete argument. After reviewing why this is the case, the book again discusses friendship at the level of the voice of the author, the instructions for community life, and the description of God, or, in the case of 2:14-26, of the two famous figures, Abraham and Rahab. It is in 2:1-13 that James's opposition to patronage appears most clearly, with the illustration of the rich man and the poor man who enter the gathering; and the community response to their entrance is important in James's larger discussion of faith and works.

In Chapter 6, we turn to Jas 3:13–4:10, which again conforms to the rhetorical structure of an elaboration exercise. After explaining how it does so, the chapter turns to the presence of friendship and benefaction at the three levels of author to audience, community behaviour, and the description of God. This chapter will argue, further, that the statement in Jas 4:4 is a rephrasing of a teaching of Jesus, but deliberately reworded in order to maintain the description of God as a friend.

Chapter 7 returns to the question of patronage as one of the rhetorical exigencies that the letter of James addresses, reviewing both some of the ideas discussed throughout the book, and briefly engaging other passages in James that support the notion that patronage could be one of the problems that James is tackling. This chapter also provides summary conclusions to the volume as a whole.

Overall, our work thus combines rhetorical analysis of James in the context of the social and cultural models of friendship, patronage and

---

[12] Wachob, *The Voice of Jesus*; Watson, "James 2."

benefaction. Often this manner of approaching a text is called socio-rhetorical criticism, a method pioneered by Vernon K. Robbins.[13] This approach explores the multiple textures of a text, focusing upon a variety of levels including the text itself and how it attempts to communicate, the social and cultural context in which the text is produced, as well as the ideological textures of both the world from which the text emerges and the world in which it is interpreted. Analysis of the text itself examines its "inner texture" or structure, as well as its "intertexture" – that is, how it uses antecedent oral and written materials, and how it interacts with the community of discourse from which it emerges.[14] Study of the social and cultural textures of texts employs social-scientific work and applies it to various dimensions of the ancient world in order to understand how the text is interacting with the large social and cultural features of that world. Sensitivity to the fact that the texts of early Christianity, for example, were produced in a world very different from contemporary North American society, is crucial here; the interpreter must be careful not to impose her or his values on texts that simply do not share them. Finally, this approach to understanding literature involves attention to the interests and power dynamics of the author, text and readers of texts.[15] Socio-rhetorical criticism acknowledges that no author, text nor interpreter (nor interpretive community) is completely neutral, but has a set of interests, positive or negative, that he, she or it wants to promote. It thus tries to articulate how the ideology is at work in authors, texts and readers, in hopes of understanding these three dimensions of text and interpretation with more clarity.

Socio-rhetorical analyses do not always examine every "texture" of a particular text but they are interdisciplinary in that they require attention to more than one dimension of a text. This volume does not examine the ideological texture of James, for example,[16] not because ideology is not important, but simply because this is beyond the aims of

---

[13] Vernon K. Robbins, *Tapestry of Early Christian Discourse. Rhetoric, Society and Ideology* (London and New York: Routledge, 1996).

[14] See Robbins, *Tapestry*, 115.

[15] For a concise discussion of what now is known as "ideological criticism," see Gale A. Yee, "Ideological Criticism," in *Dictionary of Biblical Interpretation* (ed. John H. Hayes; Nashville: Abingdon, 1999) 534-37.

[16] For recent analyses of ideology in James, see Wesley H. Wachob, "The Epistle of James and the Book of Psalms: A Socio-Rhetorical Perspective of Intertexture, Culture and Ideology in Religious Discourse," in *Fabrics of Discourse. Essays in Honor of Vernon K. Robbins* (ed. David B. Gowler, L. Gregory Bloomquist, & Duane F. Watson; Harrisburg, London, New York: Trinity Press, 2003) 264-80; Alicia Batten, "Ideological Strategies in James," in *Reading James with New Eyes. Methodological Reassessments of the Letter of James* (Library of New Testament Studies 342; London: T & T Clark, 2007) 6-26.

this particular study. Here, the focus is primarily on the social and cultural textures of the letter's context, and specifically on the concepts of patronage, friendship, and benefaction, the existence of which is well documented in the first century Mediterranean world. However, and as described above, the book also examines the "inner texture" of James insofar as it deals with the rhetorical structure and argumentation of several units in the letter, as well as the voice of the implied author. Further, there is attention to the "intertexture" in the same units insofar as they are using previous, and primarily scribal, traditions from Judaism and the Graeco-Roman world. Friendship, benefaction and patronage therefore become the "lenses" through which these literary dimensions of the text are examined. What I hope will become clear is that James not only speaks as a trustworthy and authoritative friend to his audience, but that he advocates aspects of friendship and benefaction among members of the community such that they will not seek the patronage of the wealthy. In stressing some of the virtues intrinsic to true friendship, James exposes the "false friendship" of patron-client relations. Central to his message is reliance upon God, a friend and benefactor who offers generous benefits without reproach. In emphasizing these particular aspects of God, James implicitly undermines the "friendships" the community has, or desires to have, with rich patrons, who also receive direct criticism throughout the letter. For James, a life embodying some of the great virtues of friendship is also one in which friendship with God is a possibility. Thus his moral exhortation and his theological message are intricately connected as he attempts to provide guidance in this potent little text.

2

Friendship in Antiquity

Introduction

As with any ancient "concept," the study of friendship in antiquity is a complicated enterprise, for notions of what it meant to be friends and discussions of *with whom* one could be friends, were varied. Although many authors spent considerable energies in explaining how true friends should behave, it is difficult to form a universal definition of friendship in the ancient Mediterranean. Rather, we must remain content with a spectrum of views, just as different assessments of the concept have emerged in subsequent ages.[1]

Scrutiny of ancient friendship must also be subject to the caveat that we should not impose modern assumptions upon early ideas. If we readily admit that there are disparities between contemporary Western perceptions of personhood and the good life, and those of antiquity, then we must also acknowledge the implication that our predecessors understood associations between human beings differently.[2]

For example, the modern acceptance of the individual self, the inner and private "real me," defined in opposition to or in alienation from society at large,[3] would be incomprehensible to ancients.[4] As Christopher

---

[1] A volume edited by Oliver Leaman, *Friendship East and West. Philosophical Perspectives* (Richmond, UK: Curzon, 1996), offers an array of studies on friendship ranging from Plato's views to modern Japanese perceptions, showing to what extent definitions of friendship depend in large part on the cultures from which they emerge.

[2] This is not to say that there are no continuities in thought between moderns and ancients, but they are difficult to determine. For some discussion of the challenges of finding correspondences between ancient ideas and modern ones, see Bernard Williams, *Shame and Necessity* (Sather Classical Lectures, 57; Berkeley, Los Angeles, London: University of California Press, 1993).

[3] A famous account of the development of sincerity as key component of this individualism is Lionel Trilling's *Sincerity and Authenticity* (Cambridge, MA: Harvard

Gill has carefully explained, when ancient writers do discuss *euthumia*, or the notion of being content with or true to oneself, they do not portray the deeper self as asocial, or detached from engagement with the community. Building on the work of Alasdair MacIntyre, Gill points out that for ancient thinkers,

> virtue cannot be understood without reference to the performance of social roles and practices. In so far as ethical life requires further grounding, this is to be found in a conception of human nature, understood as a focus for shared ethical aspirations, rather than a conception of a purely private (and supposedly "true") self.[5]

This is not to say that ancient people did not have independent thoughts, or were not critical of their societies and institutions (sometimes to the point of repudiating public life, as was the case with some philosophical schools), but that their understanding of the person was significantly shaped by an awareness of a shared humanity. "Self-realization" in antiquity would not be a purely private self-creating act divorced from any sense of common humanity, as promoted by some post-Enlightenment thinkers, most notably Friedrich Nietzsche.[6] It would take for granted the bonds with other people, and not assume, as is sometimes the case today, that we are all separate from one another.

Feelings of separation which contemporary people can experience have contributed significantly to modern ideas of friendship. Some argue that isolation produces a lonely angst which undercuts people's ability to make friends.[7] Certainly, such individualism promotes the need for self-disclosure.[8] Friends need to trust one another and they prove their trust by revealing aspects of their private lives, their per-

---

University Press, 1972). See also Charles Taylor's magisterial *Sources of the Self. The Making of the Modern Identity* (Cambridge, MA: Harvard University Press, 1989).

[4] The application of cultural anthropology to biblical studies has brought the contrast between modern individualism and ancient dyadism to the fore. See Bruce J. Malina, *The New Testament World. Insights from Cultural Anthropology* (Louisville: John Knox, 1981) 51-70.

[5] Christopher Gill, "Peace of Mind and Being Yourself: Panaetius to Plutarch," *ANRW* II.36.7 (1994) 4601.

[6] Gill ("Peace of Mind," 4634, n.143) thus notes the subtitle of Nietzsche's *Ecce Homo: How One Becomes What One Is*. For further discussion of this aspect of Nietzsche's thought, see Alisdair MacIntyre, *After Virtue. A Study in Moral Theory* (2nd ed.; Notre Dame: University of Notre Dame Press, 1984) 113-14.

[7] Stuart Miller (*Men and Friendship* [Los Angeles: Jeremy P. Tarcher, 1983] 21-22) claims that modern philosophy, with its emphasis upon the individual, has contributed to the demise of friendships among men.

[8] This aspect of modern friendship is acknowledged by most sociologists and psychologists writing on the subject.

sonal interests, and often their fears and insecurities. In antiquity, however, such a confessional stance was not a requirement for friendship. Honesty and frankness of speech were important, to be sure, but there is no evidence that friends had to divulge their inmost secrets to one another. As David Konstan writes, "plainspokenness and the liberty to express dangerous views ... are not the same as the injunction to self-disclosure."[9] Nor does one receive the impression from ancient literature that friendship was an antidote to loneliness, as if only a true friend could rescue another person from her or his solitude.

Secondly, the socio-political, economic and cultural dissimilarities between modern Western life and that of the ancient world have naturally had a powerful impact upon the complexion of human relationships. All of these differences cannot be detailed here, but one contrast which many contemporary researchers on friendship note is the shift from the essentially pre-industrial society of the ancient world to the highly industrialized present. Agriculture was one of the main sources of wealth in antiquity whereas industry, although an important part of the ancient economy, was not large-scale and could not generate a large profit for further investment.[10] There was no "class of entrepreneurs who [were] both capable of perceiving opportunities for profit in large-scale organization of manufacture and prepared to undergo the risks entailed in making the necessary investment."[11] Thus, the market was not the vast anonymous entity that it is in capitalist societies today.

Some thinkers have determined that this change from pre-industrial to industrialized, commercial society has improved the nature of friendship. Certain 18th-century Scottish Enlightenment writers understood the purpose of friendship in pre-commercial society to be simply that of helping friends and harming enemies.

> Where vital resources are not created and distributed impersonally by markets and bureaucracies, one has no choice but to be in [Adam] Ferguson's disapproving phrase, "interested and sordid" in all interactions, concerned only with whether they "empty [or] fill the pocket," be-

---

[9] Konstan, *Friendship in the Classical World*, 15.

[10] See M.I. Finley, *The Ancient Economy* (rev. ed.; Berkeley: University of California Press, 1985).

[11] Peter Garnsey and Richard Saller, *The Roman Empire. Economy, Society and Culture* (London: Duckworth, 1987) 43.

cause in such settings vital resources are obtained largely through what modern culture and theory see as personal relations.[12]

According to these Scots, the onset of commercial society provided a clear contrast between the world of business relations; a world of strangers or, at the most, acquaintances, in which one was expected to act equitably but out of self-interest, and the private world of family and friendship, where one offered unconditional service and love. Commercial society was beneficial, they argued, precisely because it made this distinction between the formal and impersonal relations of the business world and the informal and intimate spheres of friends and family. It thus promoted "personal relations that [were] normatively free of instrumental and calculative orientations."[13]

Critics of commercial capitalist society have viewed its impact upon personal relations in another way. Marx and others have argued that "commodification renders personal relations alienated and morally corrupt."[14] A person's worth becomes determined more by her economic value, that is, by how she can benefit the factory or the business, than by other characteristics. This view of a person as a commodity spreads and infects other forms of human associations, including families, religious groups and clubs.[15]

Whether one is a supporter or a critic of capitalist society, one needs to appreciate that friendship existed in many forms in pre-industrial civilizations. It is inappropriate to stereotype ancient friendship as a *purely* "help friends and harm enemies" concept,[16] nor as a relationship entirely free of instrumentalism, which commerce and industry have subsequently corrupted. Friendship "in any society is bounded by a set

---

[12] Allan Silver, "Friendship in Commercial Society: Eighteenth-Century Social Theory and Modern Sociology," *American Journal of Sociology* 95 (1990) 1484. Silver notes Plato's *Meno* 71.E, in which Meno says that a man's virtue is "that he be competent to manage the affairs of his city, and to manage them so as to benefit his friends and harm his enemies, as to take care to avoid suffering harm himself."

[13] Silver, "Friendship in Commercial Society," 1474. See also Allan Silver, "Friendship and Trust as Moral Ideals: An Historical Approach," *European Journal of Sociology* 30 (1989) 274-97.

[14] Silver, "Friendship and Commercial Society," 1477.

[15] Stuart Miller (*Men and Friendship*, 20) argues that intimacy and friendship are remorselessly undercut by modern civilization.

[16] However, the notion that one would support one's friends and rejoice in the ruin of one's enemies is a consistent presupposition in Greek thought. As Mary Whitlock Blundell (*Helping Friends and Harming Enemies: A Study in Sophocles and Greek Ethics* [Cambridge: Cambridge University Press, 1989] 27) states, "unlike most of us, [the Greeks] realistically acknowledged that it is also human to be pained by our enemies' success and take pleasure in their downfall."

of alternative relationships that mark off its specific dimensions and properties,"[17] but these alternative relationships are many and complex in all periods of history. There is no single narrative or development of friendship; rather, it ebbs and flows with the changing circumstances of the human community.

This chapter will explore some of the ways in which Greek, Roman, Jewish and Christian writers understood friendship. The language of friendship has a long and rich history among the ancient Greeks, reaching far back into the Archaic period and possibly even earlier. Although it would be impossible to examine this entire history here, an appreciation of some of this background is essential for understanding the contours of friendship in the first century. We will focus on the appearance and use of key terms associated with friendship, some of the virtues and characteristics of friends, as well as the notion of friendship with God, as this idea is significant to the letter of James.

Φιλία/Φίλος

Homer's poetry is the oldest extant evidence of friendship language and ideas,[18] although there is great disagreement among classical scholars as to precisely how the poet understood this type of relationship. He does not use the word φιλία, but he does employ φίλος in both the *Iliad* and the *Odyssey*. Many argue that he uses φίλος in one or both of the following ways: in the possessive sense of referring to one's own, and/or as an emotive adjective, as in "dear" or "loving."[19] When it

---

[17] Konstan, *Friendship in the Classical World*, 6.

[18] As Homer's works contain materials that predate the poetry's present form, which was established around the 8th century BCE, the friendships and friendship language which appear in them may reach far back into the dark age.

[19] For a survey of the scholarly positions on the use of φίλος, see John T. Fitzgerald, "Friendship in the Greek World prior to Aristotle," *Greco-Roman Perspectives on Friendship*, 13-34; James Hooker, "Homeric φίλος," *Glotta* 65 (1987) 44-65. Hooker (64) argues that φίλος went through changes in meaning throughout the development of the epic traditions: "the meaning of φίλος in Homer ranges from a strongly-marked affectionate use, through a strongly-marked possessive use, to a weak possessive use." David Robinson ("Homeric φίλος. Love of Life and Limbs, and Friendship with One's θυμός," *'Owls to Athens.' Essays on Classical Subjects Presented to Sir Kenneth Dover* [ed. E.M. Craik; Oxford: Clarendon, 1990] 97-108) takes a different view, stating that Homeric φίλος is never possessive, but either emotive or used to describe one's ἦτορ, κῆρ, and θυμός as friends. Arthur W.H. Adkins ("Friendship and 'Self-Sufficiency' in Homer and Aristotle," *CQ* 13 [1963] 33) emphasizes the possessive nature of φίλος although he grants that there is some degree of affection for things that are φίλοι (yet he will not accept the English words "dear" or "friend," and all that they entail, as accurate equivalents). Adkins writes that for the ancient Greek in Homer's world, the φίλοι "are his [the Greeks'] own: all else is hostile or indifferent, and the possessive affection he feels for what is φίλον is based on the

comes to Homer's substantive use of the word, disagreement falls along similar lines. Scholars who interpret the adjective φίλος in a possessive sense understand it substantively to be someone who is either one's own, one's relative or a member of one's group. Other classicists who attribute an emotive sense to the adjective φίλος likewise think that the noun means "friend,"[20] contrary to the first set of interpreters who claim that this notion of a φίλος only emerged later within Greek literature.

Regardless, Archaic Greek literature, including Hesiod and Theognis, uses other terms for "friend" such as ἑταῖρος[21] and it is not until the classical and later periods that φίλος becomes the "standard" word used. During the classical period, however, there is debate about to what type of relationship the word refers, and what the difference between φίλος and φιλία is. It is widely appreciated that "friendship" is too specific a translation for φιλία because this word can encompass a variety of relationships. That there is φιλία between two or more people need not connote friendship but simply a reciprocal relationship.[22] Φιλία can exist between humans, but also between gods and humans, as we will see. It connotes neither an exclusive relationship nor one that can only exist between non-kin. Many who examine ancient friendship think that φίλος is likewise applicable to a wide variety of relationships. That is, not only can a loyal friend be a φίλος, but a brother or a sister, or a mother or a father. Thus φίλος and φιλία are often discussed together, as if they both refer to the same range of meanings. For example, in explaining why the help friends/harm enemies code is much broader than it may first seem to moderns, Blundell states that

> the Greek *philos* (translated as 'friend,' 'beloved' or 'dear') and *philia* (translated as 'friendship' or 'love'), go well beyond our concept of

need and desire for self-preservation." Jean-Claude Fraisse (*Philia. La Notion de l'Amitié dans la Philosophie Antique*, 39) states this more emphatically: "Est *philon* ce qui ne peut être séparé de moi sans que je cesse d'exister, ou du moins de mener l'existence qui est ma raison d'être."

[20] For an outline of the scholarly positions, see Fitzgerald, "Friendship in the Greek World," 16-18.

[21] See Hesiod, *Works and Days*, 707-13; Theognis, *Eleg.* 1.95. Konstan (*Friendship*, 33), however, argues that during the Archaic period, the term φίλος is reserved for the most intimate circle of friends.

[22] Classicists disagree about the level or even presence of emotional or affectionate feelings between those in a φιλία relationship. See David Konstan, *The Emotions of the Ancient Greeks. Studies in Aristotle and Classical Literature* (Toronto, Buffalo, London: University of Toronto Press, 2006) 169-84.

friendship to cover a complex web of personal, political, business and family relationships, each of which when violated may turn to enmity.[23]

Similarly, in his dissertation on φιλία and χάρις in Euripidean drama, S.E. Scully talks about φιλία and φίλος interchangeably, assuming that they refer to the same domain of associations.[24]

Recently, Konstan has challenged the previous consensus that this breadth of relationships is signified by both nouns. He argues that φιλία can denote affection between both kin and non-kin but that the "concrete noun *philos* (distinguished more or less unambiguously from the adjective meaning 'dear' when modified by the definite article) applies specifically to the more narrow bond of friendship."[25] Even the adjective, φίλος, can apply to a wide variety of kin and non-kin who are "dear" to one another, but when the noun appears, indicated by the article in front of it, it denotes a much more specific association which can only exist between non-kin.[26] Konstan has analysed a variety of classical sources and found that the authors were very careful to make distinctions between family members and those who are not biologically related. "Where kin and acquaintances unrelated by family ties are contrasted, *philoi* clearly designates the class of friends."[27] He points out that Aristotle, who as far as we know was the first to produce a methodical study of friendship, includes many types of bonds, familial and otherwise, within the category of φιλία, but when he discusses mother-child φιλία he avoids the noun φίλος altogether:

> As has been said, there are three kinds of *philia*, according to virtue, utility, and pleasure, and these in turn are divided into two, the one set according to equality, the other according to surplus. Both sets are *philiai*, but friends [*philoi*] are those according to equality; for it would be absurd for a father to be a friend [*philos*] to his child, but of course he loves [*philei*] him and is loved [*phileitai*] by him (*Eth. Eud.* 7.4.1-2 [LCL]).[28]

Thus φιλία can encompass a diversity of relationships, but φίλος, when used as a noun, generally refers to a biologically unrelated

---

[23] Blundell, *Helping Friends and Harming Enemies*, 39.
[24] See S.E. Scully, *Philia and Charis in Euripidean Tragedy* (Ph.D. dissertation; University of Toronto, 1973) 15-51. For a discussion of other writers who take this approach, see David Konstan, "Greek Friendship," *AJP* 117 (1996) 71-72.
[25] Konstan, "Greek Friendship," 75. See also Konstan, *The Emotions*, 170.
[26] Konstan ("Greek Friendship," 84, n.3 1) acknowledges that occasionally there are exceptions.
[27] Konstan, "Greek Friendship," 73; cf. Konstan, *Friendship in the Classical World*, 53-56.
[28] Translated by H. Rackham (London: Heinemann; Cambridge, MA: Harvard University Press, 1935). See Konstan, *Friendship in the Classical World*, 68.

person. Sometimes family members can prove to be true φίλοι, but that does not mean that the noun φίλος normally includes kin.[29] Although this study will include a discussion of φιλία, it focuses on the more narrowly defined idea of a φίλος.

By the first century φίλος is the primary word for "friend" and is used in a wide variety of contexts, including official documents, letters, inscriptions, philosophical literature, Hellenistic Jewish texts, the New Testament and other early Christian literature. Within the past decade, increasing attention to the use of friendship language in a range of scriptural contexts suggests that φίλος and its cognates were more significant for some Jewish and Christian writers than was previously acknowledged.[30] Although classical Hebrew had no consistent vocabulary for friendship,[31] the translation of Hebrew biblical texts into Greek and the creation and addition of other documents reveals that Hellenistic Jews expressed interest in friendship as a topic to be discussed. The word φίλος appears 91 times in the apocryphal/deuterocanonical books, with 62 of those occurrences as the translation of a Hebrew original.[32] Some Hellenistic Jewish texts, such as the Maccabbean books, refer to φίλος quite often,[33] and Ben Sira discusses friendship at length. With regard to the New Testament, it has recently been observed that φιλέω and φίλος were more significant for some early Christian groups than has previously been recognized. Many have supposed that the ancient Christians understood ἀγαπάω to be a higher form of love than φιλέω, a supposition largely based upon the fact that Paul uses ἀγαπάω so often, and only uses φιλέω once. However, Luke-Acts uses φιλέω-related words more than cognates of ἀγαπάω, and the latter only occur in Acts. There are several examples of Lukan Q material which use the word φίλοι while the same material in Matthew does not.[34] The Gospel of John employs ἀγαπάω more than φιλέω, but

---

[29] Konstan, *Friendship in the Classical World*, 59.

[30] See, for example, Jeremy Corley, *Ben Sira's Teaching on Friendship* (BJS 316; Atlanta: Scholars, 2002), the essays in *Friendship, Flattery and Frankness of Speech*, as well as Carolinne White's *Christian Friendship in the Fourth Century* (Cambridge: Cambridge University Press, 1992).

[31] Pizzolato, *L'idea di amicizia*, 222.

[32] See Gregory E. Sterling, "The Bond of Humanity: Friendship in Philo of Alexandria," *Greco-Roman Perspectives on Friendship*, 204. n. 5.

[33] See G. Stählin, "φίλος, φιλή, φιλία," *TDNT* IX (1974) 154-55.

[34] Ann Graham Brock ("The Significance of φιλέω and φίλος in the Tradition of Jesus Sayings and in the Early Christian Communities," *HTR* 90 [1997] 396-401) identifies these examples: Matt 10:28 and Luke 12:4-5; Matt 8:8 and Luke 7:6; Matt 18:12-13 and Luke 15:4-6. Also compare Mark 13:12 and Luke 21:16, in which Luke contains a refer-

does not resist φιλέω nor φίλος, some instances of which appear to have emerged from source material or tradition, while others likely served the author's objectives.[35] Perhaps this emphasis upon ἀγαπάω has contributed to the neglect of φίλος and its cognates in early Christian literature. Be that as it may, studies on the role of friendship, particularly within Paul's letters and Luke–Acts, are increasing.

Virtues of Friends

An examination of friendship in antiquity reveals a common set of virtues regularly associated with friends. These virtues, to some extent, transcend linguistic and religious boundaries.

Gustav Stählin states that "the very fact that φίλος and φιλία occur predominantly in the originally Greek texts of the LXX shows that we have here a concept which is fundamentally alien to the OT world."[36] When φίλος appears in the apocryphal/deuterocanonical books, 62 times rendering a Hebrew word, the Hebrew is not consistent.[37] The most common Hebrew original is רע but this word is often translated into Greek as πλησίον, which can connote a variety of things including "neighbour," "another," "friend," "companion," and "paramour."[38] Other Hebrew original words include אהב (e.g. Esth 5:10), מרע (Prov 12:26) אלוף (Prov 16:28), and חבר (Dan 2:13, 17).[39]

Although Hebrew had no consistent vocabulary of friendship, this does not mean that the idea of an intimate and loyal bond between people did not exist for the ancient Israelites. The relationship between Jonathan and David ranks as a great friendship, comparable to that between other famous pairs of friends because of its intensity. 1 Sam 18:1 states that the "soul (נפש) of Jonathan was bound to the soul (נפש) of David and Jonathan loved him as his own soul (נפש)." This latter statement is repeated a few times in 1 Samuel (1 Sam 18:3; 20:17), and is reminiscent of Deut 13:7, which refers to "your friend (רע) who is as

---

ence to φίλων, while Mark makes no mention of it. Φίλοι occurs 9 more times in Luke (11:5, 6, 8; 14:10, 12; 15:9; 23:2) and 3 times in Acts (10:24; 19:31; 27:3).

[35] Brock, "The Significance," 399, 405–406.

[36] Stählin, "φίλος," See also, Treu, "Freundschaft," RAC 8, 423–26.

[37] Gregory E. Sterling, ("The Bond of Humanity," 204, n. 5) has provided a very helpful tabulation of the number of times in which φίλος appears in the LXX and the different Hebrew words from which it has been translated.

[38] Johannes Fichtner, "πλησίον in the LXX and the Neighbour in the OT," TDNT VI (1968) 312–14.

[39] The Theodotion text of Daniel uses φίλος for חבר but the LXX does not. For discussion of the translation of Hebrew words into φίλος, see Stählin, "φίλος," 154–56.

your own soul (נפש)." Jonathan gives David his own robe, armour and weapons, thereby, in Stählin's view, making David the "alter ego of his friend [Jonathan]."[40] When David laments the deaths of Saul and Jonathan, he says of Jonathan, "I am distressed for you, my brother Jonathan; greatly beloved were you to me; your love (אהבה) to me was wonderful, passing the love of women" (2 Sam 1:26). Such a strong profession of love for a friend recalls the intense relationship between Homer's Achilles and Patroclus, such that Achilles returned to a battle in which Patroclus had been killed, not because of the call of duty, but to avenge the death of his friend.

In a number of instances, the Hebrew Bible associates the quality of חסד, which has been translated as "loving loyalty"[41] or "faithful love," with friendships between people and between humans and God. This is true of the friendship between Jonathan and David, for when they make a covenant of friendship, Jonathan says: "If I am still alive, show me the faithful love (חסד) of the Lord; but if I die, never cut off your faithful love (חסד) from my house" (1 Sam 10:14-15a). Norman Habel thus suggests that "in David's bond of friendship with Jonathan there was a strong relationship between human *hesed* and the divine *hesed* of Yahweh expressed through a human being towards a friend."[42] The book of Job also links חסד with friendship, although not the חסד of God. Marvin H. Pope has translated Job 6:14 as "A sick man should have the loyalty (חסד) from his friend (רע), though he forsake fear of Shaddai,"[43] which indicates how, for the author of Job, human loyalty was a prerequisite for friendship, even in moments of alienation from the divine.[44] Unfortunately Job's friends cannot live up to this requirement, and refuse to commiserate with Job in his anger and frustration at God.

Throughout Proverbs there are various statements about friendship, including references to those who only pretend to be friends. Proverbs 18:24 states: "Some friends play at friendship but a true friend (אהב) sticks closer than one's nearest kin." Fair weather friends are plentiful during prosperity (19:6) but when people face destitution, their friends

---

[40] Stählin, "φίλος," 156.

[41] See William Hugh Brownlee, *The Dead Sea Manual of Discipline* (BASORSup 10-12; New Haven: American Schools of Oriental Research, 1951) 48.

[42] Norman Habel, "'Only the Jackal is my Friend.' On Friends and Redeemers in Job," *Int* 31 (1977) 230.

[43] Marvin H. Pope, *Job. A New Translation with Introduction and Commentary* (AB 15; New York: Doubleday, 1965) 49.

[44] Habel ("'Only the Jackal is my Friend,'" 230) writes that for the author of Job, "to be a friend is to be cohuman in a dehumanized situation where a despairing man has lost his religion as a source of inner support."

disappear (19:7). The true friend, however, will stand fast despite the hard times that the other encounters. To hate a friend (רע) is even to sin (חטא) according to Prov 14:21a while the second half of the proverb states that to have compassion on the poor is to be blessed. Such a pairing of ideas strongly suggests that to be a friend is to have compassion for others especially when they face poverty and despair.[45]

Turning to the oldest extant Greek source for friendship, the *Iliad*, we see a bond between Achilles and Patroclus that manifests an association between two people which far exceeds in intensity their associations with others. Homer describes these two characters primarily as ἑταῖροι, which can mean a variety of things, including comrades and shipmates,[46] and thus the mere designation ἑταῖροι does not distinguish Achilles's and Patroclus's friendship from their associations with other warriors. However, Homer does describe Patroclus as Achilles's πολὺ φίλτατος ἑταῖρος "dearest companion by far" (17.411,655),[47] and as many have observed, there is plentiful evidence of the depth of feeling between Achilles and Patroclus, from Apollo's wonder at Achilles's love for Patroclus (24.44-52),[48] to the "metaphorical assimilation" (for example, Patroclus dies in Achilles's armour) between the two which "calls to mind Aristotle's image of the friend as another self,"[49] a notion which we will explore later. Also of note here is the degree to which the word πιστός appears in the context of describing one's dearest companions,[50] to the point of πιστός becoming a standard word associated with friends in this literature.

This emphasis upon loyalty continues in Theognis, who offers a substantial number of complaints and pieces of advice about friends who have been duplicitous or disloyal. In fact, it appears that for Theognis, friendship has broken down. "Few *philoi* have a trustworthy mind ... [and] the poet seeks in vain for a *pistos hetairos* free of deception (*dolos*)

---

[45] A.S. Aglen ("Friend" in *Dictionary of the Bible* [ed. James Hastings; Edinburgh: T & T Clark, 1903]) 68.

[46] See Franz Dirlmeier, Φίλος und Φιλία im vorhellenistischen Griechentum, 22.

[47] See Konstan, *Friendship in the Classical World*, 33.

[48] See David M. Halperin, *One Hundred Years of Homosexuality* (New York, London: Routledge, 1990) 84.

[49] Konstan, *Friendship in the Classical World*, 42. For more of a discussion of the "assimilation" between Achilles and Patroclus, see Dale S. Sinos, *Achilles, Patroklos and the Meaning of* Philos (Innsbrucker Beiträge zur Sprachwissenschaft 29; Innsbruck: Institut für Sprachwissenschaft der Universität Innsbruck, 1980) 55-68.

[50] See Christophe Ulf, *Die homerische Gesellschaft: Materialen zur analytischen Beschreibung und historischen Lokalisierung* (Munich: C.H. Beck, 1990) 136.

like himself."[51] So often does Theognis decry the disloyalty of these persons that it can be assumed that loyalty must have once been a prized feature of true friendship. Now, according to Theognis, such faithfulness is a rarity. As Fitzgerald observes, Theognis's views likely contributed to the notion that one could only have a few loyal friends, as opposed to the larger groups of comrades and shipmates who appear in Homer's epics.[52]

An emphasis upon trust and faithfulness continues in Greek tragedy. Although Aeschylus deals with friendship the least, he does think that friends have certain obligations to one another. For example, in *Prometheus Bound*, Prometheus, lashed to the rocks as a punishment for saving humanity from Zeus's plan to annihilate the human race, laments Zeus's doings, for he, Prometheus, had assisted in securing Zeus's victory as the king of heaven. Although Prometheus is aware of his wrongdoing in thwarting Zeus's destructive plan, he is still enraged that he, a φίλος of Zeus (306), should be treated so harshly. His statement that he is a friend of Zeus may be ironic,[53] but it reveals the presupposition that friends had an obligation to help, not punish, one another. After Zeus has doomed him to eternal suffering, Prometheus cries out in agony upon the rocks,

> [s]uch profit did the tyrant of Heaven have of me and with such foul return as this did he make requital; for it is a disease that somehow inheres in tyranny to have no faith in friends (φίλοισι) (*Prometheus Bound* 223-28 [LCL]).[54]

Thus it appears that Zeus's actions are proof that the king of the gods did not place sufficient trust in his friends. Friends were supposed to be reliable, and to offer support which was expected to be reciprocated. In this case, Zeus is so angered by Prometheus's care for humanity that he disregards the help that Prometheus had extended to him in the past and thus fails, at least in Prometheus's view, to be a proper friend.

The idea that friends should aid one another is plain in Euripides's plays as well, notably in *Orestes*. In this tragedy, Orestes makes statements about the importance of mutual aid between friends in times of trouble. He tells Menelaus that "in desperate need, ought friends to help their friends. When Fortune gives her boons, what need of

---

[51] Walter Donlan, "*Pistos Philos Hetairos*" *Theognis of Megara: Poetry and Polis* (ed. Thomas J. Figueira & Gregory Nagy: Baltimore and London: Johns Hopkins, 1985) 227.

[52] Fitzgerald, "Friendship in the Greek World," 31.

[53] Scully, *Philia and Charis in Euripidean Tragedy*, 24.

[54] Translated by Herbert Weir Smythe (Cambridge, MA: Harvard University Press; London: Heinemann, 1922).

friends."[55] The true test of friendship is whether they will help when needed most. As Jean-Claude Fraisse states, for Euripides, "si l'ami est un bien, il l'est au moment où tous les autres biens disparaissent."[56] Friends should go to the limit, even to the point of giving their life for the sake of their friend. Orestes refers to Agamemnon, who "verily sold his life for thee [Menelaus], as friends (φίλοισι) should do for friends (φίλους)"[57] This statement reveals that a family member may indeed act as a friend, although the definition of a friend, as discussed earlier, does not normally include kin.

The latter point is underlined in the play when Orestes celebrates the loyalty of his friend, Pylades, who arrives to help Orestes after the latter had been condemned to death for the murder of his mother, Clytemnestra. When Pylades indicates that he wishes to stand by Orestes, Orestes declares, "Herein true is that old saying – '*Get thee friends* [ἑταίρους] *not kin alone.*' He whose soul to thy soul cleaveth, though he be not better than a thousand kinsfolk this is for thy friend [φίλος] to win."[58] Orestes is indicating that a true friend, someone who will prove reliable in a time of need, is more likely not related by blood.

Although friendship is assumed to be a noble bond in Euripides's work, he also reveals the dark side of such loyalty. In *Orestes*, Pylades and Orestes may be remarkably loyal to one another, but this fidelity becomes "pathological" when it is "elevated above all other ties and obligations."[59] In this case, the pair plan to murder Orestes's aunt, Helen, take Menelaus's daughter hostage and destroy the Argos palace, all because these people refuse to support them. For Orestes and Pylades, personal bonds of friendship exceed all other bonds.

Moving to the philosophical realm, Xenophon's defense of Socrates, the *Memorabilia*, presents a conversation that the teacher had about friendship. Whether or not the discussion took place, the dialogue reveals some of the ideas current at the time. For one thing, it is clear that friendship is an important bond, for as Socrates states, "... surely there is no other possession that can compare with a good friend (φίλος ἀγαθός)."[60] Socrates makes this statement because he is dismayed by people who neglect their friends. He laments the fact that people do

---

[55] Euripides, *Orest.* 655-57 (LCL; trans. Arthur S. Way: London: Heinemann; Cambridge, MA: Harvard University Press, 1912).

[56] Jean-Claude Fraisse, *Philia*, 77.

[57] *Orest.* 652.

[58] *Orest.* 804-806.

[59] Konstan, *Friendship in the Classical World*, 60.

[60] Xenophon, *Mem.* 2.4.5 (LCL; trans. E.C. Marchant; London, Cambridge, MA: Harvard University Press, 1923).

not take proper care of their friends and forget them in times of need. A good friend is one who offers aid and support, no matter what the situation.

> If generosity is called for, he does his part: if fear harasses, he comes to the rescue, shares expenses, helps to persuade, bears down opposition: he is foremost in delighting him when he is prosperous and raising him up when he falls (*Mem.* 2.4.6).

In this sense, Xenophon's report concurs with the tragic poets' requirement that friends be faithful and loyal.

Xenophon then continues on to describe a conversation he claims Socrates had with Critobulus over how to determine or test the qualities which make a man worth having as a friend. A desirable friend must be a good person; he must be self-controlled, loyal and fair.[61] One must also examine how the potential friend treats other people – not what he says, but what he has done (ποιέω). If the individual proves worthy, then one must set about procuring his friendship, not by flattering him (which would repel him) but by being a good person oneself. Socrates thus says to Critobulus, "Courage, Critobulus; try to be good, and when you have achieved that, set about catching your gentleman."[62] Two friends, therefore, must both be virtuous people. A bad person cannot be friends, even with a good person.

Xenophon grants that human beings have a natural propensity for evil, but despite their susceptibility to strife, envy, jealousy, anger and hatred, friendship still slips in, and "unites the gentle natures."[63] Included in this section of the discussion is a wonderful description of friendship in which friends share their food, drink and wealth, do not allow anger to get out of control, reject jealousy (ὁ φθόνος) and supply one another's needs.[64] However, that one is extraordinarily moral in one's treatment of friends does not mean that one cannot have enemies. The notion of helping friends and harming enemies is very present. Socrates, planning to aid Critobulus in obtaining friends, tells him that he must let Socrates inform the prospective friend that Critobulus has made up his mind "that a man's virtue consists in outdoing his friends in kindness and his enemies in mischief."[65] Thus, despite the outpouring of goodness that is required for friends, Xenophon remains in a world which enthusiastically promotes the deception of enemies.

---

[61] *Mem.* 2.6.5.
[62] *Mem.* 2.6.28.
[63] *Mem.* 2.6.21-22. For a brief discussion of this section, see Fraisse, *Philia*, 113-14.
[64] *Mem.* 2.6.22-23.
[65] *Mem.* 2.6.35.

Another defender of Socrates, Plato, presents a different Socratic perspective in the *Lysis*, although there is some continuity with the *Memorabilia*. In this dialogue, Socrates observes that he does not know how one person becomes a friend of another, although he acknowledges that there are people, like the two boys Lysis and Menexenus, who are friends.[66] What ensues is an inquiry into how people become friends in which Socrates begins by leading Menexenus through a series of questions centring on the adjective φίλος, which can have both active and passive senses, "loving" and "loved." Socrates rejects the notion that φιλία can exist when only one side of the relationship is loving or being loved as well as a relationship in which there is reciprocal love. The latter rejection of mutual love as a basis for friendship is not clearly argued,[67] but Socrates discards it all the same and at this point, the discussion flounders.

However, the dialogue continues on, resorting to the notion that like is attracted to like and in moral terms, in which the good are attracted to the good. The bad cannot be friends with the bad, argues Socrates, for they simply do harm to one another. Therefore, only the good can be friends,[68] an idea reminiscent of Xenophon and possibly an authentic opinion of the historical Socrates.[69] However, if the good are self-sufficient, as Socrates thinks they are, how can they be friends when they do not need one another nor miss one another when absent?[70] This statement is followed by a series of complicated arguments in which Socrates attempts to solve this dilemma. It is noteworthy that throughout these arguments ἐπιθυμία "twice accompanies the term *philiā*, as if it made little difference which [was] used."[71] Plato does not distinguish these terms, as he does in other writings,[72] and at a certain point appears to conflate ἔρως, ἐπιθυμία and φιλία when he states that the aim of these three things is to acquire what is οἰκεῖος, "one's own" or "akin" to one. But then he again focuses upon friendship, claiming that if Lysis and Menexenus are friends to one another, or φίλοι, then they must be οἰκεῖοι to one another. This "akin-ness" must be recip-

---

[66] Plato, *Lysis* 212A (LCL; trans. W.R.M. Lamb; London: Heinemann; New York: Putnam, 1930).

[67] W.R.M. Lamb (*Lysis*, 39, n.2) notes that "Plato cannot be said to have disposed of this third proposition [mutual love as a basis for friendship]."

[68] Plato, *Lysis* 214E.

[69] Jonathan Powell, "Friendship and its Problems in Greek and Roman Thought" (*Ethics and Rhetoric*, ed. H. Hine, C. Pelling and D. Innes; Oxford: Clarendon, 1995) 35.

[70] Plato, *Lysis* 215B.

[71] A.W. Price, *Love and Friendship in Plato and Aristotle* (Oxford: Clarendon, 1989) 7.

[72] See W. Joseph Cummins, "*Eros, Epithumia*, and *Philia* in Plato," *Apeiron* 15 (1981) 10-18.

rocal; however, which would mean that like would be friends with like, or the good with the good. Socrates had already rejected this notion earlier on, and thus the discussion ends in failure, for "what a 'friend' is, we have not yet succeeded in discovering."[73]

Despite the disappointing end of the *Lysis*, Plato has presented a number of features of friendship which were important throughout the classical and Hellenistic periods. The notion that only good people could be friends, which was also raised by Xenophon, became common, as did the idea that friends have a certain "akin-ness" or affinity, although other writers do not use the term οἰκεῖος. Moreover, Plato has raised the important problem of what friendship can contribute to someone who has achieved εὐδαιμονία, a word that is difficult to translate but approaches something like "happiness" or the "objective, optimal condition for human beings."[74] Why should such a person need friends? As we shall see, this issue was not a problem for Plato's successor, Aristotle.

Aristotle was the first to offer a systematic analysis of φιλία, or the character of reciprocal ties between people.[75] One of the varieties of φιλία that he discusses is that between friends or φίλοι. He explores this subject in book 7 of the *Eudemian Ethics*, books 8 and 11 of the subsequent *Nicomachean Ethics*[76] and parts of the *Magna Moralia*, the *Rhetoric* and the *Politics*. Thus, as the examination of φιλία absorbs significant sections of Aristotle's ethical writings,[77] there is today an abundance of secondary literature on the topic and there are many points of swirling debate.

At the beginning of book 8 of the *Nicomachean Ethics*, Aristotle states that friendship "is one of the most indispensable requirements of life. For no one would choose to live without friends..."[78] According to Aristotle, human beings are political creatures (πολιτικόν) and are

---

[73] Plato, *Lysis* 223B.

[74] Powell, "Friendship and its Problems," 34. Glenn Lesses, "Austere Friends: The Stoics and Friendship," *Apeiron* 26 (1993) 59, n. 10. For more on this word, see Richard Kraut, "Two Conceptions of Happiness," *The Philosophical Review* 88 (1979) 167-97.

[75] Of note is the point that for Aristotle, φιλία is not an abstract idea that can be separated from each friend's love. See Konstan, *The Emotions*, 178.

[76] The common view is that the *Eudemian Ethics* is the earlier set of lectures and was later replaced by the *Nicomachean Ethics* (Julia Annas, "Plato and Aristotle on Friendship and Altruism," *Mind* 86 [1977] 532).

[77] John M. Cooper ("Aristotle on the Forms of Friendship," *Review of Metaphysics* 30 [1977] 619) notes that friendship takes up approximately one fifth of both the *Eudemian Ethics* and the *Nicomachean Ethics*.

[78] Aristotle, *Eth. Nic.* 8.1 (LCL; trans. H. Rackham; London: Heinemann; Cambridge, MA: Harvard University Press, 1934).

meant to share their lives with one another.[79] Like many ancients prior to the rise of Christian monasticism, Aristotle probably would have perceived life in isolation, separate from the rest of society, to be "the extreme of suffering."[80] Essential to a happy life is to live with other people, to care about them, receive their care, and to participate in building a good society. Friendship figures importantly in the expression of such a life: "the happy man requires friends."[81]

Aristotle made distinctions between three kinds (εἶδος) of friendship based upon the grounds for the friendship. Two people could have a friendship rooted in utility, in pleasure or in character. These three types all require mutuality but there is a certain hierarchy among them in that character friendship is the perfect form, for it exists between persons of virtuous character.[82] Friendships based upon utility or pleasures centre upon how useful or pleasing one friend can be to another. The friends "do not love each other in themselves, but insofar as some benefit accrues to them from each other."[83] Character friendship, on the other hand, grounds itself in wishing the best for the friend for the friend's sake, and not for the sake of what the friend can do for you.[84] Indeed, a character friendship brings mutual usefulness and pleasure to the relationship, but these benefits are not the basis for the tie.

Thus for Aristotle, the best friendship is that between two good people. However, one might ask, could such a friendship exist between any two good people, or is there something more specific which draws particular human beings together? Aristotle states quite clearly that character friendship is rare, for there are not many virtuous people, but he also says that one cannot have too many friends as such a situation would inevitably lead to conflicting loyalties. Moreover, he argues that the intimacy present within friendships of character takes time to develop and is a difficult thing to obtain.[85] Presumably then, one could not simply become intimate friends with the next good person who comes along, for such a friendship would require considerable time and effort to develop.[86]

---

[79] *Eth. Nic.* 9.9.3.
[80] Konstan, *Friendship in the Classical World*, 16.
[81] *Eth. Nic.* 9.9.3.
[82] *Eth. Nic.* 8.3.6.
[83] *Eth. Nic.* 8.3.1
[84] *Eth. Eud.* 7.6.3.
[85] *Eth. Nic.* 8.6.2.
[86] As Konstan (*Friendship in the Classical World*, 76) writes: "The idea that one might transfer one's love to the next more virtuous person who comes along is not Aristotelian, though such a man will normally be the object of good will on the part of others."

Aristotle is fully aware of the issue Plato raised concerning whether a happy, self-sufficient person has need of friends, for he raises it explicitly in both of his major ethical treatises.[87] However, this issue is not problematic for Aristotle as his understanding of a happy person is a person who has friends. He writes:

> But it seems strange that if we attribute all good things to the happy man (εὐδαίμονι) we should not assign him friends, which we consider the greatest of external goods. Also if it be more the mark of a friend to give than to receive benefits, and if beneficence is a function of the good man and of virtue, and it is nobler to benefit friends than strangers, the good man will need friends as the objects of his beneficence (*Eth. Nic.* 9.9.1).

For Aristotle, having friends not only proffers obvious joys and pleasures, it facilitates mutual benefaction. Friendship promotes goodness in people for they have someone *to be good to*. Jonathan Powell suggests that for Aristotle there may be "a particular ἀρετή that goes with friendship, the quality of being a good friend to one's friends."[88] Friendship is thus not incongruous with a self-sufficient, good life but an essential component of that life.

This emphasis upon virtues, especially loyalty, faithfulness, generosity, a willingness to suffer for one's friend, and a desire for the best for the friend *for the friend's sake*, remains strong in writings on friendship up to, during and after the emergence of Christianity, and crosses linguistic and religious boundaries. Greek novelists, such as Chariton, narrate the courageous commitments of friends such as Polycharmus in *Chaereaa and Callirhoe*. Although the tale focuses upon the love story between a young man, Chaereas, and his wife Callirhoe, throughout the entire story, Chaeareas is continually protected and repeatedly saved by his friend, Polycharmus. When Chaereas believes that he has accidentally killed his wife (thinking, wrongly, that she had committed adultery) and wants to commit suicide, Polycharmus, "his closest friend [φίλος ἐχαίρετος], as in Homer Patroclus was of Achilles,"[89] prevents him from doing so. Throughout the entire novel, Polycharmus shows all the signs of a true friend: he accompanies Chaereas on dangerous expeditions, he protects Chaereas from external harm, continually

---

[87] *Eth. Eud.* 7.12.1; *Eth. Nic.* 9.9.1.

[88] Powell, "Friendship and its Problems," 37.

[89] Chariton, *Chaer.* 1.5.2 (LCL; trans. G.P. Goold; Cambridge, MA, London: Harvard University Press, 1995). This text is cited by Ronald F. Hock, "An Extraordinary Friend in Chariton's *Callirhoe*: The Importance of Friendship in the Greek Romances," *Greco-Roman Perspectives on Friendship*, 148.

comforts him, and on more than one occasion restrains the distraught young man from killing himself.[90] Polycharmus also expresses his willingness to die with Chaereas, a characteristic of friendship discussed by Aristotle and other authors. Moreover, "that only Polycharmus among Chaereas's friends shared his many reversals in fortune (8.8.7) underscores the rarity of true friendship, another familiar convention."[91] At the end of the story, having rescued Callirhoe from Babylon, Polycharmus, Chaereas and Callirhoe return to their home in Syracuse, where Polycharmus is publicly declared a "loyal friend" (φίλος πιστός)[92] of Chaereas and Chaereas presents his friend with gifts (including Chaereas's sister for a wife!).

Various philosophical groups prized such virtues of friendship as well. Epicurus reputedly said that

> the wise man is not more pained when being tortured [himself, than when seeing] his friend [tortured]: [but if his friend does him wrong], his whole life will be confounded by distrust and completely upset (*Sent. Vat.* lvi-lvii).

As well, Epicurus understands friendship to be a source of practical aid: "He is no friend who is continually asking for help, or he who never associates help with friendship,"[93] although usefulness is not the basis for friendship: "All friendship is desirable in itself, though it starts from the need of help."[94] Moreover, Diogenes Laertius attributes Epicurus with saying that on occasion, the wise man will die for a friend.[95]

The chief aim of life among the Stoics was to achieve εὐδαιμονία, as it was among many other ancient philosophers. However, in addition to wholeness and self-sufficiency, the Stoics placed particular emphasis upon virtue as an essential requirement for εὐδαιμονία, for "virtue is the state of mind which tends to make the whole of life harmonious."[96] The happy person, then, must be a virtuous person for whom all other things, including health, beauty, wealth, fame etc. ... are a matter of

---

[90] Hock ("An Extraordinary Friend,"148-57) details all of these aspects of Polycharmus's friendship with Chaereas.
[91] Hock, "An Extraordinary Friend," 156.
[92] *Chaer.* 8.8.12; Hock, "An Extraordinary Friend," 155.
[93] Epicurus, *Sent. Vat.* xxxix.
[94] Epicurus, *Sent. Vat.* xxiii.
[95] Diogenes Laertius, *Lives of Emminent Philosophers* 10.120 (LCL; trans. R.D. Hicks; London: Heinemann; New York: G.P. Putnam, 1925).
[96] Diogenes Laertius, *Lives* 7.89.

indifference.⁹⁷ These latter things are not rejected by the Stoics; rather, they simply do not rank as prerequisites for εὐδαιμονία in the manner that virtue does. For the Stoic, the wise person must be self-sufficient and as such, detached from the external changes in circumstances that life inexorably brings.

Although the Stoics accept and promote friendship, it is also ultimately a matter of indifference in comparison to virtue. Only those who are virtuous, the wise, can have and be friends as they are the sole people capable of the moral commitment required for friendship.

> Friendship, they [the Stoics] declare, exists only between the wise and good, by reason of their likeness to one another. And by friendship they mean a common use of all that has to do with life, wherein we treat our friends as we should ourselves. They argue that a friend is worth having for his own sake and that it is a good thing to have many friends. But among the bad there is, they hold, no such thing as friendship, and thus no bad man has a friend (*Lives* 7.124).

The Stoics, as is clear from Diogenes, echo many of the typical characteristics of friendship, including the notion of similarity between friends (they both must be virtuous) and the idea that one must treat one's friends just as one would treat one's self, even to the point of dying for the friend.⁹⁸ Yet there is a seeming conundrum here. How is one to reconcile the notion of friendship with the austere self-sufficiency of the Stoic sages? "Would someone as free from affect as the sage care sufficiently about others to be a real friend or be likely to have others take him to be a friend?"⁹⁹

Glen Lesses argues that these two things, friendship and self-sufficiency, can accommodate one another within Stoic thought. Because friendship requires that both friends are virtuous, "one could infer that what a sage values in friendship is the moral virtue of another."¹⁰⁰ Thus, not only could any moral person be friends with another moral person, "the individual and concrete personality of the friend becomes relatively unimportant for friendship."¹⁰¹ Friendship is rendered impersonal because its basis is moral virtue, and not powerful

---

⁹⁷ *Lives* 7.102-107.

⁹⁸ Epictetus, *Diatr.* 2.7.3. For more comparison between the Stoics and other Greek notions of friendship, see Hutter, *Politics as Friendship*, 124-25.

⁹⁹ Lesses, "Austere Friends," 63.

¹⁰⁰ Lesses, "Austere Friends," 70.

¹⁰¹ Horst Hutter, *Politics as Friendship: The Origins of Classical Notions of Politics in the Theory and Practice of Friendship* (Waterloo: Wilfred Laurier University Press), 128. The Stoics, unlike Aristotle and others, argue that one can have many friends if there are many virtuous people.

affection and attraction for another particular human being. Such a foundation for friendship therefore reduces the threat to one's self-sufficiency because (1) one friend cannot harm another as both must necessarily be virtuous; and (2) when one does something for a friend it is no different than "acting from a settled disposition to be virtuous"[102] – one is no more vulnerable in acting on behalf of a friend than when acting from a sense of moral duty.

What about when friends die? For the Stoics, a wise person is again indifferent to life and death.[103] The sage is not vulnerable to passionate emotions; he or she is immune to grief "seeing that grief is irrational contraction of the soul, as Apollodorus says in his *Ethics*."[104] Moreover, grief is less likely to overcome a Stoic because the basis of his or her friendship for another is again, not the particular characteristics of the other person, not a result of spending time together and nurturing the friendship, as Aristotle would have it, but a proclivity for moral virtue. It may seem harsh in our context, but for the Stoics, when friend a dies, he or she can be easily replaced by another virtuous person.[105] As Lesses aptly titles his article, the Stoics were "austere friends."

Neopythagoreans expected friends to be loyal and to provide aid in times of need. Iamblichus, *On the Pythagorean Life*[106] (which here relies upon the 4th century BCE source, *On the Pythagorean Life*, by Aristoxenus) describes the friendships between Phintias and Damon, and Cleinias and Prorus, as exemplary.[107] According to Iamblichus, Pythagoras encouraged friendship of all with all:

> friendship of gods for humans, through piety and worship based upon knowledge, ... friendship of people for one another: fellow-citizens through a healthy respect for law, different peoples through a proper understanding of nature, a man with his wife and children and brothers and intimates through unswerving partnership; in short, friendship of all for all, including some of the non-rational animals through justice and natural connection and association; even the mortal body's pacifi-

---

[102] Lesses, "Austere Friends," 71.

[103] Lesses, "Austere Friends," 71, who refers to *Lives* 7.102.

[104] *Lives* 7.118.

[105] In contrast to this Stoic perspective is the view of George Orwell ("Reflections on Gandhi," *The Penguin Essays of George Orwell* [London: Penguin, 1984] 469), who in his critique of Gandhi, wrote that part of the essence of being human is "that one does not seek perfection ... and that one is prepared in the end to be defeated and broken up by life, which is the inevitable price of fastening one's love upon other human individuals."

[106] I am using the translation of Iamblichus's *On the Pythagorean Life* by Gillian Clark (Liverpool: Liverpool University Press, 1989).

[107] Iamblichus, *VP* 234-240.

cation and reconciliation of opposite powers hidden within itself, through health and a lifestyle and practice of temperance ... (*VP* 229).

Regarding this point, Johan Thom has made the very significant observation that in each case, φιλία requires specific virtues, whether it be piety, respect, justice or temperance, and that φιλία has transcended all limits and become "truly cosmic."[108]

For the Pythagoreans, this cosmic friendship did not translate into concrete friendships with everyone. They did think that one should choose one's friends carefully, after weighing the person's character.[109] Furthermore, stories survive which reveal a strong element of exclusivity among Pythagoreans in that they would only befriend those who shared their unconventional lifestyle. Iamblichus and Porphyry (in part)[110] relate the tale of two Pythagoreans, Myllias and Timycha, a husband and wife, who are captured by the tyrant Dionysios. Dionysios offers them the joint rule of his kingdom if they will tell him why Pythagoreans would rather die than tread on beans. The two refuse to tell him and Dionysios orders Myllias to be taken away and the pregnant Timycha to be tortured, thinking that she will easily relent without her husband to protect her. Timycha, however, bites her own tongue off so that she will not "spill the beans," so to speak, and the moral of the tale is that these Pythagoreans would risk anything in order to refuse friendship with outsiders, even kings.

Such anecdotes support claims that Pythagorean friendship may have consisted more of "sectarian solidarity"[111] than personal affection. Certainly, if the other claims about Pythagoreans are true – that they made a five-year vow of silence, were strict vegetarians, and shared all their goods – it must have been difficult to extend bonds of friendship outside of the circle, for external relationships would undoubtedly threaten the solidarity of the group. It could be, as has been suggested, that the Pythagoreans' lofty notion of friendship of all for all was in reality only intended for members of their coterie.[112]

Plutarch, in contrast, did not think one could be friends with everyone in either theory or practice. True friends are rare, he thinks, for they must be constant and loyal. It is not possible to have many friends, for

---

[108] Johan C. Thom, "'Harmonious Equality': The Topos of Friendship in Neopythagorean Writings," *Greco-Roman Perspectives*, 97-99.

[109] See Thom, "Harmonious Equality," 87, who refers to the *Sentences of Clitarchus* 88.

[110] Iamblichus, *VP* 192-94. For Porphyry's *Life of Pythagoras*, see the translation by Edouard des Places (Collection des universités de France; Paris: Les Belles Lettres, 1982).

[111] Konstan, *Friendship in the Classical World*, 115.

[112] Konstan, *Friendship in the Classical World*, 15.

one cannot share so much with so many people without becoming like a chameleon or cuttlefish, which takes on the colour of whatever rock to which it clings.[113] Because friendship "seeks for a fixed and steadfast character which does not shift about," a genuine friend is "something rare and hard to find."[114] In this sense, Plutarch is quite similar to the classical writers, especially Aristotle. Indeed, among his lists of true friends, pairs such as Achilles and Patroclus, Phintias and Damon, and Orestes and Pylades, appear.[115] Plutarch objects to specific vices such as envy (φθόνος) and criticizes those who fall into emulation (ζῆλος),[116] for true friends should bear one another's successes and failures with equanimity.[117] In fact, as Troels Engberg-Pedersen argues, Plutarch appears to regard true, honest friendship as the "apogee" of a moral system; "the place where that system is realized."[118]

Cicero's fictional dialogue, the *Laelius*, draws upon these characteristics of Greek friendship.[119] For example, he echoes Xenophon's and the Stoics' conviction that friendship cannot exist except among good, virtuous people.[120] For Cicero, friendship is based upon goodwill: "if you remove good will from friendship the very name of friendship is

---

[113] Plutarch, *Amic. mult.* 96F.

[114] *Amic. mult.* 97B.

[115] *Amic. mult.* 93E.

[116] *Adul. amic.* 54C. Earlier authors, such as Aristotle, however, thought that emulation (ζῆλος) was virtuous for good people should want to possess worthy goods (*Rhet.* 2.11). See Christina Viano, "Competitive Emotions and *Thumos* in Aristotle's Rhetoric," *Envy, Spite and Jealousy. The Competitive Emotions in Ancient Greece* (ed. David Konstan and N. Keith Rutter; Edinburgh Leventis Studies 2; Edinburgh: Edinburgh University Press, 2003) 85-97. This view changes in the 4th century BCE, however, when authors begin to characterize emulation as a vice along with envy. Christopher Gill ("Is Rivalry a Virtue or a Vice?" *Envy, Spite, Jealousy*, 49) argues that this shift is in part due to changes in the notion of the human good or happiness: "when human happiness is identified with 'external goods' (or a combination of 'internal' and 'external' goods), competition for these – inevitably limited – goods is assumed to be the normal human state and the correlated rivalrous emotions are regarded as, in principle, normal, though they take virtuous or defective forms. Where happiness is located in solely in 'internal goods', which are sometimes seen as universally available, competition and the rivalrous emotions are presented as necessarily misguided."

[117] *Adul. amic.* 54C.

[118] Troels Engberg-Pedersen, "Plutarch to Prince Philopappus on How to Tell a Flatterer from a Friend," *Friendship, Flattery and Frankness of Speech*, 235.

[119] For a brief discussion of some of the connections between the *Laelius* and Greek philosophy, see J.G.F. Powell, *Cicero: Laelius, On Friendship and the Dream of Scipio* (Warminster: Aris and Phillips, 1990) 2-5.

[120] *Lael.* 18 (LCL; trans. William Armistead Falconer; London, Cambridge, MA: Harvard University Press, 1923).

gone," and "without virtue friendship cannot exist at all."[121] Like many philosophers before him, Cicero grants that such virtuous friendships are rare,[122] for there is a "dearth" of people who are "firm, steadfast and constant," all required features of a genuine friend.[123] These virtues of loyalty (*fides*) and constancy (*constantia*) are significant Ciceronian ingredients for a friendship, and he refers to these qualities on a number of occasions throughout his dialogue.[124]

Testing is another important element that determines whether a friend is genuine or not. A person may initially appear to be a friend through their generous offerings of goodwill and support, but in the end they may prove highly unreliable. As Cicero explains: "Hence it is the part of wisdom to check the headlong rush of goodwill as we would that of a chariot, and thereby so manage friendship that we may in some degree put the dispositions of friends, as we often do those of horses, to a preliminary test."[125] The philosopher is not naive; he knows that many may deliver sweet words but are ultimately unreliable, even deceitful. It comes as no surprise, therefore, that he has a particular dislike for flatterers, whom he thinks hypocritical, counterfeit and fickle: "nothing is to be considered a greater bane of friendship than fawning, cajolery, or flattery."[126] He refers to this vice more than once, and usually when he is providing a contrast to the honest and forthright speech that is required of friends. Cicero considers frank criticism, intended for the betterment of one's friend, to be "characteristic of true friendship"[127] and flattery its nemesis.

Turning to ancient Jewish writers, an important contributor to the discussion of friendship is Ben Sira. This author depends upon a variety of sources, including non-Jewish literature,[128] but he also

> vigorously oppose[s] any compromise of Jewish values and traditions (cf. 2:12) and pronounce[s] woe to those who forsook Israel's Law (4:18), with which wisdom itself, in his view, [is] to be identified (24:23).[129]

---

[121] *Lael.* 20, 21.
[122] *Lael.* 64.
[123] *Lael.* 62.
[124] See, for example, *Lael.* 65.
[125] *Lael.* 63.
[126] *Lael.* 91.
[127] *Lael.* 91.
[128] See Theophil Middendorp, *Die Stellung Jesu Ben Siras zwischen Judentum und Hellenismus* (Leiden: E.J. Brill, 1973); Jack T. Sanders, *Ben Sira and Demotic Wisdom* (SBLMS 28; Chico, CA: Scholars, 1983).
[129] Patrick W. Skehan and Alexander A. Di Lella, *The Wisdom of Ben Sira* (AB 39; New York: Doubleday, 1987) 46.

Some of Ben Sira's statements about friendship likely did not emerge from Jewish traditions,[130] but judging from the attention he pays to the topic, it is entirely compatible with his Jewish identity and convictions.

Ben Sira's advice about friendship, at least as it has been translated into Greek by his grandson, exhibits a number of similarities to Greek views of the relationship. First, as with many of the writings on friendship that we have encountered so far, Ben Sira refers to the rarity of faithful friends. A faithful friend (φίλος πιστός) is precious, provides shelter and is the medicine of life (φάρμακον ζωῆς) (6:14-16). A true friend will never betray the confidence of his[131] friend, for if he does, he has destroyed the friendship (27:16-21). Moreover, Ben Sira counsels that one should remain true to a friend when he is poor or in trouble, for when he is prosperous, he will share his wealth (22:13-26). In this instance it appears that the author has self-interested reasons for remaining true to the friend; as Patrick Skehan and Alexander A. Di Lella comment, the "advice Ben Sira gives on friendship is quite pragmatic and self-serving."[132]

Genuine friendship for Ben Sira does require, however, shared moral responsibilities. He states that firm friendship will be between two people who both fear the Lord (6:17). He gives instructions not only about loyalty to friends but on how one should speak to a friend. One should straightforwardly question a friend if there is reason to think that he had done something wrong, or said something injurious. If he had, the questioning would prevent him from doing it or saying it again (19:13-14). One thus has a responsibility to give a friend a chance to defend himself and to improve upon his behaviour, while at the same time to "make allowances for the friend's failure,"[133] for who has not sinned with his tongue (19:16b)? Friends should also be realistic and honest in the way in which they deal with one another, and remember that even if they "open their mouth against a friend" (22:22), they can be reconciled. But one should not make promises to a friend (ἐπαγγελλόμενος φίλῳ) out of shame, for this will lead to enmity (20:23),[134] nor should one display contempt toward or betray a friend,

---

[130] Sanders (*Ben Sira and Demotic Wisdom*, 29-38) argues that Ben Sira's sections on drinking and friendship show dependence upon Theognis.

[131] Ben Sira is referring to exclusively male relationships.

[132] Skehan and Di Lella, *The Wisdom of Ben Sira*, 317.

[133] Daniel J. Harrington, "Sage Advice about Friendship," *TBT* 32 (1994) 82.

[134] Ingrid Krammer ("Scham im Zusammenhang mit Freundschaft," *Freundschaft bei Ben Sira* [BZAW 244; ed. Friedrich V. Reiterer; Berlin, New York: Walter de Gruyter, 1996] 198-99) has observed how Ben Sira brings together the concepts of shame and friendship several times throughout his work. She argues that for Ben Sira there is a con-

for then the friend will leave (22:22). Although he does not explicitly refer to παρρησία, Ben Sira sounds a little similar to Philodemus, whom we will discuss in a later chapter, and who emphasizes the correction of friends, but not to the point of insult and alienation.

Returning to the emphasis upon testing, as raised by Cicero, Ben Sira too, is deeply concerned that one not make friends too hastily. A person should test a new friend, and put him through a period of trial (πειρασμός) before trusting him (6:7). Probably the optimal test of friendship is to determine whether the prospective friend will be supportive in adversity, for Ben Sira states that we cannot know our friends in our prosperity (12:8). The sage is aware of those who behave as friends when one is successful but subsequently disappear when disaster strikes (6:8; 12:9); in other words, he is quite familiar with the notion of a "fair weather friend" and hence cautions against immediately placing confidence in people who approach with friendly words.

Scholars have argued that friendship is highly significant for some of Ben Sira's social, and particularly his theological, convictions. Friedrich V. Reiterer, for example, is convinced that although friendship is subordinate to the themes of the wisdom of the aged, and fear of God, it is central to Ben Sira's notion of a good society.[135] William H. Irwin, moreover, has argued that human friendship is an analogy to Ben Sira's concept of the fear of God. Irwin demonstrates how Ben Sira's ideas of right relationship with God and right relationship with a friend are presented along similar lines, there being the requirements of faithfulness, trust, and a period of testing in both types of relationships.[136] Furthermore, Jeremy Corley has observed that "although the sage's friendship pericopes do not often mention God, they have a theological underpinning which relates his teachings on the topic to Israel's faith."[137] Friendship is obviously of great importance for Ben Sira, just as it is for his non-Jewish contemporaries. Moreover, it is theologically grounded in faith in God.

Ben Sira is not the only Jewish writer to stress the virtues of friends. The *Sentences of Pseudo-Phocylides*, for example, states that one should

---

cept of "rechte Scham" or proper shame which represents the loyalty and trust which one should have in order to preserve a friendship, as well as "falsche Scham" which is faithless and only serves to destroy relationships.

[135] Friedrich V. Reiterer, "Gelungene Freundschaft als tragende Säule einer Gesellschaft," *Freundschaft bei Ben Sira*, 133-69.

[136] William H. Irwin, "Fear of God, the Analogy of Friendship and Ben Sira's Theodicy," *Bib* 76 (1995) 551-59.

[137] Jeremy Corley, *Ben Sira's Teaching on Friendship* (BJS 316; Providence: Brown University, 2002) 218.

"love your friends until death, for faithfulness is a good thing,"[138] while the *Testament of Dan* criticizes anger, stating that the angry person is not able to acknowledge a friend.[139] References to friends and friendship are found throughout Josephus's writings.[140] Thus while Jewish texts do not elaborate on friendship as much as Graeco-Roman ones, they display familiarity and general admiration for the qualities that friends were to manifest.

Turning to the New Testament and early Christian literature, Paul's letter to the Philippians has been mined the most for friendship language and ideas, although other texts, such as Galatians and Romans, are thought to allude to the virtues of friendship.[141] In particular, the Christ hymn in Phil 2:6-11, although probably pre-Pauline, embodies the ideal of friendship, which is a willingness to suffer and die for others. The ordeal which the hymn describes, suggests L. Michael White, "is being portrayed, at least in part, as an all-surpassing act of selfless love – that is, the supreme virtue of friendship."[142] Abraham J. Malherbe explores Paul's notions of self-sufficiency and friendship in Philippians and argues that Paul's description of his own self-sufficiency in Phil 4:11 recalls Greek philosophical notions that true friendship does not emerge from need but from virtue.[143]

The most striking reference to friendship in the Gospel of John is the statement in 15:13 that there is no greater love than to lay down one's life for one's φίλος. Again, this aspect of friendship has surfaced in various ancient texts,[144] but it seems especially significant for the Johannine community,[145] as this is the behaviour expected of the Good

---

[138] van der Horst, *The Sentences of Pseudo-Phocylides*, 252.

[139] For translation and commentary, see H.W. Hollander and M. de Jonge, *The Testaments of the Twelves Patriarchs. A Commentary* (SVTP 8: Leiden: Brill, 1985) 278-80.

[140] See Karl Heinrich Rengstorf, *A Complete Concordance to Flavius Josephus*, vol. IV (Leiden: Brill, 1983) 303-307.

[141] For Paul's use of friendship *topoi* in Galatians, see Hans Dieter Betz, *Galatians* (Hermeneia; Philadelphia: Fortress, 1979) 220-37. Hans-Josef Klauck ("Kirche als Freundesgemeinschaft? Auf Spurensuche im Neuen Testament" *MTZ* 42 [1991]10) has noticed the theme of dying for one's friend in Rom 5:6-8, although he thinks that Paul has altered this by claiming that Christ died even for sinners and the ungodly.

[142] L. Michael White, "Morality between Two Worlds," 213.

[143] Abraham J. Malherbe, "Paul's Self-Sufficiency," *Friendship, Flattery and Frankness of Speech*, 136-37.

[144] For example, Aristotle, *Eth. Nic.* 9.8.9; Epictetus, *Diatr.* 2.7.3; Plutarch, *Adv. Col.* 8.111b.

[145] For an evaluation of this theme in John, see Josephine Massyngbaerde Ford, *Redeemer, Friend and Mother: Salvation in Antiquity and in the Gospel of John* (Minneapolis: Fortress, 1997) 168-86.

Shepherd (10:11, 15, 17-18) and then it is presented again in 1 John 3:16, as something community members must be willing to do for one another. Mitchell observes how the stress upon love for community members, represented by a willingness to die for one another, is quite different from the command to love one's enemies. This emphasis may have emerged from the sectarian nature of this community and the threat of persecution which may have required members to die for one another.[146]

Early Christian non-biblical literature also displays a high regard for the virtues associated with friendship, although during the fourth century and later, some Christians tended to avoid the classical words for friendship, φιλία and *amicitia*, in favour of ἀγαπή and *caritas*.[147] Despite this decline of classical words for friendship, aspects of Greek notions of friendship still surface among Christian writers, but they are sometimes made secondary to Christian ideas. For example, Clement of Alexandria is striking in his emphasis upon friendship as an important part of Christian discipleship, and he accepted Aristotle's taxonomy of friendships. He writes, "the Lord did not say, 'give,' or 'provide,' or 'benefit,' or 'help,' but 'make a friend (φίλος);' and a friend is made not from one gift, but from complete relief and long companionship."[148] For this early Christian writer, friendship (at least, friendship with other Christians) clothed in classical philosophical garb was not only acceptable, it was precious.

By the fourth century, aspects of the so-called "pagan" concept of friendship had become problematic for some Christian writers, while others were able to integrate friendship into their Christian understanding of human relationships. There is no evidence that Christian doctrine directly clashed with Greek notions of friendship; rather, some

---

[146] Mitchell, "Greet the Friends by Name," *Greco-Roman Perspectives on Friendship*, 258-59. Sharon H. Ringe (*Wisdom's Friends. Community and Christology in the Fourth Gospel* [Louisville: Westminster John Knox, 1999] 64-83) has also observed how friendship is related to the ecclesiology of the Johannine community.

[147] Robert Joly, *Le Vocabulaire chrétien de l'amour est-il original?* Φιλειν et ἀγαπᾶν dans le grec antique (Brussels: Presses Universitaires, 1968) has studied the history of the word φιλέω and found that it declines in usage in non-Christian literature *before* the rise of the church. Konstan ("Problems," 102 n. 39) notes, however, that despite this decline, some early Christian writers "perceived a tension between the abstract nouns *agapé* and *philia* in ways foreign to pagan texts, and that these same writers tended to avoid the term *philos* (or *amicus*) in contexts relating to Christian love."

[148] Clement of Alexandria, *Quis div. salv.* 32 (LCL; trans. G.W. Butterworth; Cambridge, MA: Harvard University Press; London: Heinemann, 1968).

tensions arose over specific values associated with friendship and the ideas and sentiments that some Christians wished to emphasize.[149]

The word "some" is important here, as Christians from the same time and region did not always share similar views. Some of the church fathers wholeheartedly embraced friendship. A good example is the contrast in ideas of two Cappadocians, Basil of Caesarea and Gregory of Nazianzus, whose friendship became a model for subsequent Byzantine writers.[150] Gregory uses φίλος regularly and refers to "pagan" sources as authorities on friendship with no compunction.[151] In a letter to Sophronios,[152] he celebrates the fact, as did the Stoics, that friends are united by virtue, while in his letter to Palladios he says "If someone asked me, 'What is the best thing in this life?' I would respond, 'Friends.'"[153] Gregory also discusses friendship in Christian terms. In a letter which was probably addressed to Gregory of Nyssa, he states that all who live according to God and who follow the same gospel are friends (φίλοι) and relations.[154] Nor did Gregory see any incongruity between the Christian emphasis upon loving everyone and an intimate personal relationship between two particular individuals. Carolinne White sums up this dimension of Gregory's perspective very well:

> Even [Gregory's] belief that it was possible and legitimate to love some men more strongly than others is expressed in Christian terms and he appears not to have seen any conflict between man's duty to love all men and his desire for close friendships. In Ep. 147 he justifies his special love for Nicoboulos by saying that he is following God's example, for did not God, the creator of all, choose one race as his own but was not deemed unjust for so doing? Such special love could co-exist with a more general, extensive philanthropy which the very nature of Christ, the members of whose body all Christians are, teaches us to practice.[155]

---

[149] Konstan, "Problems," 104.

[150] Raymond Van Dam, "Emperor, Bishops, and Friends in Later Antique Cappadocia," *JTS* n.s. 37 (1986) 73 n. 99, who refers to F. Tinnefeld, "Freundschaft in den Briefen des Michael Psellos. Theorie und Wirklichkeit," *JOEByz* 22 (1973) 151-68.

[151] White (*Christian Friendship*, 70-72) traces the influence of classical authors, including Homer, Hesiod, and Theognis, upon Gregory's views of friendship, while Konstan ("Problems," 104) demonstrates the Aristotelian and Stoic influences upon Gregory.

[152] Gregory of Nazianzus, *Ep.* 39.1 (*Saint Grégoire de Nazianze. Lettres* (2 vols.; ed. and trans. Paul Gallay; Paris: Les Belles Lettres, 1964, 1967).

[153] *Ep.* 103.1.

[154] *Ep.* 11.2.

[155] White, *Christian Friendship in the Fourth Century*, 72.

Gregory was thus able to fuse both classical and Christian concepts together in his view of friendship.[156]

Basil also draws upon some of the classical notions of friendship, as we will see below, but he was a little more suspicious of close friendships as he thought that they might interfere with Christian community life. This may have been a factor in the sometimes difficult relationship between Basil and Gregory. Basil was suspicious of close friendships in the coenobitic communities because he thought that they could "lead to a loss of equality among the members of that community and a consequent growth of mistrust and jealousy, even of hatred."[157] Although Basil appears to have maintained a sincere affection for Gregory, Gregory understood that Basil proposed things to him not for Gregory's sake alone, but for the sake of the church. This lead to feelings of betrayal in Gregory, as if Basil did not give priority to their friendship, and Gregory, in turn, did things which provoked Basil's resentment. The reasons for all of Basil's and Gregory's battles may never be entirely clear, but it seems likely that at least one was this differing attitude toward friendship, and its importance in relation to allegiance to the community of Christians as a whole. Moreover, it is of note that Basil often uses the language of brotherhood instead of that of friendship, and substitutes ἀγάπη for φιλία. This is likely because Basil would prefer to be identified as a brother in the faith, rather than as a friend who has earned his status because of his own merits.[158] The classical notion of friendship emphasized the virtuous nature of each friend, but for Basil, such an emphasis may have clashed with his notion of Christian humility and thus he wished to avoid an association with friendship.[159]

Like Gregory of Nazianzus, other famous Christians from the fourth century did not resist classical notions of friendship. However, they did not allow theories of friendship to jeopardize their commitment to Christ and to the Church. Ambrose of Milan's *De officiis ministrorum* models itself upon Cicero's *De officiis* and *Laelius*, although Ambrose also uses biblical texts to support his views of how Christian clergy should behave. The bishop devotes considerable space to friendship in

---

[156] See also, David Konstan, "How to Praise a Friend. St. Gregory of Nazianzus's Funeral Oration for St. Basil the Great," in *Greek Biography and Panegyric in Late Antiquity* (eds. Tomas Hägg and Philip Rousseau; Transformation of the Classical Heritage 31; Berkeley and Los Angeles: University of California Press, 2000) 160-79.

[157] White, *Christian Friendship in the Fourth Century*, 82.

[158] Konstan, *Friendship in the Classical World*, 161.

[159] As Basil (*Ep.* 56) writes: "and if we are filled with the conceit of empty pride and arrogance, then we are fallen into the sin of the devil from which there is no escape."

this document, and he refers to it with the words *amicitia* and *caritas*, as if the two terms were interchangeable. He also encourages openness and even the disclosure of personal intimacies among friends, which would promote "a harmony of sentiment and collective loyalty within a community organized around a shared vision of life,"[160] again reminiscent of the philosophical schools. However, Ambrose is very clear that one's friendships should "never interfere with one's love of and service to God. The claims of God must always take precedence."[161] Thus despite his recognition and admiration for the classical descriptions of friendship, Ambrose places a limit upon such relationships if they threaten one's allegiance and love of God, or, one would surmise, if they disrupted community life.

John Chrysostom displays awareness and acceptance of friendship as evidenced in his treatise, *De Sacerdotio*, which begins: "I had many genuine and true friends (φίλοι), men who understood the laws of friendship, and faithfully observed them."[162] In his second homily on 1 Thess 2, Chrysostom praises true friendship, which is obtained between those who possess "one soul" (ὁμόψυχοι), and who would willingly die for one another. However (and particularly after he joined the priesthood), friendship is still subordinate to the spiritual love of God, for "it alone is indissoluble."[163]

The examination of Jerome's life and writings under the rubric of friendship leads to some almost bittersweet observations. Here was a person who placed a high value upon friendship, but then came to distrust it because he believed that his friends had failed him. He may have only had a "superficial knowledge" of Greek literature,[164] but he was probably well acquainted with and admiring of Cicero and other Latin writers, as he paraphrases the *Laelius* with the words, "A friendship which can cease is never genuine," and Horace, when he refers to a friend as being a "part of my soul."[165] Jerome did have numerous close friendships throughout his life and appears to have truly needed

---

[160] Konstan, *Friendship in the Classical World*, 152.

[161] Elizabeth Clark, *Jerome, Chrysostom, and Friends. Essays and Translations* (Studies in Women and Religion 1; New York and Toronto: Edwin Mellen, 1979) 42, with reference to Ambrose, *De off. min.* 3.132. See also, White, *Christian Friendship in the Fourth Century*, 127.

[162] Chrysostom, *De Sac.* 1.1 (The Nicene and Post-Nicene Fathers, first series, vol. 9 [ed. Philip Schaff; trans. W.R.W. Stephens & T.P. Brandram; New York: Christian Literature Company, 1889]).

[163] Konstan, *Friendship in the Classical World*, 162.

[164] Clark, *Jerome, Chrysostom, and Friends*, 43.

[165] Jerome, *Ep.* 3; cited by White, *Christian Friendship in the Fourth Century*, 139.

people, as many of his letters reflect sincere affection for their recipients.[166] The problem was that Jerome, a notoriously difficult person, mistrusted those who did not agree with him, a fact which, in turn, alienated his friends.[167] When he increasingly sought an ascetic life of solitude, he became more disparaging of friendship. Thus, there is no evidence that Jerome specifically repudiated classical definitions and descriptions of friendship; rather, he regarded human relationships, at least in theory, as unreliable and secondary to a life of solitary asceticism.

Augustine, particularly in his later writings, emphasized *caritas* more than *amicitia*, but this does not mean that classical descriptions of *amicitia* could not inform his view of *caritas*, nor that human friendship was not important to him. Eoin Cassidy has shown that aspects of classical friendship influenced Augustine's view of Christian *caritas*.[168] Although Augustine's vision of Christian love was extended to all, and required no merit or testing, the intimacy, reciprocity and equality characteristic of Greek and Roman portrayals of friendship were key elements in his understanding of *caritas*.[169] For Augustine, such intimacy was also extended to Christ, with and through whom all Christians were joined. As he wrote to his friend Marcianus, "I did not really have you as a friend (*amicus*) until I clove to you in Christ."[170]

The person who had the greatest difficulty reconciling friendship and Christianity was the late fourth century Christian, Paulinus of Nola. In a letter to Pammachius, Paulinus contrasts their friendship (*amicitia*), which Konstan interprets to mean, "our version of what is usually called friendship,"[171] with their spiritual friendship (*caritas*) "which is produced by God as its source and is joined in a brotherhood of souls."[172] Similarly in his 51st epistle, Paulinus writes: "We have become known to each other not by human friendship but by divine grace and it is by the inner depths of Christ's love that we are joined."[173] The classical notion that true friendship was based upon

---

[166] See White, *Christian Friendship in the Fourth Century*, 130.

[167] White, *Christian Friendship in the Fourth Century*, 129.

[168] Eoin Cassidy, "The Recovery of Classical Ideal of Friendship in Augustine's Portrayal of *Caritas*," *The Relationship between Neoplatonism and Christianity* (ed. Thomas Finan & Vincent Twomey; Dublin: Four Courts, 1992) 127-40.

[169] See also, White, *Christian Friendship in the Fourth Century*, 185-217.

[170] Augustine, *Ep.* 258.1 (LCL; trans. James Houston Baxter; Cambridge, MA: Harvard University Press; London: Heinemann, 1930).

[171] Konstan, *Friendship in the Classical World*, 158.

[172] Translation of Paulinus's 13th epistle is by Konstan, *Friendship in the Classical World*, 158.

[173] Translation by White, *Christian Friendship in the Fourth Century*, 155.

virtue may also have been problematic for Paulinus, just as it was for Basil. Mutual admiration for one another's fine character was thought to be typical of Greek and Roman noble friendships, for such virtue bound friends together and maintained their bond. For Paulinus, however, the Christian should be modest and humble, and to presume to be virtuous would be arrogant. He portrays himself as a sinner in his letters, and consistently declares himself unworthy of the love that others have for him.[174] Such an emphasis is consistent, however, with the understanding of Christian *caritas*, which is offered to people regardless of their achievements.

In sum, we observe that up to, during and after the first century, qualities such as loyalty, generosity, reliability, equanimity, and sometimes a willingness to suffer and die for a friend are fairly consistently valued in the writings on friendship, whether they are found in Archaic Greece, the classical and Hellenistic ages, the Hebrew Bible, Hellenistic Judaism, the New Testament or early Christianity. The notion that true friends must be virtuous people and that friendship is not easy – that it requires a certain period of testing – also emerges. Hellenistic Jewish Christians such as Paul appealed to the virtues of friendship in his letters probably because he knew that this would be an effective means of communicating with his churches. Many patristic writers, moreover, embraced classical notions of friendship, but by the fourth century, there is some hesitancy in placing too much emphasis upon these virtues. Some Christian clerics, such as Basil, thought that intimate friendships based upon virtues could upset community life, or, as with Paulinus, they could distract from a life of humility. But overall, these characteristics of friendship were sufficiently widespread such that it would not be strange or unreasonable to think that the author of James, wherever he was writing from in the Mediterranean basin, would be familiar with such virtues.

One aspect of friendship closely related to these virtues was frank speech. However, given that the contexts for discussing this particular aspect of friendship was often that of flattery and the behaviour of clients in patron-client relationships, I will address the topic of frank speech in a subsequent chapter that explores the relationships between friendship, patronage and benefaction. But before moving to that chapter, it is important to discuss a few other aspects of friendship that emerge reasonably consistently in antiquity.

---

[174] Konstan, *Friendship in the Classical World*, 160.

"One Mind/Soul"

First, an intriguing expression that emerges often is that true friends share "one soul" or "one mind" (μία ψυχή). Just as friends share similar virtues, they are understood to think the same. This is anticipated in Homeric literature, although the precise phrase does not appear. In the *Iliad*, Agamemnon tells Odysseus that they think the same things (4.360-61), while in the *Odyssey* Nestor describes his friendship with Odysseus as one in which they were of one mind (3.126-29).[175] The idea is also alluded to in the Hebrew Bible, where, as we have seen, the notion of sharing a life or a soul (נפש) with a friend existed for the biblical writers, witnessed most explicitly in the description of David and Jonathan, whose souls were bound together (1 Sam 18:1).

The Greek phrase does emerge, however, with Aristotle. Aristotle uses strong language to describe friends: a friend is another self (ἄλλος αὐτός) and a person should feel "towards his friend in the same way as towards himself."[176] Aristotle quotes the proverb, "Friends have one soul (μία ψυχή) between them,"[177] which was apparently well-known.[178] In the *Eudemian Ethics*, this phrase underlines the fact that a man should relate to his friend just as he relates to himself:

> And wishing for the other to exist, and associating together, and sharing joy and grief, and 'being one spirit' (μία ψυχή) and being unable even to live without one another but dying together – for this is the case with the single individual, and he associates with himself in this way, – all these characteristics then belong to the good man in relation to himself (*Eth. Eud.* 7.6.8-13).

Such an understanding of friendship has many ramifications for how friends should be treated.[179] For example, a friend must forgo money if it means that his friend will gain, he must give up honours and offices

---

[175] See Fitzgerald, "Friendship in the Greek World," 21-23.
[176] *Eth. Nic.* 9.4.5.
[177] *Eth. Nic.* 9.8.2; *Eth. Eud.* 7.6.10.
[178] Electra describes her brother, Orestes, as her μία ψυχή in Euripides's *Orest.*1046.
[179] The notion of a friend as another self also has consequences for the understanding of Aristotle's moral philosophy as a whole. Some scholars argue that ultimately, Aristotle is interested in each person achieving his or her own εὐδαιμονία and thus that his moral theory is egoistic, whereas others think that Aristotle is interested not only in personal εὐδαιμονία but the εὐδαιμονία of friends as well. This interpretation understands Aristotle as an altruist and the idea that a friend is another self and thus should be treated as well as one treats one's own self is often used to support it. See Dennis McKerlie, "Friendship, Self-Love, and Concern for Others in Aristotle's Ethics," *Ancient Philosophy* 11 (1991) 85-100.

for his friend's sake, and indeed, friends should surrender their lives for one another, just as they should for their country.[180]

Likewise, Plutarch says that in friendship, there "must be no element unlike, uneven, or unequal, but all must be alike to engender agreement in words, counsels, opinions, and feelings, and it must be as if one soul (μία ψυχή) were apportioned among two or more bodies."[181] Philo also refers to the idea. He cites Deut 13:7 when he states that "in Moses' view a friend is so near that he differs not a whit from one's own soul, for he says, 'the friend, who is equal to thy soul.'"[182] Paul also refers to the notion of being "one soul" (μία ψυχή) with the Philippians (1:27), he asks them to be "fellow souls" (σύμψυχοι) in 2:2 and he ascribes to Timothy the status of being "of equal soul" (ἰσόψυχος) with himself (2:20).[183] Related to the "sameness of soul" concept is the notion that friends think the same thing, and Paul uses this idea twice, in 2:2 when he asks the Philippians to complete his joy by being of the same mind, and in 4:2, when he requests the same of Euodia and Syntyche. "In both cases, he is using the cultural idiom to exhort the Philippians in general, and Euodia and Syntyche in particular, to be friends."[184] In addition, the phrase appears in Acts to describe the early believers, who were ψυχὴ μία (4:32). Finally, Gregory of Nazianzus depicts his friendship with Basil as two bodies bound by "one soul" (μία ψυχή),[185] and even Basil, whom we saw was less at ease with individual friendships, comments that the saying "the friend is another self" was wise.[186]

The notion of sharing a soul also appears in Latin literature. Cicero writes that the friend is "another self" and that "the effect of friendship is to make, as it were, one soul [*unus animus*] out of many."[187] He objects to fickleness and changeability of character precisely because such inconsistency would prevent the unification of souls, as there would be no enduring loyalty or sincerity (*veritas*), "without which the word

---

[180] *Eth. Nic.* 9.8.9.
[181] *Adul. amic.* 96E.
[182] *Her.* 83.
[183] See Fitzgerald, "Philippians," 145.
[184] Fitzgerald, "Philippians," 146.
[185] Gregory of Nazianzus, *Or.* 43.20 (*Grégoire de Nazianze, Discours 42-43* [SC 348; ed. and trans. Jean Bernardi; Paris: Éditions du Cerf, 1992]).
[186] Basil, *Ep.* 83. For Basil's letters I am using the translation by Roy J. Defferrari (LCL; London: Heinemann; New York: Putnam: Cambridge, MA; Harvard University Press, 1926-34).
[187] *Lael.* 80; 92.

friendship can have no meaning."[188] Like Aristotle and Plutarch, Cicero thought that two friends could mingle their souls, such that one soul could be made out of two.[189] Minucius Felix reflects upon the positive aspects of friendship when he thinks about his departed friend, Octavius. Minucius remembers how he and his cherished friend shared similar likes and dislikes as if "a single mind" (*unam mentem*) had been divided into two.[190] Ambrose of Milan calls the friend a "second self" and states that it is natural for one to search for another with whom one can join souls.[191]

Thus this mingling of minds or souls becomes a significant idea by the first century, and continues on into the early Christian depictions of friendship. Although it does not appear in the letter of James, this phrase is significant background for exploring what the author might be getting at with the use of the phrase δίψυχος ("double-souled"), which a later chapter will address.

"All in Common"

Linked to the notion of friends sharing a mind or soul, is the idea that friends would share material goods in common. The saying attributed to Pythagoras – "friends have everything in common" – circulated widely in antiquity[192] but most of the sources for his words are from classical and Hellenistic sources. Philo refers to the phrase in his description of the Essenes and the Therapeutae,[193] and Paul, especially in Philippians, emphasizes κοινωνία, using the word or one of its cognates six times (1:5,7; 2:2; 3:10; 4:14-15) throughout the letter.[194] Gregory of Nazianzus refers to the proverb, "the possessions of friends are in common" (κοινὰ τὰ τῶν φίλων) as the "rule of friendship."[195] Likewise, when he writes of friends giving and receiving, Dio Chrysostom quotes the proverb "'Common are the possessions of friends'" and concludes

---

[188] *Lael.* 92.

[189] *Lael.* 81.

[190] Minucius Felix, *Oct.* 1.3 (LCL; trans. Gerald H. Rendall [based on the unfinished version by W.C.A. Kerr] Cambridge, MA: Harvard University Press; London: Heinemann, 1960).

[191] Ambrose, *Off.* 3.22.133 (*Omnia quae extant opera* 7 [Collectio SS. Eccleisiae Patrum 60; ed. D.A.B. Caillau; Paris: Apud Parent Desbarres, 1839]).

[192] Diogenes Laertius (*Lives* 8.10) claims that the historian Timaeus of Tauromenium (4th-3rd cent. BCE) attributes these sayings to Pythagoras.

[193] For the Essenes, see *Prob.* 85-87; for the Therapeutae, see *Contempl.* 13-17.

[194] See Fitzgerald, "Philippians,"146.

[195] *Ep.* 31.1.

that "when the good have good things, these will certainly be held in common."[196]

The author of Acts has perhaps one of the most famous references to this phrase, as the early believers are said to have shared "all things in common" (ἅπαντα κοινά) (2:44; 4:32). In a close study of friendship traditions in Luke-Acts Alan Mitchell concludes that the evangelist deployed these traditions as a vehicle "to encourage upper status people in the community to benefit those beneath them."[197] Luke promoted friendship within the early church communities to the extent that he wanted those of different degrees of wealth and status to bridge their differences and become friends with one another. Concretely for Luke, friendship meant that those of greater means would have to give up some of their wealth for the sake of the entire Christian community. Such a practice was not unheard of, but as has been mentioned, ἅπαντα κοινά, despite its wide circulation, did not necessarily manifest itself in the form of renouncing one's wealth for the sake of another. Philosophers such as Aristotle, Cicero, Seneca and Plutarch invoked the saying κοινὰ τὰ φίλων, and advocated generosity toward others, but not to the extent that they would forsake their own personal wealth, nor in order to obliterate the status divisions which existed in their society. Theirs was an ethic of friendship, but one largely limited to a world of educated elites who wanted to preserve their ability to help their friends, and thus maintain their rights to private property.[198]

Mitchell provides seven reasons in support of his thesis that Luke is going farther than the philosophers referred to above, and advocating a friendship community which destroys distinctions in wealth and status.[199] First, Luke expects wealthier Christians to help the less fortunate with no expectation of a return (Lk 6:34-35; 14:12-14; Acts 20:35). Next, in the two summaries in Acts 2:44-47 and 4:32-37, Luke uses egalitarian friendship language, such as the maxims about sharing a soul or mind, and sharing possessions, to emphasize unity and harmony in the Christian community. Third, in these summaries Luke alludes to traditions from the LXX, for example, the union of heart and soul (Deut 4:29; cf. Acts 4:32) which would place "the equality of the

---

[196] Dio Chrysostom, *De Regn*. 3.110 (trans. J.W. Cohoon; LCL; Cambridge, MA: Harvard University Press; London: Heinemann, 1961).

[197] Alan C. Mitchell, "'Greet the Friends by Name': New Testament Evidence for the Greco-Roman *Topos* on Friendship," *Greco-Roman Perspectives on Friendship*, 239.

[198] These philosophers' positions are sketched by Mitchell, "'Greet the Friends by Name,'" 244-46 and also in his article, "The Social Function of Friendship in Acts 2:44-47 and 4:32-37," *JBL* 111 (1992) 262-64.

[199] Mitchell, "'Greet the Friends by Name,'" 248-57.

friendship ideal in terms of religious obligation."[200] Then, Luke uses the image of Barnabas (Acts 4:36-37), a landowner, laying the money he made from the sale of his field at the apostles' feet. This is a striking image of status reversal, for Barnabas was likely a wealthy person while the apostles were poor fishers who had given up their possessions to follow Jesus (Lk 18:28). Mitchell's fifth piece of evidence is the example of Ananias and Sapphira, who, contrary to Barnabas, secretly attempt to keep a portion of the proceeds from their sale of land and die as a result (Acts 5:1-11). It is here, Mitchell suggests, that Luke may be leveling a critique at those who, such as the philosophers mentioned above, justified their personal wealth by stating that they needed it in order to help their friends. This rationalization is not acceptable to Luke. Sixth, Peter performs what is described as an act of benefaction (Acts 4:9) in Acts 3:1-10 when he heals a cripple, but unlike a typical benefactor, he expects nothing in return. This behaviour conforms well to Luke's description of believers in Lk 22:25-26 which contrasts authoritative benefactors with community leaders, who, rather than control others, must serve the rest of the community members. Finally, Luke provides various examples of people traversing social boundaries in Acts. As Mitchell points out, "the picture is one of people from differing statuses joining together, and, often, those of a higher status aiding those of a lower one."[201] Thus, if Mitchell is correct, Luke promoted the friendship ethic to such a degree that it could extend across social divisions, and, moreover, required the wealthier friends to forfeit their own personal property for the sake of the community of friends.

Friendship and Fictive Kinship Language

Attention to papyri and to inscriptions from ancient associations indicates that in addition to φίλος and φίλοι, friends would use fictive kinship language to refer to one another. Here Peter Arzt-Grabner's analysis of Greek papyri is very informative. He observes that ἀδελφός refers regularly in letters to people who are not biologically related such as business partners, officials and friends. He cites first century letters that clearly indicate that the "brother" is the sender's friend, one in particular referring to members of the recipient's biological family thus

---

[200] Mitchell, "'Greet the Friends by Name,'" 252.
[201] Mitchell, "'Greet the Friends by Name,'" 256-57.

2. Friendship in Antiquity

suggesting a close relationship between the sender and receiver.[202] After examining a wide spectrum of papyri, Arzt-Grabner concludes that the use of "brother" or "sister" was not a "standard" feature of a specific social relationship or that there was a specific causal relationship from one group to another for using these terms. Rather, business partners, officials and friends seem to have used fictive kinship terms to express "closeness, solidarity and some kind of bond of engagement."[203] "Brother" never emerges as an alternative to "friend" but "it is *used sometimes for* a *close* friend or partner or colleague."[204] Arzt-Grabner also indicates that there are "almost no certain examples for a metaphorical use of ἀδελφή."[205] This observation is interesting when we turn to James, for Jas 2:15 clearly refers to an ἀδελφή in a metaphorical sense.

Kinship language appears in inscriptions for ancient associations as well. Philip Harland's studies of Greek inscriptions reveal that often the association's members would refer to themselves as φίλοι, and that "friends" and "brothers" were used "almost interchangeably" within the evidence for Egyptian groups.[206] For Harland, the existence of familial language within associations of the Greek East (e.g. "brothers" for the members or "father" for the benefactor of the association) and the comparison of its use in papyri and other sources indicates that groups did not use such language purely formally or woodenly, but that "when a member of a guild called a fellow 'brother,' that member was (at times) expressing in down-to-earth terms relations of solidarity, affection, or friendship, indicating that the association was a second home."[207]

The question of why fictive kinship language is sometimes preferable to ancient writers when they are writing to or of a "friend" remains. Why not simply use φίλος all the time? Here, Harland refers to the

---

[202] Peter Arzt-Grabner, "'Brothers' and 'Sisters' in Documentary Papyri and in Early Christianity," *RivB* 50 (2002) 192-95. Papyri using "brother" for "friend" include *BGU* VIII 1874; *POxy* VII 2148; *SB* V 7661; *POxy* XLII 3057; *SB* XIV 11644.

[203] Arzt-Grabner, "'Brothers,'" 202.

[204] Arzt-Grabner, "'Brothers,'" 202.

[205] Arzt-Grabner, "'Brothers,'" 187.

[206] Philip A. Harland, "Familial Dimensions of Group Identity: 'Brothers' (Ἀδελφοί) in Associations of the Greek East," *JBL* 124 (2005) 500. In n. 27 Harland provides a list of associations from the Greek East (especially Asia Minor) that use φίλοι. These are *IGLAM* 798; *IIasos* 116; *IMagnaMai* 321; *IDidyma* 502; *IMylasa* 571-75; *TAM* V 93; *ISmyrna* 720; *MAMA* III 580, 780, 788; *IPontBithM* 57; *IPrusaOlymp* 24; *IAsMinLyk* I 69. This listing also appears in Harland's earlier book-length study (*Associations, Synagogues, and Congregations. Claiming a Place in Ancient Mediterranean Society* [Minneapolis: Fortress, 2003] 33 n. 4 [285] where he points out that the association would often designate itself as "the friends."

[207] Harland, "Familial," 513.

work of Reidar Aasgaard, who in turn, relies upon Plutarch for an explanation of why sibling language might be more effective than that of friendship.[208] Although friendship was a very important form of relationship for Plutarch, "most friendships are in reality shadows and imitations and images of that first friendship which Nature implanted in children toward parents and in brothers toward brothers."[209] Plutarch distinguishes between friendship and siblingship. This distinction helps us understand why many groups in the ancient world, including early Christian ones, would employ family language alternately or as a supplement to the language of friendship: it would further the bonds of solidarity and support that such groups sought.

Friendship with God

Thus far we have dealt with friendship on the human plane, but given the fact that James makes a direct statement that "friendship with the world is enmity with God" (Jas 4:4), attention to the possibility of human/divine friendship in ancient literature is requisite. We see that this idea appears in a variety of contexts although it does not receive nearly as much attention as friendship between humans.

Homer, for example, does not limit feelings of affection to human beings. Certain individuals in the epics, particularly kings and other leaders, enjoyed a special association with the gods, as Franz Dirlmeier has shown.[210] Such figures earned the title Διὶ φίλος. This is not to say that they were friends in the manner in which Achilles and Patroclus were, but simply that they were more "dear" or more "loved" by certain gods than most people. Often, those more dear to the gods had semi-divine parentage or had made considerable sacrifices to the gods.[211] Maurice Vidal, moreover, argues that the title was given to Homeric heroes not to indicate some sort of mystical bond between the god and the human, but to underline specific qualities of the hero, such as strength or beauty or wisdom.

> Dès lors, tout homme supérieur par quelque côté aux autres mortels sera par là semblable aux dieux (θεοειδής ἀμτόθεος, ἰσόθεος), divin lui-même (θεῖος), de race divine (διογενής, διοτρεφής) et aimé des

---

[208] See Reidar Aasgaard, *'My Beloved Brothers and Sisters!' Christian Siblingship in Paul* (Early Christianity in Context; London/New York: T & T Clark, 2004) ch. 6.

[209] Plutarch, *Frat. Amor* 479 D (LCL; trans. W.C. Hembold; Cambridge, MA, London: Harvard University Press, 1939).

[210] See Franz Dirlmeier, "ΘΕΟΦΙΛΙΑ - ΦΙΛΟΘΕΙΑ," *Philologus* 90 (1935) 57-77, 176-93.

[211] See Scully, *Philia and Charis in Euripidean Tragedy*, 27.

2. Friendship in Antiquity

dieux (Διὶ φίλος): tels Pâris et Hélène pour leur beauté, don d'Aphrodite, Agamemnon ou Achille pour leur force et leur royale prestance ..."[212]

There could be great affection between gods and humans, but such affection did not constitute a friendship of equals nor even like-mindedness between the two. Indeed, in most cases being loved by the gods reflected the particular outstanding characteristics of the hero in question.

The notion of human friendship with God does appear, however, in the Hebrew Bible. Exod 33:11 states that God would speak face to face with Moses, "as one speaks to a friend" (רע), and 2 Chron 20:7 refers to Abraham as God's friend (אהב), as does Isa 41:8 (אהב is also used here in reference to Abraham). The Exodus reference to friendship may serve to emphasize Moses' role as a personal mediator between God and Israel, as throughout Exodus 32–34, "the twofold connection [of Moses] with Yahweh, as intimate friend and as designated mediator, is exhibited and exploited."[213] The designation of Abraham as God's friend may find its origins in Gen 18:17 which describes the "exceptional character of Abraham's relationship to God."[214] Abraham is also an exemplar of trust and faith in God, and it is likely for this reason that the epithet "friend of God" is applied to him more often in later Jewish and some early Christian literature.[215]

The Greek translators of the Hebrew texts and Hellenistic Jewish authors found such a notion entirely acceptable. On the one hand, they translate the Exod 33:11 passage with the word φίλος – God spoke to Moses as one speaks to a friend, but even more compelling is Wis 7:27, which says that in every generation wisdom passes into holy souls (ψυχάς) and makes them friends of God (φίλους θεοῦ) and prophets (προφήτας). The passage continues: "for God loves nothing so much as the person who lives with wisdom" (Wis 7:28). To be a friend of God is to be beloved by God, but why does the passage include a mention of making people prophets? For David Winston, the reference indicates that wisdom is the source of prophecy; that "in each generation [wis-

---

[212] Maurice Vidal, "La *Theophilia* dans la Pensée religieuse des Grecs," *RSR* 47 (1959) 164-65.

[213] Walter Brueggemann, *Theology of the Old Testament. Testimony, Dispute, Advocacy* (Minneapolis: Fortress, 1997) 571.

[214] Claus Westermann, *Isaiah 40-66. A Commentary* (OTL 19; trans. David M.G. Stalker; Philadelphia: Westminster, 1969) 70.

[215] See A.R. Millard, "Abraham," *ABD* I (1992) 35.

dom is] guiding the friends of God and inspiring his prophets."[216] The emphasis is upon the power of wisdom; she can do everything, including making some humans friends of God and empowering others to speak as prophets.

Apart from indicating that to be a friend of God is to be loved by God, the Wisdom passage does not provide any other details about the relationship. In fact, most texts which refer to friendship with God do not elaborate a great deal on the subject. Moreover, there is some question whether non-Jewish and non-Christian Greek thinkers would have accepted such an idea at all. Is the notion of friendship with God then confined to the Jewish and Christian realm of ideas?

The classic study on the topic of friendship with God is the 1923 article by Erik Peterson, and his ideas have been used by subsequent authors.[217] Peterson traced the idea of friendship with God through the classical Greek writings, the biblical traditions, and other Jewish and early Christian texts. He argued that that there were two streams of ideas in Greek classical antiquity, one accepting friendship between people and gods, and another, exemplified by Aristotle, which rejected it. Philo and later Christian writers, he says, were influenced by the Greek classical traditions which supported the notion of friendship with God, as well as by the biblical traditions which endorsed it.[218]

Peterson's thesis has been challenged by David Konstan, who has offered a different interpretation of the Greek classical texts upon which Peterson depends to build his argument. Konstan contends that Peterson has based his discussion upon an erroneous reading of the literature: Peterson has failed to distinguish between the adjectival and substantive use of the word φίλος. In Homeric times, we recall, mortals could be "dear" to the gods (Διὶ φίλος), but this did not mean that they were their "friends." Peterson, however, reads forms of φίλος substantively rather than as an adjective. For example, he refers to Plato's *Timaeus* 53D (ὃς ἂν ἐκείνωι φίλος ἦι) as an instance of friendship between a man and God,[219] but as Konstan explains, the passage refers to "whoso-

---

[216] David Winston, *The Wisdom of Solomon* (AB 43; Garden City, NY: Doubleday, 1979) 42-43.

[217] Erik Peterson, "Der Gottesfreund: Beiträge zur Geschichte eines religiösen Terminus," *ZKG* 42 (1923) 161-202. Luke Johnson's commentary on James (*The Letter of James*, 244) follows Peterson as does Jürgen Moltmann ("Open Friendship: Aristotelian and Christian Concepts of Friendship," *The Changing Face of Friendship* [ed. Leroy S. Rouner; Notre Dame: University of Notre Dame Press, 1994] 36).

[218] Peterson, "Der Gottesfreund," 164-65, 172-87.

[219] Peterson, "Der Gottesfreund," 163.

ever may be dear to that one [the god]," not a "friend" of God.²²⁰ Similarly, Peterson cites a passage from Xenophon's *Symposium*, which refers to οὗτοι τοίνυν οἱ πάντα μὲν εἰδόντες, πάντα δὲ δυνάμενοι θεοὶ οὕτω μοι φίλοι εἰσὶν ὥστε διὰ τὸ ἐπιμελεῖσθαι μου οὔποτε λήθω (4.47-48).²²¹ But again, this passage, as Konstan points out, does not refer to the gods as friends, but to the fact that they are friendly to the speaker; that the speaker, Hermogenes, is loved by the gods.²²²

Peterson cites some similar examples that are easily refuted by Konstan, as well as some trickier ones, which are also analysed and rejected but on different grounds. For example, the phrase φίλος θεοῦ appears in Maximus of Tyre,²²³ but Konstan and others charge that the expression is a marginal gloss that was subsequently added by a copyist who was comfortable with such an idea.²²⁴ Konstan does grant Peterson's point, however, that among the Stoics there was some talk of friendship between gods and mortals, for as a text from Pseudo-Plutarch's "Life of Homer" states: "the Stoics, who indicate that good men are friends of gods (φίλους θεῶν τοὺς ἀγαθοὺς ἄνδρας), took this too from Homer."²²⁵ Konstan also allows for the evidence from Philodemus's *On the Gods*: καλείτω καὶ τοὺς σοφοὺς τῶν θεῶν φίλους καὶ τοὺς θεοὺς τῶν σοφῶν,²²⁶ which in his view allows for the expression "friends of the gods" "in a restricted sense."²²⁷ But he goes on to quote more of Philodemus, who says "we do not seem to call such things friendship,"²²⁸ as if it is very unusual to call mortals and gods friends. Konstan also deals with Peterson's references to Epictetus's use of φίλος τοῦ θεοῦ. In Epictetus's *Discourses* 2.17.19, a hypothetical young man says that he shall be satisfied if he can "look up to heaven as a friend of God (ὡς φίλος τοῦ θεοῦ)"²²⁹ then in 4.3.9 Epictetus claims that he is a "free

---

²²⁰ David Konstan, "Problems," 92.
²²¹ Cited in Peterson, "Der Gottesfreund," 162.
²²² Konstan, "Problems," 92.
²²³ Peterson, "Der Gottesfreund," 168.
²²⁴ Konstan, "Problems," 94.
²²⁵ Pseudo-Plutarch, *Vit. Poes. Hom.* 143 (ed.; trans. J.J. Keaney and Robert Lamberton; American Philological Association. American Classical Studies 40; Atlanta: Scholars, 1996). See Peterson, "Der Gottesfreund," 161, and Konstan, "Problems," 94.
²²⁶ Col. 1.17-18; text in H. Diels, *Philodemus Über die Götter: Drittes Buch, I. Griechischer Text*, in *Abhandlungen der königlich preussischen Akademie der Wissenschaften* (Berlin: Verlag der königlichen Akademie der Wissenschaften, 1917) 16; cited in Konstan, "Problems," 94 n. 21.
²²⁷ Konstan, "Problems," 94.
²²⁸ Col.1. 19-20. Cited in Konstan, "Problems," 94-95.
²²⁹ Translated by W.A. Oldfather (LCL; Cambridge, MA: Harvard University Press; London: Heinemann, 1967).

man and a friend of God (φίλος τοῦ θεοῦ)." Peterson cites these examples as clear evidence for Greek acceptance of the idea of friendship with God,[230] but Konstan argues that in the first case Epictetus places ὡς before the expression, thereby softening it, while in the second example Konstan argues that the Stoic is using very strong language because he is "playing here on his status as a former slave."[231]

In my view, Konstan has not sufficiently refuted Peterson's evidence for the Greek acceptance of friendship with God. Indeed Peterson may have overstated his claims for the classical Greek acceptance of the idea, but that there were various individuals, especially the Stoics, who sanctioned the concept is clear.[232] Epictetus may be using strong language because he is freed from slavery, but all the same, he clearly says that he is a friend of God, meaning, as the passage continues, that he "shall obey Him of [his] own free will" (4.3.9). Moreover, Pseudo-Plutarch was aware that some Stoics accepted the idea of friendship with God, and Philodemus allowed for it, even if only in a narrowly defined way. Therefore, although the concept only appears solidly in a few Greek texts, Konstan is not entirely convincing that the "Christian interest in friendship with God derives wholly from Biblical passages."[233] Early Christian writers may have been influenced by a variety of traditions, and one must study each of them individually to determine to what extent biblical or Greek sources may have been influential.

Like the biblical writers, Philo is comfortable with the idea of a human-divine friendship. He says that the wise are friends of God (φίλοι θεοῦ),[234] and he refers to specific individuals, such as Abraham and Moses, who are friends with God.[235] An important attribute of those worthy of friendship with God is faithfulness. In the context of writing about oaths, Philo states:

> Some have said, that it was inappropriate for Him to swear; for an oath is added to assist faith, and only God and one who is God's friend is faithful (πιστὸς δὲ μόνος ὁ θεὸς καὶ εἴ τις θεῷ φίλος), even as Moses is said to have been found "faithful in all his house" (*Leg.* 3.204).

---

[230] Peterson, "Der Gottesfreund," 170-71.

[231] Konstan, "Problems," 95.

[232] It is interesting that in his subsequent book, Konstan (*Friendship in the Classical World*, 168) is a little less strong in his criticism of Peterson, claiming that Peterson "greatly overstated the case for friendship with the gods in early classical sources." In his earlier article ("Problems," 91) Konstan had bluntly stated that "Peterson ... is wrong about the classical materials."

[233] Konstan, "Problems," 96.

[234] *Her.* 21.

[235] *Sobr.* 56; *Somn.* 1.193-95.

Furthermore, Philo writes: "For if, as the proverb says, what belongs to friends is common, and the prophet is called the friend of God (φίλος ... θεοῦ), it would follow that he shares also God's possessions, so far as it is serviceable"[236] This excerpt is similar to a syllogism attributed to Diogenes the Cynic,[237] and its presence in Philo may be evidence that he was aware that there was a notion of friendship with God in non-Jewish circles.

Sterling maintains that for Philo, friendship is an important philosophical concept which enabled the ancient writer to express a Jewish universal understanding of humanity: when "Philo's thought becomes universal he uses the language of friendship."[238] Other authors, such as J. Massyngbaerde Ford, have noticed that Philo makes a "clear association between friendship and the covenant and, implicitly, redemption."[239] Neither of these dimensions of Philo's perception and application of friendship language will be explored here, but the fact that scholars have observed such things confirms the degree to which this Hellenistic Jewish author thought friendship was a crucial aspect of human and divine interaction.

The notion of friendship with God appears in various other Jewish texts. Josephus writes of Johsua's final speech to the people in which he recalls God's benefactions to them, and exhorts them to maintain God's goodwill, for "piety alone could they retain the friendship of the Deity."[240] The book of *Jubilees* states that those who do not commit sin or break the covenant "will be written down as friends" in the heavenly tablets.[241] Similarly, Abraham was found faithful by God and for that reason was recorded in the heavenly tablets as a friend of God in *Jub.* 19.9. In the *Testament of Abraham*, Abraham is called the friend (φίλος) of God, presumably because he "did all pleasing things before [God],"[242] while in the *Apocalypse of Abraham* Abraham is called "beloved" by God because he "desired to search for [God]" and

---

[236] *Mos.* 1.157 (LCL; trans. F.H. Colson; London: Heinemann; Cambridge, MA: Harvard University Press, 1935).

[237] Diogenes Laertius, *Lives* 6.27. See Konstan, "Problems in the History," 95-96.

[238] Sterling, "The Bond of Humanity," 222.

[239] Ford, *Redeemer – Friend and Mother*, 92.

[240] *Ant.* 5.116 (trans. H.St.J. Thackeray & Ralph Marcus; LCL; Cambridge, MA: Harvard University Press; London: Heinemann, 1988).

[241] *Jub.* 30.21 (trans. O.S. Wintermute in *The Old Testament Pseudepigrapha* 2 [ed. James H. Charlesworth; Garden City: Doubleday, 1985] 113-14).

[242] *Test. Abr.* A 15 (trans. Michael E. Stone; SBLTT 2 Pseudepigrapha Series 2; Missoula: SBL, 1972, 41).

subsequently he is addressed as "friend of God" by an angel.[243] Rabbinic literature also refers to Abraham as a friend of God, probably under the influence of the biblical texts.[244] The Damascus Document at Qumran, moreover, has been translated to refer to Abraham as a "friend [אהב]" of God for keeping God's precepts and not following the desire of his spirit." Likewise Isaac and Jacob "were written up as friends of God" because they also kept God's precepts.[245] Obedience and complete faith in God are the recurring qualities which earn various persons the epithet "friend" of God in this literature, although Abraham receives it most often, owing to its explicit association with him in the biblical texts.

Abraham's friendship with God appears with some regularity within early Christian writings. 1 Clement refers to Abraham twice as being called "the Friend" (ὁ φίλος, 10.1) or the "Friend of God" (17.2),[246] and so do Tertullian and Irenaeus,[247] as if this title were common knowledge.[248] Moreover, the notion of human friendship with God was acceptable within some Christian circles. Clement of Alexandria makes reference to it throughout his writings,[249] while at the same time he accepts Aristotle's three classes of friendship, the highest of which is based upon virtue.[250] This idea of a human–divine friendship was to continue to exist among fourth century Christian writers and on into the Middle Ages.

---

[243] *Apoc. Abr.* 9-10 (trans. R. Ruinkiewicz in *The Old Testament Pseudepigrapha* 1 [ed. James H. Charlesworth: Garden City: Doubleday, 1983] 693).

[244] This is the view of Florentino García Martínez, "The Heavenly Tablets in the Book of Jubilees," *Studies in the Book of Jubilees* (ed. Matthias Albani, Jörg Frey & Armin Lang; Tübingen: Mohr Siebeck, 1997) 246. Rabbinic references to Abraham (and others) as a friend of God include *b. Menah.* 53b; *t. Ber.* 7.13; *Sifre Num.* 115; *Sifre Deut.* 352; *Mek. Bo.* 18.22. In some cases, other biblical heroes are included as friends of God. See also Louis Ginzberg, *The Legends of the Jews* V (Philadelphia: Jewish Publication Society of America, 1929) 207-208.

[245] Translation of CD 3.2 is by Florentino García Martínez & Eibert J.C. Tichelaar, *The Dead Sea Scrolls Study Edition* I (Leiden, New York, Cologne: Brill, 1997) 553.

[246] For text and translation of *1 & 2 Clement* and the *Shepherd of Hermas* see *The Apostolic Fathers* (LCL; trans. Kirsopp Lake; Cambridge, MA: Harvard University Press; London: Heinemann, 1917).

[247] Tertullian, *Adv. Jud.* 2.7; Irenaeus, *Adv. Haer.* 4.14.4; 16.2.

[248] See also Pizzolato, *L'idea di amicizia*, 239-40.

[249] Clement, *Al. Prot.* 12.12.3; *Al. Strom.* 7.68.1.3.

[250] Clement, *Al. Strom.* 2.19; see Konstan, *Friendship in the Classical World*, 156.

Conclusion

This chapter has only touched upon some of the key characteristics of friendship in antiquity, but it provides the reader with sufficient background against which to compare some of the language and ideas associated with friendship in the letter of James. We have seen that qualities such as loyalty, faithfulness, being of "one mind/one soul," sharing possessions, as well as proving one's friendship through trials, were commonly associated with friendship, appearing in Graeco-Roman, Jewish and Christian sources.[251] For some writers, notably Ben Sira, the author Wisdom, Philo, Paul and a few patristic authors, friendship takes on a decidedly theological dimension, whether they are referring explicitly to friendship with God, or grounding a friendship morality in faithfulness to God. For Luke-Acts, themes associated with friendship shape the author's perception or ideal vision of the early church, whether or not it fully materialized. Thus we see that the *topos* of friendship was both widespread and quite meaningful for a diverse range of writers and communities. Before analyzing how it may have been used within the rhetoric of James, however, we need to clarify some of the distinctions between friendship, benefaction and patronage, as the language of friendship was regularly employed in the latter two forms of relationships.

---

[251] Joseph A. Marchal (*Hierarchy, Unity and Imitation: A Feminist Rhetorical Analysis of Power Dynamics in Paul's Letter to the Philippians* [Academia Biblica 24; Atlanta: Society of Biblical Literature, 2006] 35-50) is certainly correct in pointing to the aristocratic, elitist and male nature of most ancient discussions of friendship (which I take as a given), yet his treatment of friendship is rather brief (very little discussion of Hellenistic Jewish uses of the concept appear) and the purpose of his work seems more oriented towards usefulness for feminist and liberationist interpretations.

3

Friendship, Patronage and Benefaction

Introduction

The previous chapter explored primarily literary and philosophical authors who discuss aspects of ideal friends and friendships. Given the wide range of discussions of this ideal, and the pervasive use of the language of friendship, one can confidently conclude that this noble ideal had considerable rhetorical appeal among many groups by the first century CE. However, it is impossible to know to what degree friendships actually embodied these ideals, and, despite the love and affection that these texts indicate are expected of friends, many friendships included economic and political benefits that surely motivated people to develop and maintain them. Although plenty of writers stress the sacrifices friends should make for one another, numerous if not most friendships in antiquity likely had instrumental dimensions to them, albeit to varying degrees, as is probably the case with many friendships today.

We also must remember to consider friendship in light of the centrality of reciprocity for interpersonal relations in antiquity, a centrality that has been established for some time.[1] Reciprocity consists of the exchange of goods and/or services, modest or great, between persons, families or groups. In their social history of the early Jesus movement, Ekkehard and Wolfgang Stegemann discuss three forms of reciprocity: familial or balanced reciprocity, which involves persons of roughly the same social status and in which friends participate; general reciprocity between unequal partners, and negative reciprocity between

---

[1] See Karl Polanyi, *Primitive, Archaic and Modern Economy: Essays of Karl Polanyi* (ed. G. Dalton; Garden City, NY: Doubleday, 1968) and subsequently, Marshal Sahlins, *Stone Age Economics* (Chicago: Aldine-Atherton, 1972).

3. Friendship, Patronage and Benefaction

strangers and enemies.² Whether the offer of favours from friend to friend was motivated by love and concern or more self-interested motives, generosity and a response of gratitude to that generosity were key ingredients to friendship, and aided its longevity.³ Even though the motives for friendship vary, it provides both emotional and practical benefits. As Koenraad Verboven writes:

> So although emotional friendship can (and should) be distinguished from instrumental friendship from a conceptual and motivational point of view, from a normative point of view affection and utility coincide in the institution of friendship as it emerges in the Greek and Roman world.⁴

Descriptions and narrations of ideal friendship from antiquity indicate to what extent this relationship embodied virtues and noble feats, but the fact that friendships could bring material and/or social rewards must be acknowledged. And given this "exchange" element within friendship, one understands how some friendships could begin as or become purely instrumental, possibly descend into forms of manipulation, or, as we will explore subsequently, present themselves as friendships when in reality they are purely economic and social arrangements. Just as the word "friend" is used casually among persons today, even with reference to those to whom one is not particularly close, ancient people would use φίλος liberally to include relationships that reflected few if any of the characteristics described in the previous chapter.⁵

More specifically, the patron–client relationship, an asymmetrical liaison in which the patron often held sway over his or her clients,

---

² Wolfgang Stegemann and Ekkehard W. Stegemann, *The Jesus Movement: A Social History of Its First Century* (trans. O.C. Dean Jr.; Minneapolis: Fortress, 1999) 34-37.

³ Koenraad Verboven (*The Economy of Friends. Economic Aspects of* Amicitia *and Patronage in the Late Republic* [Collection Latomus 269; Bruxelles: Éditions Latomus, 2002] 35-45) describes how Roman *amicitia* was ideologically constructed around the ethical values of *liberalitas* or *benignitas, gratia, fides* and *beneuolentia* or *amor*.

⁴ Verboven, *The Economy of Friends*, 44.

⁵ As Michael Peachin ("Introduction and Acknowledgements" *Aspects of Friendship in the Graeco-Roman World* [Journal of Roman Archaeology Supplementary Series 43; Ann Arbor: Cushing-Malloy, 2001] 8) has written of the debate about whether ancient Greek and Roman notions of friendship were primarily emotional or political: "Perhaps, in the end, it would be best to presume what seems logical, namely, that there were many relationships among the Greeks and Romans which we would readily recognize as proper friendships. Simultaneously, however, there were many interpersonal bonds, which could be labeled with the words *amicitia* or φιλία, but which we would not find particularly friendly."

would often mask itself as friendship. Such an attempt at camouflage caused considerable dismay to those authors who held friendship in high esteem, and provided fodder for satirical writers. And given the fact that patronage would use the language of friendship so regularly, some have supposed that patronage and friendship were one and the same. We thus need to sort out what the differences between a patron-client relationship and a friendship, or ideal friendship, are. This is significant to the study of James, for as explained in the introduction, the letter writer is attempting to challenge the audience's temptation to rely upon wealthy patrons, and doing so by appealing to friendship. Despite the fact that the word "friend" is used for people in a patron-client relationship, the author of James, along with other ancient writers, did not think that friendship and patronage were one and the same, and in fact understands there to be a significant gap between the two.

Another form of exchange, namely that between a benefactor and an association, city or individual beneficiary, would use the language of friendship to some extent (and members of an association would refer to their group as "the friends" as we have seen). Again, scholarship has often treated benefaction as the same as patronage, because the relationship is not necessarily between equals but between a wealthy and powerful benefactor, and a group of recipients or a single person of a different social status. However, studies of benefaction, especially those that examine associations and cities in the Greek east, have concluded that Greeks of the east did not understand benefaction to be identical to patronage, the latter emerging with the rising power of Rome. Thus we will discuss the differences between patronage and benefaction. This comparison should reveal that the rhetoric of ideal benefaction[6] was much more consistent with the values and activities associated with the ideal of friendship than patronage was.

This chapter thus explores the practice of benefaction, how it compares to friendship, and how benefaction can be distinguished from patronage as well as the differences between patronage and friendship. Such a sorting out of these concepts is crucial before entering into analysis of James, for the letter appeals to the ancient ideal of friendship, especially the benefaction and friendship of God, in its attempts to argue against the potential or real influence of the rich, including rich

---

[6] Please note that I distinguish between the ideal forms of benefaction that many of our ancient writers discuss, and the concrete reality of benefaction, which is harder to ascertain. As many scholars observe, the rhetorical thrust of any text does not necessarily reflect lived reality.

patrons. Before beginning this conceptual discussion, we will pay some attention to the role of friendship within the social and political world of antiquity more generally. This is crucial, for it better enables us to understand why some contemporary scholars may view patronage and friendship to be one and the same.

Friendship, Politics and Society

Apart from the brief discussion of how friendship ideals may have had an impact on the community in Acts, we have been exploring friendship primarily on an individual basis. But the language of and practices associated with friendship were also used within larger social and political contexts. For example, Homer recognizes a form of friendship which did not require affection called φιλοξενία, or "guest-friendship." Such a friendship could be formed between people of very different social stations and between strangers, or ξένοι,[7] and it had very pragmatic goals, including political and family alliances that could last for generations. As indicated above, "reciprocity and gift-giving formed a central social institution"[8] in the world of Homer, and thus the giving and receiving of hospitality and friendship were expected. Such relationships and practices were not necessarily devoid of affection, but they were also not *built on* affection, rather, on the mutual practical benefits that such ties could bring. Likewise Hesiod, a peasant farmer, realized the need for cooperation and mutual aid among neighbours, especially when they faced the pressures of the wealthy aristocracy above them. He thus generally tends to view bonds between people from a practical perspective, akin to Homer's portrayals of guest-friendship.[9]

The question of whether loyalty to a friendship could conflict with loyalty to the state was also significant for some authors. It has been suggested that a tragic poet such as Euripides, who portrays friendships that go too far such that the friends plot evil and destructive crimes against kin and state, may be reflecting some of the developments in late fifth century Athenian politics whereby younger members of the

---

[7] For more discussion of the differences between friendship and guest-friendship, or "ritualised friendship," see G. Herman, *Ritualised Friendship and the Greek City* (Cambridge and New York: Cambridge University Press, 1987) 29-31, and Simon Goldhill, *Reading Greek Tragedy* (Cambridge: Cambridge University Press, 1986) 81-82.

[8] T. Gallant, *Risk and Survival in Ancient Greece: Reconstructing the Rural Economy* (Cambridge: Polity, 1991), 146.

[9] Pizzolato (*L'idea di amicizia*, 16-18) particularly emphasizes the economic dimension of Hesiod's concerns about friendship.

aristocracy were vying for more political power.[10] However, one should not assume that groups of φίλοι represented the small conspiratorial oligarchies which attempted to overthrow the *dēmos* during this period. Despite of the claims of Horst Hutter, who argues that friends formed political groups and that the "meaning of politics lay in the fulfillment of friendships,"[11] there is not much evidence for φίλοι playing a formal role in politics at this time. This is not to say that political supporters could not be friends with a leader, or that those who plotted to destroy a democracy could not view one another as friends. The notion of help friends/harm enemies was indeed a central presupposition of classical Greek society. Euripides's *Electra*, for example, depicts those who are supportive of the rebellious children of Agamemnon as φίλοι,[12] while in *Orestes*, as we saw, those against Orestes and Pylades are enemies. But it does not follow from these examples that politics was run by small groups of official φίλοι. Hutter equates a φίλος with a ἑταῖρος, as if the two were interchangeable, whereas an ἑταῖρος was a comrade or companion, and not necessarily (although it could be) an affectionate friend. Groups of Athenian ἑταῖροι were active as "oligarchical cells" near the end of the fifth century but according to the rhetor, Hypereides, they were subsequently banned.[13] They continued to exist in the fourth century, but at this time they served primarily as social clubs which fostered mutual aid between private individuals.[14] Despite the wealth of classical philosophical writings on friendship, there is little evidence that it was *primarily* a political concept even though it could serve political ends.[15]

One might think that Sophocles's *Antigone* could challenge this latter statement. In this play, Creon, the ruler of Thebes, declares,

> ... I condemn the man who sets his friend (φίλον) before his country. For myself, I call to witness Zeus, whose eyes are everywhere, if I perceive some mischievous design to sap the State, I will not hold my tongue; nor would I reckon as my private friend a public foe, well

---

[10] Konstan, *Friendship in the Classical World*, 61.

[11] Hutter, *Politics as Friendship*, 25.

[12] See David Konstan, "*Philia* in Euripides' Electra," *Philologus* 129 (1985) 176-85.

[13] Hypereides, *Eux.* 3.7-8. See M.H. Hansen, *The Athenian Democracy in the Age of Demosthenes: Structure, Principles and Ideology* (trans. J.A. Crook; Oxford: Oxford University Press, 1991) 281; cf. Lynette G. Mitchell and P.J. Rhodes, "Friends and Enemies in Athenian Politics," *Greece and Rome* 63 (1996) 11-30.

[14] Demosthenes, *Con.* 54.7, 14-20, 30-40.

[15] Powell ("Friendship and its Problems," 32) writes that the function of one-to-one political friendships "does not seem to receive so much emphasis or attention" in democratic Athens as it does in Archaic Greece.

3. Friendship, Patronage and Benefaction 61

knowing that the State is the good ship that holds our fortunes all: farewell to friendship, if she suffers wreck (*Ant.* 182-88 [LCL]).[16]

In this instance Creon is worried that friends of the dead Polyneices will band together and return to sack Thebes. He has stated succinctly that civic loyalty lies far and above loyalty to φίλοι, as if friendship could be a threat to state stability. "Such suspicion of personal attachments among one's subjects is part of the characterization of the tyrant, who sees plots brewing in all associations not directly under his control."[17] Creon's anxiety is not evidence that pockets of friends regularly attempted to usurp the state, but a testimony to his tyrannical paranoia.

According to Aristotle, friendship did not pose a threat to the political world of his day. For Aristotle,

> friendship appears to be the bond of the state; and lawgivers seem to set more in store by it than they do by justice, for to promote concord, which seems akin to friendship, is their chief aim, while faction, which is enmity, is what they are most anxious to banish. And if men are friends, there is no need of justice between them; whereas merely to be just is not enough – a feeling of friendship is also necessary. Indeed the highest form of justice seems to have an element of friendly feeling in it (*Eth. Nic.* 8.1.4).

Φιλία, we have observed, can include all kinds of mutual affection, including kinship ties, civic ties, and intimate bonds between φίλοι. Sometimes treaties between nations were called φιλία, just as a foreign ally could be called a φίλος.[18] For Aristotle, the closer the ties of φιλία, the stronger the claims of justice,[19] for feelings of affinity promoted justice and fairness. He could not envisage friendship in conflict with the state because in his view, one was coextensive with the other. Political authority in Aristotle's day was understood to be the "institutionalized will of the δῆμος,"[20] and not a remote force, disinterested in the general will of the populace. If a man was delinquent in his duties to the state, he was likely neglectful of his friends as well. Political conflicts were not caused by allegiances to

---

[16] Translated by F. Storr (Cambridge, MA: Harvard University Press; London: Heinemann, 1912).
[17] David Konstan, "Friendship and the State," *Hyperboreus* 2 (1994/95) 10.
[18] Konstan, *Friendship in the Classical World*, 83.
[19] *Eth. Nic.* 8.9.3.
[20] Konstan, "Friendship and the State," 8.

personal friendships, but by a deficiency of moral substance.[21] Indeed, Aristotle thought that "civic, and not just personal, friendship [was] an essential component in the flourishing human life"[22] and comments that a good leader is one who promotes friendship among citizens of the state.[23]

Not all members of the state are equals and Aristotle grants that φιλία may exist between unequals, as is the case in φιλία between a father and son, for example, or between a husband and wife.[24] Aristotle states at one point that the three types of friendship between φίλοι which he has distinguished, namely those based on utility, pleasure or character, are friendships of equality, "for both parties render the same benefit and wish the same good to each other."[25] However, he also recognizes that disparities arise between friends and that friends may not always be equal, because one friend may give much more than he receives and vice versa. Aristotle thus spends considerable time discussing proportional friendship and its relationship to the law, prompting Frederic M. Schroeder to comment that the philosopher "paves the way for the obligation between patron and client and a redefinition of friendship along these lines in the postclassical period."[26] However, this is not to say that patronage and friendship were confused, at least in rhetoric, at the time of the Athenian democracy, for as Paul Millet has written:

> It seems a plausible hypothesis that the democratic ideology, with its emphasis on political equality, was hostile to the idea of personal patronage, which depended on the exploitation of inequalities in wealth and status.[27]

---

[21] As Konstan ("Friendship and the State," 7) notes, "a good person will be responsive to obligations wherever φιλία obtains, whether in personal friendships or in the realm of civic society."

[22] Cooper, "Aristotle on the Forms of Friendship," 648. See also John M. Cooper, "Political Animals and Civic Friendship," in *Aristoteles' "Politik"* (ed. Günther Patzig; Göttingen: Vandenhoeck & Ruprecht, 1990) 220-41.

[23] *Eth. Nic.* 8.1.4.

[24] Aristotle reflects the standard view of women as inferior to men. Julie K. Ward, however, thinks that Aristotle's views on friendship, despite his obvious sexism, have the potential to inform contemporary feminism. See her article, "Aristotle on *Philia*: The Beginning of a Feminist Ideal of Friendship?" *Feminism and Ancient Philosophy*, 155-71.

[25] *Eth. Nic.* 8.6.7.

[26] Frederic M. Schroeder, "Friendship in Aristotle and Some Peripatetic Philosophers," *Greco-Roman Perspectives on Friendship*, 45.

[27] Paul Millett, "Patronage and Its Avoidance in Classical Athens," *Patronage in Ancient Society*, 17. Millett does grant, however, that patronage and friendship could be confused in practice for friendship was "one of the obvious ways in which patronage could be disguised in order to make it acceptable" (p. 33).

3. Friendship, Patronage and Benefaction 63

For Aristotle, if a huge disparity emerges between φίλοι, whether it is economic or in the realm of character, their friendship will inevitably break. Likewise, humans cannot be friends with gods, who are far superior, and princes cannot be friends with people below their stature.[28] Although Aristotle may have some wonderful things to say about friendship, his ideas of with whom one can be friends are limited by his deeply hierarchical society.

Not surprisingly, Aristotle's student, Theophrastus, mirrors many of his teacher's ideas. For example, he accepted Aristotle's taxonomy of friendship, that is, the categories of friendship such as character friendship, pleasure friendship and utility friendship. However, Theophrastus did argue that these types of friendships could exist when one friend was superior to the other.[29] Aristotle had rejected character friendship between a prince and his subjects, whereas Theophrastus suggested that

> the ruler and the ruled may also become virtuous friends, and in other respects they will be friends, but while being friends they will maintain what is lawful, the one being inferior to the extent dictated by law, and the other being superior.[30]

Similarly, friendships based upon pleasure or utility could occur between superior and inferior people – even a husband and wife could be friends!

Unlike his teacher, Theophrastus had a burning concern for what to do if one's allegiance to the law – to the state, conflicted with loyalty to a friend. For Theophrastus, there was no simplistic answer; rather, one must use practical wisdom in each set of circumstances to determine whether the advantages to the friend outweigh the damage to one's reputation.[31] If they did, then one should support the friend; if they did not, one's "honour has without doubt the greater weight."[32]

Theophrastus's reasoning here is not particularly striking or surprising but what is significant is the fact that he addresses the possibility of such a scenario at all. It could be that he thought Aristotle had left this issue undeveloped, and thus attempted an elaboration of the problem;[33] however, changes in the political climate of Greece likely had a signifi-

---

[28] *Eth. Nic.* 8.7.3-6.
[29] See Schroeder, "Aristotle and Some Peripatetic Philosophers," 45.
[30] See W.W. Fortenbaugh, P.M. Huby, R.W. Sharples, & D. Gutas, eds., *Theophrastus of Eresus: Sources for his Life, Writings, Thought and Influence*, vol. II (PhilAnt 54,2; Leiden: E.J. Brill, 1992) 355.
[31] Pizzolato, *L'idea di amicizia*, 68.
[32] Fortenbaugh, Huby, Sharples, Gutas, *Theophrastus of Eresus*, 359.
[33] Konstan, "Friendship and the State," 8, n. 18.

cant impact as well. We remember that for Aristotle, friendship ties and loyalty to the state were generally coterminous. "Social relations, including friendship, were not separated off from political obligations in classical Athens because the distinction between society and the state was, like the state itself, inchoate."[34] Theophrastus, however, lived on the cusp between the classical and Hellenistic periods, a time of momentous political changes in Athens. At the end of the fourth century BCE, the Athenian δῆμος had lost its power to Macedonian supported powers, and in 317/16 Demetrius of Phaleron, a "Macedonian-backed puppet dictator,"[35] who had studied with Theophrastus at the Lyceum, came to power. No longer could all well-to-do Athenians engage in politics, rather, many felt disenfranchised from the world of the state, as it was now held up by foreign might. Participation in national politics was not perceived by all as a natural endeavour but more of a duty, and the focus of many lives became the personal as opposed to the public. As Peter Green suggests, "the movement toward a private rather than a public existence may have been intensified by the removal of full political freedom, by subservience to autocratic (and more often than not, external) government ..."[36] Green goes on to point out that there were many factors contributing to such a movement and that it was not universal – not everyone felt alienated from politics. However, the shifts in authority no doubt played a role in discouraging many from the political realm.

Moreover, with the decline of the δῆμος, separate institutional domains, such as the museum and the law courts, emerged and represented "instances of distinct realms of knowledge and authority."[37] Formerly, the δῆμος had expressed this authority and laws and art had been subservient to it, but during the Hellenistic and Roman periods this "centre" had disappeared, to be replaced by multiple spheres of authority and culture. Likewise friendship "came to be represented as a separate domain of relations in potential conflict with duty and ... with obligations to the state."[38] Although Theophrastus was likely quite sympathetic to Demetrius (remember that Aristotle had tutored Philip of Macedon), he must have sensed that civic loyalty no longer came

---

[34] Konstan, "Friendship and the State," 8.

[35] Peter Green, *Alexander to Actium. The Historical Evolution of the Hellenistic Age* (Berkeley, Los Angeles: University of California Press, 1990) 36.

[36] Green, *Alexander to Actium*, 40.

[37] Konstan, "Friendship and the State," 14.

[38] Konstan, "Friendship and the State," 15.

easily to all. In such an atmosphere, antagonism between loyalty to friends and duty to the state could readily emerge.

Historians have observed how the decline of Athens, political turmoil, and the displacement of peoples affected the way in which individuals perceived the good life during the Hellenistic age. With less political and financial freedom, it could be argued that some people sought "freedom of the soul."[39] This quest was not solely caused by the changed political conditions, but they were significant, as many were disillusioned with political life and saw no opportunities for participation in government. Civic ties no longer possessed the important position which they had held for Aristotle's conception of human flourishing, and space opened up for the development of intimate friendships within the various philosophical schools, of which we have already seen some examples.

Despite the potential rifts between friendship and political life, different types of evidence reveal that φίλος continued to be used as both an official and a non-official term. Katherine G. Evans has surveyed a random sampling of Greek documentary papyri and inscriptions for the use of the words φίλοι and φιλία. Out of an examination of 18,000 documents, only 203 used friendship terminology, and some of these texts were composed well beyond the Hellenistic period. However, Evans did find evidence that the word φίλος was used to describe officials in Ptolemaic Egypt in the last three centuries BCE. These officials included "first friends" and "friends" of the king who served as advisors and in various administrative capacities throughout the Egyptian dominion. Evans also found evidence for the Roman use of φίλος as an official position. Three papyri mention the "friends" of the Roman prefect, each of which indicate that the φίλοι of the prefect served in advisory and judicial positions in deciding the outcomes of legal proceedings.[40]

Gabriel Herman has also called attention to honorary decrees in which specific persons at court are referred to as φίλοι. Herman points out that it is not always clear what φίλος means when it appears in these decrees; does it refer to an equal person, which φίλος usually implies, or to an inferior who performs services for the ruler?[41] It seems to Herman that sometimes φίλος is understood to be a technical term, referring to a servant or official of the king, while at other times it may

---

[39] Green, *Alexander to Actium*, 53.

[40] K.G. Evans, "Friendship in Greek Documentary Papyri and Inscriptions," *Greco-Roman Perspectives on Friendship*, 188-89.

[41] Herman, "The 'Friends' of the Early Hellenistic Rulers," 111.

be an informal friend. The official notion of φίλος appeared in evidence from the Hellenistic kingdoms, and was often applied to ethnic Greeks, who, finding themselves in foreign lands, were dependent upon their leaders for their survival:

> the *philoi* ... held their wealth and status almost entirely at the rulers' discretion; for the Greek déracinés in particular, it was a matter of life and death to maintain a ruler's favour.[42]

Many Greeks were highly critical of this hierarchical relationship in which the φίλοι would do their best to keep their rulers happy, and thus much philosophical and satirical literature lampoons these φίλοι as flatterers and parasites. The connection between friendship and flattery will be discussed in more detail further on, but it is interesting to note for the time being that the same people who are honoured in decrees as φίλοι of rulers are simultaneously caricatured and ridiculed by other Greek writers. These φίλοι may be high ranking officials and generals, but they still receive biting criticism from many authors. As Herman comments: "to have a high rank in a king's court meant to be rated low in Greek public opinion."[43] Certain thinkers, such as Plutarch, disapproved of the designation φίλοι to those who ingratiated themselves to their superiors.[44] But despite this criticism, the official rank of friend is to be found in many Hellenistic courts.[45]

Turning to Rome, Cicero was fully aware that advantages, often political advantages, were gained from friendship, but gain or privilege was not the sole purpose of such a bond, as the previous excerpts from the *Laelius* should have made clear. However, the *Laelius* is principally a discussion of the highest form of friendship – that between virtuous people – whereas Cicero was aware that other, "ordinary" friendships could exist. These "ordinary" associations often materialized within the political arena, in which virtuous friendships were extremely rare,[46] and could break down when the persons involved changed their dispositions or tastes, or, significantly, when disagreements arose about the

---

[42] Herman, "The 'Friends' of the Early Hellenistic Rulers," 115.
[43] Herman, "The 'Friends' of Early Hellenistic Rulers," 122.
[44] Plutarch, *Adul. amic.* 51D.
[45] Frank Walbank, "Monarchies and Monarchic Ideas," *Cambridge Ancient History* 7.1 (eds. F.W. Walbank, A.E. Astin, M.W. Frederiksen, & R.M. Olgivie; Cambridge: Cambridge University Press, 1984) 69. Walbank discusses one of the earliest references to a friend as an official of the king, which is in a letter from Lysimachus to the city of Priene, which Walbank dates to c. 285 BCE.
[46] *Lael.* 64.

state.[47] The latter issue seems to have been of particular concern to Cicero, just as it was to Theophrastus. What was one to do when one's state allegiance clashed with one's friendships?

Although he discusses the problem with respect to ordinary friendships, Cicero was deeply familiar with Roman politics and undoubtedly witnessed men destroying deep bonds of friendship because of their political ambitions and loyalties. The assassination of Julius Caesar occurred during the last year of Cicero's life, and was probably another reason why he meditated upon the nature of friendship during that year, and as a result composed the *Laelius*. Ultimately, for Cicero, loyalty to friends could not justify a crime against the state. To violate or sin against one's country was dishonourable and evinced a lack of virtue. He writes: "Therefore it is no justification whatever of your sin to have sinned on behalf of a friend; for, since his belief in your virtue induced the friendship, it is hard for that friendship to remain if you have forsaken virtue." And then:

> Therefore let this law be established in friendship: neither ask dishonourable things, nor do them, if asked. And dishonourable it certainly is, and not to be allowed, for anyone to plead in defence of sins in general and especially of those against the State, that he committed them for the sake of a friend (*Lael.* 38; 40).

Aulus Gellius tells us that Cicero had read Theophrastus's treatise, *On Philia*, but had not dealt as thoroughly with the problem of loyalty to friends versus loyalty to the state as had Theophrastus.[48] Cicero does grant that a person may overlook certain kinds of dishonourable behaviour in friends, but there are limits to such allowances. Here Gellius wishes that Cicero would be clearer about what these limits are. We know that Cicero is against placing the value of a friendship over faithfulness to the state,[49] but he does not spell out in detail the types of misdemeanors which he would tolerate in a friend.

The question of conflict between loyalty to friends and loyalty to the state thus had become a significant issue by the time that Rome had come to power. Aristotle's view that the two naturally went together was by no means the norm, for now intimate friendships could exist

---

[47] *Lael.* 77f.
[48] Aulus Gellius, *Noct. Att.* 1.2.3.10-20.
[49] *Lael.* 61. Brunt ("*Amicitia*," 380-81) points out that Cicero was representing the Roman tradition: "the good man was true to his friends, but not to the extent that he was bound to assist them in doing wrong, and above all not in dereliction of the supreme duty to the fatherland, than which there could be no graver example than the imposition of despotic rule."

among people who were alienated in some way from the state. Authors such as Cicero do not place loyalty to friends above loyalty to the state but they could easily imagine how a conflict between the two could emerge.

The use of the language of friendship in political contexts to refer to officials or generals who catered to the wishes of wealthy providers, and the simultaneous ridiculing of these same individuals, indicates that by the Hellenistic period, φίλος was regularly used to refer to people who were not friends in the ideal sense. That is, they would not qualify as friends for authors such as Plutarch, or the tragic poets, for they did not uphold the types of virtues that were discussed earlier on. However, such an employment of friendship language indicates that it must have had significant rhetorical power within political and economic contexts. This is especially significant with regard to benefaction and patronage.

Benefaction

By the first century, the practice of benefaction ("euergetism") was deeply embedded within ancient Mediterranean society. Benefaction fitted firmly into the reciprocity system of the ancient world whereby a benefactor provided finances or other types of assistance to individuals or groups, usually in exchange for some type of gratitude and honours.[50] Evidence of benefaction is widespread, from philosophical writings to public monuments. Inscriptions regularly delineated the type and size of benefactions provided, and praised the giver for his or her various virtues. For example, an inscription from Delos set up by an association of Dionysiac artists praises the benefactor Kraton for his financial assistance and for displaying "love of goodness" (καλοκαγαθία) and "piety" (εὐσέβεια). The inscription indicates, moreover, that Kraton will be crowned each year and that statues of him will be set up and crowned as well. This strongly suggests that Kraton is continuing to provide for the artists as they are honouring him year after year.[51]

The above inscription indicates that human benefactors did not inevitably place their beneficiaries in a submissive role, for inscriptions often state how the recipients have fulfilled their obligations to the

---

[50] Ideas from this section appear in my article, "God in the Letter of James: Patron or Benefactor?" *NTS* 50 (2004) 257-72.

[51] See *IG* XI/4 1061 in F. Hiller Gaertringen *et al.* (eds.), *Inscriptiones graecae, consilio et auctoritate Acadaemiae Litterarum Borussicae editae* (14 vols.; Berlin: de Gruyter, 1873-).

benefactor, thus indebting their benefactor to them.[52] The benefactor was under pressure to maintain his or her honour by repeated donations to the receiving group. As Philip Harland has pointed out, "failure to meet expectations, especially at critical times, could result in shame and, more concretely, angry mobs seeking revenge against wealthier inhabitants ... Publicized contributions by the wealthy to the polis and its inhabitants ensured the maintenance of a person's position and prestige within the city, while also staving off the potential for such conflicts."[53] Although certainly benefaction occurred within a system, in this case, of generalized reciprocity whereby the participants were not of the same social status, the exchange was not completely controlled by the more powerful party because the recipients, in their ability to uphold their part of the bargain through honours etc., are able to exert pressure on the benefactor insofar as she or he is concerned about her or his overall status within the community. Moreover, and as Harland has indicated, continued donations were a means of maintaining one's security.

In addition, the public proclamation of the benefactor's contributions and "good will" enabled groups to jostle other potential benefactors to open up their wallets. An inscription from Athens,[54] for example, honours an individual named Sophron who has apparently founded the *thiasos* and has provided for it. The inscription makes it clear, however, that one of the reasons why the group will crown Sophron is to provoke a rivalry among other potential benefactors. Prospective donors would know that they would receive thanks for their contributions, and this public proclamation of their generosity would impel them to provide. Thus the fulfilment of obligation by a group to its benefactor was not only a means of preserving the benefaction, but also a method of attracting assistance from elsewhere.

In some of the philosophical discussions of benefaction, however, the ideal benefactor is someone not spurred on by wishes for recognition of his or her generosity. Seneca, for example, says that the benefactor should not be motivated by a desire for repayment, for "to help, to be of service, is the part of a noble and chivalrous soul; he who gives benefits the gods, he who seeks a return, money-lenders,"[55] although the ideal beneficiary should undoubtedly want to return the

---

[52] See *SEG* 26.1282.
[53] Harland, *Associations, Synagogues and Congregations*, 100.
[54] *IG* II² 1297.
[55] Seneca, *Ben.* 3.15.4.

benefit.[56] Earlier on, Aristotle had written about a magnanimous man, who is disposed to bestow benefits, and who repays a benefit with interest because he does not want to be placed in the role of beneficiary.[57]

Whether or not this ideal image of the benefactor was often manifested by human beings, it forms the backdrop for the characterization of both human and divine benefactors. Such figures are often referred to as "father" as they parallel the selfless behaviour of parents who continue to raise children despite the risk of ingratitude or other disappointments from their offspring.[58] Indeed benefaction was a key attribute of parents, and various philosophers praise the benefaction of parents and remind children of their responsibility to show gratitude for the receipt of parental beneficence. Iamblichus, for example, says that "our parents alone are the first in benefactions" and that "we cannot go wrong if we show the gods that we do good to our parents."[59] Such selfless providers showed concern (πρόνοια) for the good of either children or for communities and are regularly praised for such thoughtfulness and care.[60] "Father" imagery in particular appears with some regularity in tributes to founders and saviours, in conjunction with epithets such as σωτήρ, εὐεργέτης and κτιστής,[61] and as T.R. Stevenson points out, this characterization of a human or divine benefactor "rests upon the recognition of the procreative/tutelary power and entails the selfless use of that power."[62]

Gods are regularly described as benefactors. Seneca writes of the continual and lavish beneficence of the gods,[63] and complains that humans are deficient in comparison to the gods when it comes to benefaction.[64] Inscriptional evidence also regularly points to the gods as providers of good things. An inscription from Philadelphia for a private cult of Zeus asks the gods to provide "health, salvation, peace" among other benefits for the cult leader, Dionysius, and his family. Earlier in

---

[56] *Ben.* 1.4.3.

[57] *Eth. Nic.* 4.3.1f.

[58] See Seneca, *Ben.* 1.1.10.

[59] Iamblichus, *VP* 38.

[60] See J.R. Harrison, "Benefaction Ideology and Christian Responsibility for Widows," *NewDocs* 8 (1997) 106-16.

[61] See T.R. Stevenson, "The Ideal Benefactor and the Father Analogy in Greek and Roman Thought," *CQ* 42 (1992) 430.

[62] T.R. Stevenson, "Social and Psychological Interpretations of Graeco-Roman Religion: Some Thoughts on the Ideal Benefactor," *Antichthon* 30 (1996) 18.

[63] *Ben.* 4.3.3.

[64] *Ben.* 1.10.5; 4.26.1; 7.31.2.

3. Friendship, Patronage and Benefaction

the inscription it makes it clear, however, that if the participants violate certain purity regulations the gods will curse them. As the inscription states: "The gods will be gracious to those who obey, and always give them all good things, whatever gods give to men whom they love. But should any transgress, they shall hate such people and inflict upon them great punishments."[65] This emphasis upon honouring the gods appropriately through proper behaviour within the cult is a reminder of the importance of viewing benefaction within a context of reciprocity, usually generalized reciprocity, given that the exchange is between people of differing social status or between humans and gods. The gods will certainly provide generous benefits, but there is an understanding that the humans will respond with requisite recognition, honours, or in this case, the observance of good conduct and purity regulations.

Texts found in both the Septuagint and among Hellenistic Jewish writers are at ease in referring to God as a benefactor. Frederick Danker has noticed that of the 22 times that the *euerg–* word family appears in the Septuagint, 14 of them refer to God.[66] In 2 Maccabees, Maccabeus's soldiers bless God with hymns and thanksgivings after God benefits (εὐεργετέω) Israel and grants them victory. Many other instances of LXX references to euergetism emerge in wisdom literature, five of which are in the Wisdom of Solomon,[67] a text which, as we saw in the previous chapter, speaks of friendship with God. Wisdom 3:5, for example, refers to the souls of the righteous that will receive great good (εὐεργετηθήσονται) because God tested (ἐπείρασεν) them. Later in the same chapter, it also refers to the benefit or gift (χάρις) that is upon God's holy ones (3:9), and as has been demonstrated by a variety of scholars, χάρις is a standard term associated with ancient benefaction.[68] In this instance those who receive χάρις do so because they trust in God.

Josephus refers to God as a benefactor as well.[69] We already saw how, in his *Antiquities of the Jews*, Josephus relates a speech of Joshua which recalls God's benefactions (εὐεργεσίας) to the people and instructs them

---

[65] SIG 985. Translation by Stephen Barton and G.H.R. Horsley, "A Hellenistic Cult Group and the New Testament Churches," *JAC* 24 (1981) 7-41.
[66] F.W. Danker, "Benefactor," *AB* 1 (1992) 670.
[67] Wis 3:5; 7:23; 11:5; 16:2, 11.
[68] See Zeba A. Crook, *Reconceptualising Conversion. Patronage, Loyalty, and Conversion in the Religions of the Ancient Mediterranean* (BZNW 130; Berlin, New York: Walter de Gruyter, 2004); Danker, *Benefactor*; James R. Harrison, *Paul's Language of Grace in its Graeco-Roman Context* (WUNT 172; Tübingen: J.C.B. Mohr [Paul Siebeck] 2003).
[69] For listing of the number of times *euerg* words appear in Josephus, see Karl Heinrich Rengstorf, *A Complete Concordance to Flavius Josephus* (5 vols.; Leiden: Brill, 1973).

to maintain God's goodwill, for "by piety alone could they retain the friendship of the Deity" (φίλον αὐτοῖς διαμενεῖν τὸ θεῖον) (*Ant.* 5.115-116). The latter is a clear example of how God as a benefactor and God as friend can co-exist for Josephus, just as they do for the author of the Wisdom of Solomon (7:27). Such a combination seems possible on the human level as well, for in *Antiquities* 3.65 Josephus writes of the people's gratitude (εὐχαριστία) to Moses and of Raguel's admiration for Moses, who had devoted himself to saving his friends (φίλων).

Like Josephus, Philo comfortably describes God with benefaction language. Zeba A. Crook has observed how for Philo, "God is, indeed must be, the supreme benefactor because all things are God's alone; nothing else, or no one else, *has* anything to give,"[70] and discusses in particular a passage from *Legum allegoriae* 3.77-78 which is full of references to God as providing χάρις or εὐεργεσία, which are concrete benefactions and not abstract notions of grace, as Crook observes. James Harrison has pointed out, however, that Philo critiques the Hellenistic notion of benefaction whereby the benefactor provides, and the beneficiaries respond with praise and honour. For Philo, benefaction from God is not identical to those benefactors so often celebrated in inscriptional evidence. God does not "hawk his goods in a commercial enterprise."[71] God is a different sort of benefactor, whose character is motivated by "an unconditional generosity" and not an expectation of return.[72] Harrison draws parallels between Philo's approach and that of Seneca, who also characterized the ideal benefactor as decidedly not prompted by the possibility of a repayment, similar to the parental images discussed earlier. But we must still understand Philo's approach to benefaction within the context of reciprocity, for those who are worthy to receive God's beneficence are deemed worthy of it through their piety or other forms of activity. Philo may be critical of the common practice of benefaction that he sees going on around him, but when he discusses God as a benefactor, albeit a uniquely generous and unselfish one, he does not assume that God provides to those who are not worthy of such beneficence.

Philo also links benefaction with friendship. Several passages are relevant here, the first one clearly contrasting a wealthy man with a true benefactor. After describing the miserable and worthless rich man who wastes his money on pleasure, Philo instructs: "You will contribute freely to needy friends (φίλων), will make bountiful gifts to

---

[70] Crook, *Reconceptualising Conversion*, 87.
[71] Harrison, *Paul's Language of Grace*, 131. See Philo, *Cher.* 122-23.
[72] Harrison, *Paul's Language*, 131.

serve your country's wants, you will help parents without means to marry their daughters ... you will all but throw your private property into the common stock and invite all deserving of kindness to take a share."[73] Moreover, references to friendship with God emerge in the context of references to benefaction. A striking passage from *De Sobrietate*, in which Philo writes of Noah's blessing of Shem, is worth quoting in full.

> It is the Lord and God of the world and all that is therein, whom he declares to be peculiarly the God of Shem by special grace (χάριν). ... For while the words "Lord and God" proclaim Him master and benefactor (εὐεργέτης) of the world which is open to our senses, to that goodness which our minds perceive He is saviour and benefactor (εὐεργέτης) only, not master or lord. For wisdom is rather God's friend (φίλον) than His servant. And therefore He says plainly of Abraham, "shall I hide anything from Abraham My friend (φίλου)?" [Gen 18.17]. (*Sobr.* 54-56)

Philo continues on to describe how he who has "this portion" has registered "God as his father" and become by adoption "His only Son," possessing all the riches, and who "reaps the praise which is never debased by flattery ..." (*Sobr.* 56). Philo asks how this fortunate beneficiary should respond to God's generosity and responds: "What should he do but requite his Benefactor (εὐεργέτην) with the words of his lips with song and with hymn? ... For it is meet that he who has God for his heritage should bless and praise Him, since this is the only return that he can offer, and all else, strive as he will, is quite beyond his power " (*Sobr.* 58). God is clearly both benefactor and friend in this passage. The text also illustrates that despite God's tremendous generosity, there is still an expectation that the beneficiaries, as worthy as they are, will respond with blessings and praise for God and thus the reciprocal relationship remains in effect.

Crook has indicated that "χάρις does not occur between actual friends"[74] but the above evidence indicates that this word can appear in the context of friendship, and that friends can offer benefits and express gratitude for them even if this exchange is not necessary for the relationship.[75] Aristotle says that "things that create friendship are doing a

---

[73] *Fug.* 29.

[74] Zeba A. Crook, "Reflections on Culture and Social-Scientific Models" *JBL* 124 (2005) 520.

[75] As Konstan (*Friendship in the Classical World*, 81) puts it: "Clearly the Athenians felt strongly about returns for favors granted and made material claims on gratitude owed. But in none of the above passages is the demand for reciprocity of services connected with

favour (χάρις) and doing it unasked, and not making it public after doing it."[76] Moreover, in the context of discussing how friends share possessions in common, Dio Chrysostom comments that "he who shows his friends (φίλοις) a favour (χαριζόμενος) rejoices both as giver and receiver at the same time."[77] Seneca says that there is nothing to prevent him from giving a gift to a friend, while joining others in agreeing that friends have all things in common,[78] while Plutarch states that "graciousness [χάρις] and usefulness go with friendship."[79]

Inscriptional evidence points to an overlap between friendship and benefaction terminology, although here the benefactors or φίλοι are human beings, given that the notion of friendship with God was much less common in Greek thought. For example, an Athenian inscription from 306-305 BCE honours Timosthenes of Carystus, who "continues to be a friend (φίλος) to the people of Athens" and who "did not withdraw friendship (φιλίας) and was continually benefiting in public the people of Athens."[80] This benefactor likely did not embody the ideal benefactor or the ideal friend, but again it illustrates the fact that for these Greeks, friendship and benefaction could overlap, just as they could for Josephus and Philo.

Benefaction and friendship were by no means the same, and we must remember that ideal friendship existed within the context of balanced reciprocity in which the parties were equal, whereas benefaction occurred within a generalized form of exchange. However, the ideal image of a benefactor as a generous and sometimes selfless provider could overlap with that of the ideal friend, for indeed both images shared these characteristics. Perhaps it is this overlap that made it easy for Greeks to think of their benefactors as friends? Moreover, did the fact that benefactors of Greek cities were not all powerful in that they had to continue to provide in order to maintain honour or keep the peace enable people to think of them more as friends than as ruthless rulers?

---

friendship. This is not to say that Athenians could not be disappointed by a friend's ingratitude, but rather that the notion of *kharis* as the obligation to reciprocate kindnesses was not specifically associated with relations between *philoi*."

[76] *Rhet.* 2.4.29.

[77] *De Regn.* 3.110.

[78] *De Ben.* 7.12. In addition, Pseudo-Plutarch's *Life and Poetry of Homer* links God's beneficence to the community of friends who not only hold all in common, but are dear to the gods, a phrase discussed in Chapter 2. See Harrison, *Paul's Language of Grace*, 187.

[79] *Adul. amic.* 51B.

[80] *IG* II² 457. Translation by P. Harding, *From the End of the Peloponnesian War to the Battle of Ipsus: Translated Documents* (Cambridge: Cambridge University Press, 1985) 154.

Hellenistic Jewish authors are also at ease in mixing up benefaction language with that of friendship, particularly when they cast God as a benefactor *extraordinaire*. God's generosity receives emphasis. Sometimes it is very clear that the recipients of God's χάρις have benefited because of their loyalty to God or some particular act, and thus it is not necessarily a free χάρις that God bestows, or a χάρις that can be taken for granted or remain unacknowledged by the recipients. Authentic friendship with this benefactor God is entirely possible, although the authors do not intimate that humans are somehow equal to God. Thus we see that there is evidence within the Hellenistic tradition that the concepts of friendship and benefaction could overlap, at least rhetorically, on both the human and the divine planes. This overlap exists even though the two types of relationships originated separately and continued to maintain distinctive characteristics, especially with regard to status. The next question is thus to determine where patronage fits within this ancient conceptual and social landscape.

Patronage

Although its precise origins are obscure, by the first century, the practice of patronage was deeply entrenched in the Mediterranean area and discussions of it are now regularly found in studies of the world of the New Testament.[81] Patron-client relations were generally long term liaisons between unequals; that is, between a wealthy patron and one or more poorer clients who would provide services, and especially honours, in exchange for land, food, work, protection or whatever it was that the patron could provide.[82] Often this exchange could slide into explicit exploitation as the patron, being the more powerful participant in the relationship, could determine the nature of the relationship and could demand more and more from his or her clients.[83] Understandably, the client often had to resort to flattery in order to preserve or obtain provisions, protection or whatever was needed from the patron for the client's survival.

Some classical and biblical scholars have understood patronage and benefaction to be the same thing, for certainly they have much in

---

[81] For example, see K.C. Hanson & D.E. Oakman, *Palestine in the Time of Jesus: Social Structures and Social Conflicts* (Minneapolis: Fortress, 1998) 63-97.

[82] See Richard Saller, *Personal Patronage under the Early Empire* (Cambridge: Cambridge University Press, 1982) 1.

[83] See P. Millett, "Patronage and Its Avoidance in Classical Athens," *Patronage in Ancient Society* (ed. A. Wallace-Hadrill; Leicester-Nottingham Studies in Ancient Society 1; London/New York: Routledge, 1989) 16.

common and both draw upon the language of friendship, as we shall see presently with regard to patronage. Both phenomena also involve an exchange between parties, either towards an individual or group, endure over long periods of time, and involve people of differing social status (although benefaction can occur between friends, as discussed, even though it need not, as ideally friends share all in common). Additionally, there are examples of ancient persons – generally wealthy males – who functioned as both patrons and benefactors. But this does not mean that the two things were universally understood to be identical, at least in the first century.[84]

First, whereas evidence for benefaction reaches back into Greek classical writers and inscriptions, patronage is particularly associated with Roman power and politics,[85] and only well into the imperial period does it come to pervade the Mediterranean. As the Roman administration spread throughout the Greek east, the Greeks would honour this new power in the language and categories that they knew – that of benefaction. Thus, this does not mean that the Greeks understood the "Roman rule over them as patrocinium (as the Romans did)."[86] Moreover, as the Romans took control in the eastern provinces, the phrase "common benefactor" (κοινός εὐεργέτης) begins to appear as a new epithet for the Roman rulers. According to Andrew Erskine, the emergence of this phrase indicates that the Greeks did not perceive Roman power in the same manner that they had understood that of the Hellenistic kings. Comparison of the use of κοινός εὐεργέτης in Greek inscriptions to that of Egyptian papyri indicates that it was used

---

[84] The most thorough argument I have seen for the importance of the distinction is Stephan Joubert's *Paul as Benefactor: Reciprocity, Strategy and Theological Reflection in Paul's Collection* (WUNT 124; Tübingen: Mohr Siebeck, 2000) 17-72. Crook (*Reconceptualising Conversion*, 60-66) has challenged Joubert, arguing that although there are differences between patronage and benefaction, one cannot distinguish "patronage and benefaction too starkly based on any standard"(p. 65). Crook then uses the terms together throughout parts of his book, but at some points uses benefactor or patron. In the case of James, Crook thinks that God is a "patron" in Jas 4:1-6 because "friend" (4:4) is a term used for clienthood. However, "friend" is also used in the context of benefaction, and as we have seen, has a rich background in Hellenistic Jewish literature.

[85] For a discussion of the "foundation myth" of patronage, see Verboven, *The Economy of Friends*, 57-62. As he says, "patronage ... emerges as a culturally distinct phenomenon in Roman society not because there were any technical requirements about how such relations had to be formed and maintained, but because there existed an ideological mould ascribed to the *maiores* classifying relations based on reciprocity and loyalty between unequal partners as patron client relations" (p. 61).

[86] Stephan Joubert, "One Form of Social Exchange or Two? 'Euergetism,' Patronage, and New Testament Studies," *BTB* 31 (2001) 22.

in reference to the king, Ptolemy, who was all-powerful for the Egyptian peasant. In the Greek east, the phrase was not used for the Greek kings because no one rivaled them. However, when Rome assumed control, its strength could not be matched and the Greeks knew it. Therefore "common benefactor" reflects what was perceived to be an unbeatable power. For Erskine, not only did the Greeks now view Rome as the benefactor, they were "obedient to Rome and subordinate to it, just as the peasant was to the Ptolemies."[87] The language of benefaction thus continues to appear in Greek inscriptions honouring Roman officials, but the nature of the relationship was not necessarily understood in the same manner as it was between the Greeks and their kings.

Scholars such as Erich Gruen have argued that the Romans did not understand their control over the Greek east in terms of patronage, but were simply building upon the already established practice of benefaction.[88] However, G.W. Bowerstock had observed how from the time of Sulla (c. 80 BCE), "the word *patron* emerges on inscriptions as a regular conjunct with *euergetes* and *soter*, it is a Latin word thinly disguised as Greek, and it connotes a characteristically Roman institution."[89] Claude Eilers has examined inscriptions from North Africa in which civic generosity and *patronatus* coincide. In 11 of 21 cases the patron and the benefactor are the same person. The remaining 10 inscriptions, however, name one person as the patron (usually a Roman official who dedicated the inscription) and another as the financial provider or benefactor.[90] As Eilers points out, if generosity and liberality had become part of the ideology of patronage, one would expect to see more overlap between those referred to as benefactors and those as patrons: "apparently, being a *patronus* of a city was not closely linked to material generosity."[91] Although patronage and euergetism could coincide, and indeed, both roles were occupied by the wealthy, generosity is not a key attribute of patronage as it is of benefaction. Moreover, it is not clear that the Romans wanted to substitute patronage for benefac-

---

[87] Andrew Erskine, "The Romans as Common Benefactors," *Historia* 43 (1994) 86.

[88] Erich S. Gruen, *The Hellenistic World and the Coming of Rome* (Berkeley: University of California Press, 1984) 158-200.

[89] G.W. Bowerstock, *Augustus and the Greek World* (Oxford: Oxford University Press, 1965) 12. For an example of an inscription honouring someone as a πάτρωνα, see *SEG* 37.959.

[90] Claude Eilers, *Roman Patrons of Greek Cities* (Oxford Classical Monographs; Oxford: Oxford University Press, 2002) 100-01.

[91] Eilers, *Roman Patrons*, 101.

tion. Rather, "patronage was added to the Hellenic system of services and honours, *euergesiai* and *timai*, without merging with it."[92]

Finally, a difference between patronage and benefaction important to observe is that patron client relations were those in which the client(s) *could not repay* the benefit provided by the patron. "A client was by definition unable to solve his debt of honour to his patron."[93] This inability to return the favour is what made a person a *cliens*, which was a degrading term in itself.[94] Martial likens such a situation to slavery, asking the patron Gallus why, if he does not get any richer by the client's crucifixions, he does not simply remit the ordeals.[95] J.E. Lendon quotes Fronto who compares the favours of a protégé to that of a client. The difference between the exchange is that over time, Fronto and his protégé stop counting the favours, whereas clients could never stop counting.[96] Clients were forever indebted to their patrons, and thus the possibility of exploitation was often on the horizon. All the client could do was dream that some terrible disaster would befall the patron, for only then "by some imagined act of derring-do, could the client perform such great service as would free him."[97]

Patronage was different from benefaction, therefore, in that it was by definition between unequals, and placed the client forever in the patron's debt. Benefaction certainly could place a recipient in a submissive role, but not by definition, and inscriptions attest to the fulfillment of obligations and honours by beneficiaries, thereby exerting pressure on the benefactor to continue to provide.[98] Moreover, benefaction was particularly associated with magnanimity, liberality and even selflessness, whereas patronage need not be characterized by such attributes. The fact that patrons came to be described with such virtues, or that they were honoured as both patrons and benefactors, need not lead one to conclude that patronage and benefaction were one and the same thing.

---

[92] Jean-Louis Ferrary, "The Hellenistic World and Roman Political Patronage," *Hellenistic Constructs: Essays in Culture, History, and Historiography* (ed. P. Cartledge, P. Garnsey & E.S. Gruen; Hellenistic Culture and Society 26; Berkeley: University of California Press, 1997) 110.

[93] Verboven, *The Economy of Friends*, 62.

[94] See Saller, *Personal Patronage*, 8-11.

[95] Martial, *Ep.* 10.82.

[96] Fronto, *Ad Ver.* 1.6.2. J.E. Lendon, *Empire of Honour. The Art of Government in the Roman World* (Oxford: Oxford University Press, 1997) 67.

[97] J.E. Lendon, *Empire of Honour*, 67.

[98] See *SEG* 26. 1282.

Patronage, Friendship, and Flattery

Here it is worth recalling the text from Philo in which the author describes the fortunate recipient of God's benefaction, who sings praises to God, but does not resort to flattery,[99] clearly indicating that to attempt to flatter God would be inappropriate, to say the least. For Philo, God is not a patron who can be seduced by the fawning of humans. This does not mean that people did not necessarily praise and attempt to flatter benefactors, but rather that the ideal benefactor should not be predisposed to saccharine words. In contrast, the image of the flatterer is strongly associated with patron-client relations as the client would seek the patron's favours, and so-called "friendship," through flattery. We thus turn to the topic of flattery and how it relates to friendship and patronage as ancient discussions of it in particular reveal how authors did not view true friendship and patronage to be the same. In fact, some writers were very sensitive and perhaps even embittered by the fact that patrons and clients would dare refer to one another as a "friend."

Philo's disapproval of flattery[100] joins that of other writers. The flatterer (κόλαξ) in fact receives much criticism and ridicule in ancient literature, from authors such as Theophrastus, Maximus of Tyre and others, and was considered to be a false friend.[101] True friendship, many authors argued, was characterized by "frank speech" (παρρησία) while the flatterer was associated with the client, who pathetically attempted to gain more benefits from a patron.

The first century BCE Epicurean, Philodemus of Gadara, who lived at Herculaneum, wrote an essay on frankness, Περὶ παρρησία, which explains how one is to go about speaking firmly and honestly, but not cruelly, to fellow disciples or friends. This straightforward and often reproving talk was intended for the edification of one's friends and it was directly opposed to flattering speech, a thing detestable to many philosophers. The goal of frank criticism was the moral improvement of the addressee and the relationship of the speaker to the listener was somewhat akin to that of a physician and patient.[102] Philodemus uses the verb θεραπεύω, for example, to indicate that the friends must

---

[99] Philo, *De. Sobr.* 56.
[100] See also Philo, *Conf.* 48.
[101] For Theophrastus, see Fortenbaugh *et al.*, *Theophrastus of Eresus*, 2.373; Maximus of Tyre, *Or.* 14.18.
[102] See Norman W. De Witt, "Organization and Procedure in Epicurean Groups," *CP* 31 (1936) 205-11.

"treat" one another for their errors.[103] With some friends or pupils, one had to be harsher, depending upon their character, but one must be careful not to overly chastise the young because they "might become irritated" and hate everyone; indeed, "the use of inconsiderate frank speech ... severs the social relations among friends of the community."[104] This frank criticism, although sometimes hard to take, was ultimately the "sign of a genuine friend," while the flatterer "gives himself away by a self-interested adulation that is exploitative rather than altruistic."[105]

The diametric opposition between friendship and flattery was not always an issue in the history of Greek friendship. During the Archaic and Classical ages, flattery was considered to be a vice but it did not figure as a problem in friendship relations as friends were generally equals. Moreover, παρρησία was understood more as a political right to freedom of speech rather than the personal quality of candour. As Arnaldo Momigliano put it, with the defeat of Athens by Philip of Macedon, "Menander replaced Aristophanes, and *parrhesia* as a private virtue replaced *parrhesia* as a political right."[106] During Hellenistic times, however, so-called "friendships" became common between unequals and were thus more susceptible to exploitation, that is, people would pretend to be friends to those either above or beneath them, but then prove themselves untrue when the ostensible "friend" was in trouble. Such relations were further complicated by the system of patron-client relations, and as mentioned above, a worrisome and somewhat irritating feature of this system was the fact that many clients would attempt to become friends with their patron through smooth talk, flattery, and sometimes even imitation of frank speech, for the sole purpose of attracting the patron's consideration. Philosophers of friendship, such as Philodemus, found these flatterers particularly revolting, as not only were they selfish and deceitful, but they threatened to undermine and pervert true friendship.

---

[103] "... that he can be treated, either by us or by another of his fellow-students" (*Lib.*, fr. 79; trans. David Konstan, Diskin Clay, Clarence E. Glad, Johan C. Thom & James Ware; SBLTT 43; Graeco-Roman 13; Atlanta: Scholars, 1998).

[104] Clarence E. Glad, "Frank Speech, Flattery and Friendship in Philodemus," *Friendship, Flattery and Frankness of Speech*, 39-40.

[105] David Konstan, "Friendship, Frankness and Flattery," *Friendship, Flattery and Frankness of Speech*, 7.

[106] Arnaldo Momigliano, "Freedom of Speech in Antiquity," *Dictionary of the History of Ideas: Studies of Selected Pivotal Ideas*, vol. II (ed. P.P. Wiener; New York: Charles Scribner's Sons, 1973-74) 260. This citation appears in Konstan, "Friendship, Frankness and Flattery," 9.

These attitudes towards flattery are echoed by Plutarch. Plutarch does not think that one should have too many friends, for undoubtedly some of those so-called friends will not be true friends, but those seeking some type of selfish gain. Consider the following excerpt from *On Having Many Friends*:

> In the houses of rich men and rulers, the people see a noisy throng of visitors offering their greetings and shaking hands and playing the part of armed retainers, and they think that those who have so many friends must be happy. Yet they can see a far greater number of flies in those persons' kitchens. But the flies do not stay on after the good food is gone, nor the retainers after their patron's usefulness is gone (94B [LCL]).[107]

As Edward O'Neil observes, Plutarch may have the system of patron-client relations in mind here, as he describes people who appear to be friends but in reality are only out for themselves.[108] True friends, according to Plutarch, are rare, for they must be constant and loyal.

O'Neil has surveyed the *topoi* in Plutarch's writings on friendship which the moralist shares with many other philosophers of friendship.[109] Rather than reiterating all of these themes, I want to focus upon Plutarch's adamant distinction between friends and flatterers, which he makes most forcefully in his essay, *How to Tell a Flatterer from a Friend*.[110] Here again we see the nexus of friendship, frankness and flattery which we observed in the writings of Philodemus.

For Plutarch, the true friend is someone who will use παρρησία in a tactful, considerate manner for the benefit of his or her friend.[111] The flatterer, however, is a fake; a person who pretends to be friends, who may use frank speech in order to convince the listener that he or she is a sincere friend, but who is in fact a dangerous individual.[112] As described earlier, the flatterer is a chameleon-like person who is fickle, changing all the time, eagerly dancing around swearing oaths and solic-

---

[107] Translated by Frank Cole Babbit (London, Cambridge, MA: Harvard University Press, 1928).

[108] Edward N. O'Neil, "Plutarch on Friendship," *Greco-Roman Perspectives on Friendship*, 109.

[109] O'Neil ("Plutarch on Friendship," 113-22) shows how Plutarch must have been familiar with some of the typical goods that are typical of true friendship, including goodwill, intimacy, frankness, kindness, pleasure, usefulness and like-mindedness.

[110] Translation by Frank Cole Babbitt (LCL; London: Heinemann; Cambridge, MA: Harvard University Press, 1928).

[111] *Adul. amic.* 71B.

[112] Troels Engberg-Pedersen, "Plutarch to Prince Philopappus on How to Tell a Flatterer from a Friend," *Friendship, Flattery and Frankness of Speech*, 71.

iting witnesses to support him whenever he is accused of anything. The friend, however, is the complete antithesis of the flatterer, and does not require such formalities or ministrations.[113] The language of noble friendship is simple (ἁπλοῦς) and void of phoniness and posturing.[114]

Flatterers, moreover, are obsessed with and covetous of status and will dishonestly seek to improve their reputations or gain wealth by exploiting the trust and sincerity of other people through the emulation of friendly behaviour. Plutarch calls them apes.[115] True friends, in contrast, do not possess envy (φθόνος) for one another nor are they inclined to fall into emulation (ζῆλος),[116] for they bear one another's successes and failures with equanimity.[117] In fact, as Troels Engberg-Pedersen argues, Plutarch appears to regard true, honest friendship to be the "apogee" of a moral system; "the place where that system is realized."[118] Frank speech or criticism is a means towards this end of friendship, whereas flattery is destructive of it; flattery "perverts" friendship and the moral system which it represents.[119]

For Engberg-Pedersen, "How to Tell a Flatterer from a Friend" is a plea for a moral expression based upon trust, permanence of character, loyalty and sincerity – all things that are constitutive of friendship. This expression faced the threat of erosion by the highly status-conscious practice of patronage, which placed all people within a hierarchy. Andrew Wallace-Hadrill has summed up this latter system of human relations:

> From the point of view of the society, patronage represented a flexible method of integration and simultaneously of social control; that is not to say that it was always effective, nor indeed a particularly attractive system to live in. From the point of view of the individual patron, the ability to persuade others of his power to secure access to benefits was the basis of social credibility. The ideology thus both results from and morally underpins the social system.[120]

Such a scheme for society did not promote genuine friendship, for people were constantly scrambling to either climb up the status ladder or at least, not fall off of it – and they apparently employed all of the skills of the flatterer to do so. They fawned upon the wealthy and

---

[113] *Adul. amic.* 62D.
[114] *Adul. amic.* 62C.
[115] *Adul. amic.* 52B.
[116] *Adul. amic.* 54C.
[117] *Adul. amic.* 54C.
[118] Engberg-Pedersen, "Plutarch to Prince Philopappus," 75.
[119] Engberg-Pedersen, "Plutarch to Prince Philopappus," 72.
[120] Andrew Wallace-Hadrill, "Patronage in Roman Society: From Republic to Empire," *Patronage in Ancient Society*, 85.

powerful, offering phony "sage" advice or sweet compliments if required, all in the hopes of obtaining some small favour or distinction, or of exploiting the generosity of the person whom they had lured into their nets. There was no place for trust, sincerity, intimacy, simplicity or loyalty here, only cunning and guile.

But what likely irritated Plutarch more than all else was the fact that within this world of patronage, patrons and clients were often described as φίλοι. The flatterer imitated the friend, employing frank speech in his duplicity, and was therefore sometimes extremely difficult to detect, "as in the case with some animals to which Nature has given the faculty of changing their hue, so that they exactly conform to the colours and objects beneath them."[121] Such a designation of patrons and clients as friends "should be seen as a sham. It reflects an attempt to conceal the real ties, which were strongly hierarchical and status-determined."[122]

In his emphatic demonstration of the differences between friendship and flattery, and of the need to be able to distinguish between the two, Plutarch may be engaging in a larger social and political argument within which friendship and flattery represent, indeed embody, opposite poles. Genuine friendship delineates a society of trust and permanency, whereas flattery exemplifies the world of patronage in which people are obsessed with their own status and potential gains. As Engberg-Pedersen suggests, whenever we observe this nexus of friendship, flattery and frankness of speech within ancient texts, there is likely "a concern about the status system and a set of counter-values."[123] This is not to say that Plutarch, a well-to-do person, wanted to equalize wealth or obliterate all status distinctions, but simply that he was frustrated by the threat flattery posed to his noble ideal of friendship and the behaviour which characterized such an association.

Although Latin developed a separate vocabulary for patronage, this blurring of patron-client and friendship relations was also problematic for some Roman authors, just as it was for Plutarch. Unlike the Greek word φιλία, which describes relationships of affection between any two or more people, regardless of their biological connection, Latin had a more precise word for friendship, *amicitia*. This term refers to a relationship between two friends or *amici*, although the precise nature of the relationship could vary. Some scholars have claimed that *amicitia*

---

[121] *Adul. amic.* 51D.
[122] Engberg-Pedersen, "Plutarch to Prince Philopappus," 78.
[123] Engberg-Pedersen ("Plutarch to Prince Philopappus," 79) refers specifically to early Christian texts.

was simply a practical association, devoid of affection and intimacy,[124] or they have suggested that there is no distinction between a patron-client association and one of friendship.[125] Others, such as Richard Saller, have argued that the distinction between a client and a friend is sometimes so small that they could both be examined within the framework of patronage. He writes:

> To discuss bonds between senior aristocrats and their aspiring juniors in terms of "friendship" seems to me misleading, because of the egalitarian overtones that word has in modern English. Though willing to extend the courtesy of the label *amicus* to some of their inferiors, the status-conscious Romans did not allow the courtesy to obscure the relative social standings of the two parties. On the contrary, *amici* were subdivided into categories: *superiores, pares* and *inferiores* (and then lower down the hierarchy, humble *clientes*). Each category called for an appropriate mode of behaviour, of which the Romans were acutely aware (Pliny, *Ep.* 7.3.2, 2.6.2; Seneca, *Ep.* 94.14). The central question ... is whether *amici inferiores* can appropriately be analysed under the heading of patronage. Resemblances between the behaviour of aristocratic *amici inferiores* and *clientes* suggest that such an analysis would be a reasonable way of proceeding.[126]

Indeed, as Saller argues, there is some overlap between *amicitia* and *clientela* in the Roman world. Sometimes, both elements were present within a relationship as friendships could exist between persons of unequal stations in life.[127] But Roman friendship is not wholly reducible to a patron-client association, nor to a mere practical association. Peter Brunt writes that

> the range of *amicitia* is vast. From the constant intimacy and goodwill of virtuous or at least like-minded men to the courtesy that etiquette normally enjoined on gentlemen, it covers every degree of genuinely or overtly amicable relation. Within this spectrum purely political connections have their place, but one whose all-importance must not be assumed.[128]

---

[124] This is the view of Ronald Syme, *The Roman Revolution* (Oxford: Oxford University Press, 1939) 157.

[125] Konstan ("Patrons and Friends," 328) refers to Nicholas Horsfall (*Poets and Patron: Maecenas, Horace and the Georgics, Once More* [North Ryde, 1981] 5) who writes: "the line between *amicus* "friend" and *amicus* "client" should not be drawn, now or at any point later in the relationship."

[126] Richard Saller, "Patronage and Friendship in Early Imperial Rome: Drawing the Distinction," *Patronage in Ancient Society*, 57.

[127] See Konstan, *Friendship in the Classical World*, 136-37.

[128] Peter Brunt, "*Amicitia* in the Late Roman Republic," *The Fall of the Roman Republic* (Oxford: Clarendon, 1988) 381.

Moreover, and as discussed earlier, a patron-client relation necessarily placed the client in a situation in which he or she could not return the benefit or favour in equal amounts to the patron, thereby making the client permanently subservient to the patron unless some sort of serious mishap allowed the client to repay with some great feat or brave act. Thus, even though Roman patronage may have used similar language, and operated within a similar ethical exchange framework that involved loyalty and gratitude, from an emic point of view, "Roman patronage was not a mere variant of *amicitia*," although, from an etic point of view it could be described as a "lop-sided *amicitia*."[129] Moreover, the word *amicitia* may have been used broadly, but it does not mean that the characteristics of loyalty, honesty and trustworthiness were no longer important aspects of friendship, even in associations which were more political than intimate. Some Latin authors make it very clear that they understand there to be a difference between *amicitia* and *clientela*. But before we turn to those writers, let us recall Cicero's *Laelius de amicitia*, which reveals to what extent intimate friendship based upon virtue prevailed as a noble phenomenon in the world of this period.

Cicero's *Laelius* is solid evidence that the notion of a friendship based upon goodwill and virtue was a noble idea during the late Roman Republic. As mentioned above, however, *amicitia* could encompass intimate associations or mutual relations of *politesse*. In Rome, friendships existed between persons of both equal and unequal statures and could involve an exchange of goods and services.[130] It is for this reason that friendship in its Roman form *could be* indistinguishable from a patron-client relationship. Barbara Gold writes that "the word *amicus* is a perfect locus for discussing patronage, since it is a nicely ambiguous word which applies equally well to political allies or personal intimates, to the patron or the client."[131] Indeed, Roman society was exceptionally stratified, and people were often vying for the attentions and friendships of the wealthy and powerful. Sometimes a client of a wealthy person was also a friend, especially among the poets and their

---

[129] Verboven, *The Economy of Friends*, 62.

[130] As Konstan (*Friendship in the Classical World*, 128) writes: "... helpfulness is traditionally the mark of a friend and services may be interpreted as a sign of good will or amicableness. Mutual support is the point at which the vocabularies of friendship and exchange of benefits intersect, and Cicero moves naturally between the two issues, defending his integrity on both the counts of refraining from offending a supposed friend and of being conscientious in respect to any genuine debts of gratitude he may owe."

[131] Barbara K. Gold, *Literary Patronage in Greece and Rome* (Chapel Hill, London: University of North Carolina Press, 1987) 134.

"great friends" who gave the artists material wealth, fame and influence in exchange for "the gift of poetic immortality," that is, poetic tributes to the rich person's qualities.[132]

However, we have argued that this does not mean that patronage and friendship were one and the same. Friendship required honesty and goodwill between the two *amici*,[133] even if they were of separate social stations, or were not particularly close. Friends offered frank criticism; they did not flatter one another in order to gain advantages, as Plutarch made so utterly clear. Thus when both friendship and patronage existed together, tensions might surface as the friends could not always be sure whether the other's action sprang from *bona fide* friendship or another, possibly manipulative, strategy. Moreover, friends occasionally became clients, for as Peter White observes, "an exchange that was badly balanced over time might also work to clientize a friend."[134]

Konstan has examined the works of two Roman poets, Horace and Juvenal, with a focus upon this issue of friendship and patronage. In Juvenal's fifth satire, for example, the poet ridicules a certain Trebius, who fancies that he will attain the friendship of the wealthy patron, Virro. Juvenal exposes the fact that in reality, all Trebius will achieve is a client status and will "be as humble and indifferent to the eyes of Virro as the mob that lines up to salute him each day."[135] Trebius is invited to Virro's home for a meal but Virro treats him horribly, uncovering to what extent Virro does not consider Trebius a friend, but a mere hanger-on, whom he can humiliate and exploit. Juvenal concludes his satire by informing Trebius what his imagined friendship with Virro will be like: "If you can endure such things, you deserve them; some day you will be offering your head to be shaved and slapped: nor will you flinch from a stroke of the whip, well worthy of such a feast and such a friend."[136]

Some have interpreted this satire to equate friendship with patronage,[137] whereas Konstan has shown that Juvenal refers to friends and friendship throughout the satire with his tongue firmly placed inside of

---

[132] See Peter White (*Promised Verse: Poets in the Society of Augustan Rome* [Cambridge, MA, London: Harvard University Press, 1993] 14-27) for a discussion of patterns of exchange between the Augustan poets and their wealthy friends.

[133] Konstan, "Patrons and Friends," 336.

[134] White, *Promised Verse*, 31.

[135] Konstan, "Patrons and Friends," 336.

[136] Juvenal, *Sat.* 5.170-73 (LCL; trans. G.G. Ramsay; London: Heinemann; Cambridge, MA: Harvard University Press, 1950).

[137] See Richard LaFleur, "*Amicitia* and the Unity of Juvenal's First Book," *ICS* 4 (1979) 171.

his cheek. Part of Juvenal's humour resides in his portrayal of the "friendship" between these two characters as an absurd tale of abuse and manipulation. The irony lies in the tension between this absurdity and the notion of friendship as "a relationship based upon mutuality and generosity."[138] Trebius and Virro play at being friends, but in reality their association is based upon utility. Virro, the more powerful of the two, actually exploits Trebius, making their so-called friendship all the more counterfeit. Rather than likening friendship to patronage, Juvenal lays bare the hypocrisy of those who pretend to be friends but are in truth manipulating one another for their own interests.

Horace's eighteenth epistle also underlines the contrast between friendship and patronage. Horace spends the bulk of this letter advising its addressee, Lollius, a man of candour (Horace calls him *liberrime*)[139] on how to be an accommodating client. Lollius's natural disposition is to be straightforward and unafraid of speaking with frank speech (*libertas*) but Horace is seemingly against such honesty and pushes him in the opposite direction "to the point of endorsing the kind of assumed expressions and attitudes characteristic of the flatterer."[140] But then suddenly Horace changes his course and counsels Lollius to seek the quiet life; to read and to question the wise. He states: "Those who have never tried think it pleasant to court a friend in power; one who has tried dreads it."[141] The poet exhorts Lollius to seek his own way, to be free from the anxiety and fears that catering to a patron produces. He asks Lollius, "What will make you a friend to yourself?"[142] and states that the path, he, Horace, has taken is that of a secluded, unencumbered life, in which he may not "waver to and fro with the hopes of each uncertain hour."[143]

This letter demonstrates, then, that a life of independence is not compatible with the life of a client; of someone who must indulge the whims of a patron and adjust his or her behaviour based upon the fancies of the wealthy and powerful. In the first part of the letter, Horace referred to Lollius's patron as a "rich friend,"[144] "great friend,"[145] and

---

[138] Konstan, "Patrons and Friends," 337 n.29.
[139] Horace, *Ep.* 18.1 (LCL; trans. H. Rushton Fairclough; London: Heinemann; Cambridge, MA: Harvard University Press, 1942).
[140] Konstan, "Patrons and Friends," 339.
[141] *Ep.* 18.90.
[142] *Ep.* 18.101.
[143] *Ep.* 18.110.
[144] *Ep.* 18.24.
[145] *Ep.* 18.44-45.

"worshipful friend"[146] but again, the designation "friend" is likely ironic in the sense that this "friend" is far from the frank and good spirited person that an ideal friend is understood to be. Lollius may think that he has a friend in his patron, but in actuality he has only someone who will force him to quell his instinct to speak forthrightly, forcing him, instead, to speak in an ingratiating and pleasing manner. Such behaviour is counter to Lollius's dispostion for independence and thus Horace ends the letter with a plea for the quiet life, dependent upon no one but oneself.

Thus in Rome, friendship was still perceived by some as a relationship based upon mutual goodwill and honesty, as Cicero's reflections upon the subject illustrate. However, friendships did exist among people of differing social classes. It was common for patrons and clients to call one another *amici* even when the ideals of generosity and frankness did not manifest themselves in the relationship. It is this sort of pretension that the poets Horace and Juvenal sharply criticize, for they believe, like Plutarch, that it is hypocritical to call someone a friend whom one does not treat with genuine affection and goodwill. In practice, friendship could and did overlap with patronage, but they should not be conflated as one and the same.

Conclusion

This chapter has dealt with a variety of interrelated issues. First, that friendship was important politically and economically at certain points and in particular environments is without question. However, its use in such contexts does not mean that the lofty ideal image of friends as two people who act selflessly and generously towards one another did not exist. In fact, the use of this language of friendship in primarily political contexts illustrates the esteem with which the concept of friendship was held by ancients.

Second, given the previous statement and the centrality of reciprocity to ancient social relations, it is easy to understand how "friend" is used within the exchange systems of both benefaction and patronage. These two forms of exchange overlap with one another in a variety of ways, but they are also distinct. Benefaction, or at least the ideal forms of it, is associated with the virtue of generosity, and in this way it overlaps with the ideal of friendship. The noble benefactor should not be motivated by a desire for return, although it would be dishonourable for a beneficiary not to express gratitude. Moreover, when benefactors

---

[146] *Ep.* 18.73.

provided for associations and cities, they were not all-powerful, despite their wealth and status. Once the beneficiaries had fulfilled their obligations, the benefactor was often compelled to keep providing, and not to do so could even invite risk. The patron, however, appears to have had more power over his or her client(s), for the very definition of clienthood was to be unable to repay the debts incurred. Thus clients were extremely vulnerable to their patron's whims and often resorted to flattery for their own survival. Such behaviour was a far cry from ideal friendship, in which friends spoke plainly and directly to one another. Thus one can understand why writers such as Plutarch became so frustrated when they saw patrons and clients pretending to be friends, when in fact, they manifested one of the furthest things from it.

The foundationally distinct but overlapping concepts of benefaction and patronage, and their relationship to friendship, have now been exposed. We shall now turn to the text of James itself to determine to what extent these themes and practices help illuminate the arguments that the author is attempting to make.

4

The Exordium: James 1:2-18

Introduction

Having surveyed aspects of the history of friendship and some of the similarities and differences between friendship, patronage and benefaction, we now turn to an analysis of James. The next three chapters will examine three sections of the letter where I think that the social and cultural phenomena just discussed play significant roles. Reading these sections of James in light of friendship, patronage and benefaction can aid in better understanding what the author is attempting to convey. I also think, as do other authors, that these passages form discrete rhetorical units within the letter. Thus these chapters will examine not only the presence of friendship, patronage and benefaction within the language and social world of James, but how these textures function within the rhetoric, or inner texture, of the texts under examination. Before beginning this discussion the present chapter will briefly review the status of James both as a letter and as a rhetorically sophisticated document. It will not dwell on these issues, however, as they have been thoroughly discussed by other authors and there is something of a consensus emerging that James is a carefully crafted document,[1] although there is no agreement as to its overall literary or rhetorical structure.[2]

---

[1] A notable exception is the view of Wiard Popkes, who does not think that James is shaped by an overall literary structure, but by the various traditions that are incorporated into the document. See his *Der Brief des Jakobus* (THKNT 14; Leipzig: Evangelische Verlagsanstalt, 2001) 54-57.

[2] For a survey of contemporary studies of the structure of James, see Taylor, "Recent Scholarship on the Structure of James," 86-115.

James as a Letter

The debate about James as a letter recalls the work of Adolf Deissmann, whose studies of the ancient letter were conducted nearly a century ago. Deissmann classified letters into true letters, which are private and address concrete situations, and epistles, which are public, highly literary, and artistic. James, he argued, clearly falls into the latter category, as it lacks the detail required for a specific situation; rather, James is a "pamphlet addressed to the whole of Christendom."[3] Similarly, Martin Dibelius's influential commentary on James viewed the document as a string of discontinuous ethical admonitions, with no evidence of an "epistolary situation," the only "letter" characteristic being the prescript in Jas 1:1.[4] These observations led him to conclude that James is not an actual letter, but another genre, namely paraenesis.[5]

However, studies of ancient epistolography have shown that the ancient letter was a tremendously flexible and varied form of communication, and Deissmann's classification of letters into "real letters" and epistles has been criticized as a far too narrow, and indeed misleading, means of describing the great diversity of extant ancient letters. For example, there are epistles which could also be classified as "real letters" and some "real letters" bear characteristics of epistles.[6] Indeed, as David Aune has declared, apart from Deissmann's categorization, which Aune deems problematic, "few typologies of Greco-Roman or early Christian letters have been proposed and none widely adopted."[7] Other genres of literature could be framed within some of the conventions of a letter and could function as a letter, despite the fact that they do not bear all or even many "real letter" characteristics.[8] For example, essays could be framed by epistolary introductions and conclusions, and thus serve as

---

[3] Adolf Deissmann, *Light from the Ancient East* (trans. Lionel R. M. Strachan; New York: George H. Doran, 1927; repr., Peabody, MA: Hendrickson, 1995) 242-43.

[4] S. R. Llewellyn ("The Prescript of James," *NovT* 39 [1997] 385-93) has argued that Jas 1:1 was a later addition, and that perhaps this originally "loose compilation of sayings" comparable to the *Gospel of Thomas* and Q, was preserved "because it was given the ostensible form of the letter [with the addition of the prescript] at some later stage in its transmission."

[5] Dibelius, *James*, 2-3.

[6] Wachob, *The Voice of Jesus*, 5 n. 12. David E. Aune, *The New Testament in Its Literary Environment* (LEC 8; Philadelphia: Westminster, 1987) 165-66.

[7] David E. Aune, *The New Testament*, 161.

[8] As Aune (*The New Testament*, 170) writes, "epistolary prescripts and postscripts could be used to frame almost any kind of composition. The epistolary conventions of many letter-essays, philosophical letters, and novelistic and fictional letters functioned frequently in this way."

"letter essays," and philosophers would use the letter form as a means of instructing their students.[9] Such letters are not private nor do they necessarily focus upon a particular epistolary situation, but they are generally categorized as letters, albeit "literary" letters.

Many today consider James to be a "literary" letter which was not addressed to a private individual but probably to a number of communities, as indicated by the initial reference to the "twelve tribes in the diaspora" (1:1). In this way, James is comparable, as Karl-Wilhelm Niebuhr has argued, to ancient Jewish encyclicals, such as the Aramaic diaspora letters dispatched by members of the Gamaliel family,[10] and the encyclicals preserved within 2 Maccabees,[11] which were addressed to more than one group and could serve a variety of religious or administrative purposes.[12] It also, however, is analogous to what Fred O. Francis calls "secondary letters," or letters which "lack situational immediacy."[13] Francis observes that "secondary letters," often found within historical narratives such as the letter in 1 Macc 10:25 and the one within Josephus's *Antiquities* (8.50-54), have double opening statements, as James has,[14] and they end abruptly, with no epistolary close,[15] another feature of James. These characteristics also appear in many independent Hellenistic private and public letters,[16] and several letter collections leave out opening greetings and closing salutations altogether.[17] Some Hellenistic Jewish letters, such as the apocryphal Letter of Jeremiah, which is not embedded in a historical narrative, has

---

[9] See Aune, *The New Testament*, 165-69; and Abraham J. Malherbe, *Moral Exhortation, A Greco-Roman Sourcebook* (LEC 4; Philadelphia: Westminster, 1986) 79-85.

[10] See Karl-Wilhelm Niebuhr, "Der Jakobusbrief im Licht frühjüdischer Diasporabriefe," *NTS* 44 (1998) 420-43. For the texts and translations of these letters, see Dennis Pardee, *Handbook of Ancient Hebrew Letters* (SBLSBS 15; Chico, CA: Scholars, 1982) 186-96.

[11] See 2 Macc 1:1-9; 1:10-2:18.

[12] See Baasland, "Literarische Form," 3646-84; Ropes, *The Epistle of St. James*, 127-28; Wachob, *The Voice of Jesus*, 5-6.

[13] Francis, "The Form and Function," 111.

[14] Francis ("The Form and Function," 111) points out that in Jas 1:1-27 "there is a presentation and representation of testing, steadfastness, perfect work/gift, reproaching/anger, wisdom/words, and rich-poorer/doer. In both cases these themes laid down in the opening verses are subsequently developed in the body of the epistle."

[15] Embedded within Thucydides's narrative there are letters (7.10-15; 1.128.7) with neither opening nor closing formulae. See Aune, *The New Testament*, 169.

[16] For example Phlm 4-7 contains a double opening statement, and many Hellenistic letters, private and public, primary and secondary, end abruptly, such as 1 John. See Francis, "The Form and Function," 112, 125.

[17] Aune (*The New Testament*, 171) refers to the letters of Apollonius, for example, which all have abbreviated openings, and only four of which have closing salutations.

neither an epistolary prescript nor a closing formula.[18] Moreover, beginning with the phrase πρὸ πάντων in 5:12, James closes with a warning against the use of oaths and expressions of concern for the recipients' health and well-being. Referring to F.X.J. Exler's study of Hellenistic epistolography,[19] Francis points out how Greek letters may end with the phrase πρὸ πάντων followed by a health wish and/or an oath formula. Finally, many letters, including several New Testament letters,[20] refer to prayer in their closing. Thus James is not so devoid of epistolary features as Dibelius and others have thought, but may best be classified as a "literary" letter.[21]

James and Rhetoric

Despite Dibelius's view that James had limited epistolary features, he did grant that it was a sophisticated document, at least at the level of writing style and vocabulary. Recent scholarship on James concurs with Dibelius that the author writes in good Greek, uses rare words, and that the letter manifests various rhetorical elements, such as paronomasia (1:1, 2), parechesis (1:24), alliteration (1:2), and homoioteleuton (1:6) among others.[22] Yet Dibelius's fundamental description of James as paraenesis placed limitations upon the document that are no longer acceptable to many today. For Dibelius, paraenesis was a literary genre manifested by a series of exhortations strung together with little continuity between them and no overarching frame or theme.[23] Moreover, Dibelius thought that if something was essentially paraenetic, it was simply a loose assemblage of diverse traditions with no overall theological purpose or structure.[24]

It is likely for this latter reason that Dibelius did not apply the tenets of Greco-Roman rhetorical theory to the letter. For Dibelius, parae-

---

[18] Aune, *The New Testament*, 178.

[19] F.X.J. Exler, *The Form of the Ancient Greek Letter: A Study in Greek Epistolography* (Washington: Catholic University of America, 1923).

[20] For example, 1 Thess 5:17, 1 John 5:14-17, Phlm 22. See Francis, "The Form and Function," 125.

[21] Peter H. Davids, "The Epistle of James in Modern Discussion," *ANRW* 2.25.5 (1988) 3628-29; Johnson, *The Letter of James*, 24; Laws, *The Epistle of James*, 6; Wachob, *The Voice of Jesus*, 8.

[22] Dibelius, *James*, 37-38; see Wachob (*The Voice of Jesus*, 11-12) for a more substantial list of James's rhetorical elements.

[23] Dibelius, *James*, 5-11.

[24] Dibelius (*James*, 22) wrote that paraenesis, "by its very nature cannot at all bring together a coherent structure of theological thought." The origins of Dibelius's ideas about paraenetic literature are helpfully discussed by Wachob, *The Voice of Jesus*, 36-52.

netic literature was *by nature* unoriginal; it consisted primarily of a collection of traditions and was more interested in the transmission of materials than in their revision. As he wrote, the "first feature" of paraenesis "is a pervasive *eclecticism* which is a natural consequence of the history and nature of paraenesis, since the concern is the transmission of an ethical tradition that does not require a radical revision even though changes in emphasis and form might occur."[25] Thus Dibelius's presuppositions that James consisted primarily of paraenesis and about the nature of paraenesis itself prevented him from exploring how ancient rhetorical conventions may have been operative in James.

Dibelius understood paraenesis as a literary genre spanning Jewish and Greek cultures and grounded in ethical exhortation, which in turn, had an important role in early Christianity as it struggled to provide directives for fledgling Christian communities. There is little contention with this latter point, but historians have not been able to discover a definition of paraenesis as a technical term for a literary genre in the ancient world. In his taxonomic study of wisdom literature, John G. Gammie argues that paraenetic literature is a secondary genre of wisdom literature, with paraenesis as a sub-division of paraenetic literature. Paraenesis, therefore, "cannot be properly classified as a major literary type or even as a secondary genre."[26]

Others, such as Wesley Wachob, do not think that paraenesis is distinguishable from protreptic,[27] for indeed, both terms refer to hortatory speech. However, various studies have attempted to find differences between the two, with the result that some scholars, such as Wachob and Patrick Hartin,[28] prefer to classify James as protrepsis, while others, such as Gammie, think of it as paraenesis.[29] The issue of whether to

---

[25] Dibelius, *James*, 5.

[26] John G. Gammie, "Paraenetic Literature: Toward the Morphology of a Secondary Genre," *Semeia* 50 (1990) 41.

[27] Wachob (*The Voice of Jesus*, 51) says that "they are interchangeable terms for exhortation or horatory speech." Wachob bases his findings on the pioneering work of Theodore C. Burgess ("Epideictic Literature," *University of Chicago Studies in Classical Philology* 3 [1902] 89-248) which was apparently overlooked by Dibelius and those he depended upon for his understanding of paraenesis.

[28] For Hartin's discussion of this (largely based upon Gammie's *Semeia* article) see *A Spirituality of Perfection. Faith in Action in the Letter of James* (Collegeville: Liturgical Press, 1999) 45-49.

[29] Wachob (*Voice of Jesus*, 45) points out that Benjamin Fiore, although he admits that the modern distinction between protrepic and paraenesis is "sharper" than in antiquity, accepts Rudolf Vetschera's observation that paraenesis can include many aspects of life such as "culture, friends, enemies, good fortune" but that protreptic "hopes to lead the addressee to obtain a certain knowledge and the *aretē* included in it" (*The Function of*

categorize James as paraenesis or protrepsis cannot be solved here, but suffice it to say that debates about the literary genre and nature of James have contributed to the conclusion that we should no longer view James as a hodge-podge of sayings but as an organizationally disciplined letter, despite the fact that there are debates about the exact arrangement of that structure.

Some scholars object to the application of rhetorical analysis to letters such as James because in the ancient world, as Watson and Hauser, who build from the work of Abraham J. Malherbe, point out, epistolary theory and rhetorical theory developed separately from one another in antiquity and thus some scholars wonder if rhetoric truly affected letter writing in the ways in which other authors would like to think it did.[30] The ancient rhetorical handbooks rarely discuss rhetoric's applicability to letters, and likewise, letter writing manuals do not discuss rhetoric. It was not until the fourth and fifth centuries, moreover, that Christianity explicitly integrated rhetorical and epistolary practices.[31]

But as Wachob and others have affirmed, that rhetorical and epistolary theory was not formally integrated at the time of the composition of various texts of the New Testament does not mean that rhetoric could not have exerted an influence upon letter writing.[32] Rhetoric pervaded the cultures of the Graeco-Roman world and the authors of the New Testament did not require formal training in rhetoric in order

---

Personal Example in the Socratic and in the Pastoral Epistles [AnBib 105; Rome: Biblical Institute Press, 1986] 41). Fiore bases his comments upon the work of Rudolf Vetschera, *Zur griechischen Paränese* (Smichow/Prague: Rohlicek & Sievers, 1911-12) 7. Stanley Stowers has argued that the difference may be based upon the nature of the audience: paraenesis was directed to the converted in an effort to reinforce particular attitudes while protreptic is occasionally used in attempts to convert people. However, Stowers admits that this is not an entirely consistent feature of each term (*Letter Writing*, 91-92) and Wachob (*The Voice of Jesus*, 48) has noted that Clement of Alexandria, with his *Exhortation to Endurance or to the Newly Baptized*, did not presuppose a particular audience disposition when he titled his work a Προτρεπτικός. Gammie ("Paraenetic Literature," 53) points to a perhaps more convincing difference between the two terms that protrepsis builds a sustained argument which is much more systematic and organized than that of paraenesis, even though the latter can have a narrow focus.

[30] Duane F. Watson and Alan J. Hauser, *Rhetorical Criticism of the Bible. A Comprehensive Bibliography with Notes on History and Method* (Leiden: E.J. Brill, 1994) 121. Abraham J. Malherbe (*Ancient Epistolary Theorists* [SBLSBS 19; Atlanta: Scholars, 1988] 2) writes that epistolary theory "is absent from the earliest extant rhetorical handbooks, and it only gradually made its way into the genre."

[31] Watson, *Rhetorical Criticism*, 122.

[32] Wachob, *The Voice of Jesus*, 8. See also Burton L. Mack, *Rhetoric and the New Testament* (Guides to Biblical Scholarship; Minneapolis: Fortress, 1990) 31.

to be influenced by it, although some were likely from a well educated background. By simply living in the culture that they did, they would have come into contact with rhetoric, "for the rhetorical theory of the schools found its immediate application in almost every form of oral and written communication."[33] Moreover, Aune claims that by the third century BCE, rhetoric had come to influence letter writing,[34] and other authors have demonstrated that certain Greek writers wrote letters according to rhetorical conventions prior to the Common Era.[35] Demetrius, an otherwise unknown Greek writer who refers to Aristotle's *Rhetoric* from time to time, discusses letters in his treatise, *On Style*, which can possibly be dated to the early first century BCE.[36] Demetrius says that "the letter, like the dialogue, should abound in glimpses of character,"[37] and he continues on to describe the appropriate style and topics for letters. What is unusual, as George Kennedy comments, is that other rhetoricians do not discuss letters, as the epistolary format was used so widely in the Greco-Roman world.[38] Perhaps, as Jeffrey Reed points out, the three species of rhetoric were too limited for letter writers, despite the fact that their functions appear in letters.[39]

Despite this lack of ancient discussions of rhetoric as it relates to letter writing, there is now a wealth of rhetorical studies on the New Testament letters even though there remain some who are skeptical of rhetoric's applicability.[40] But when it comes to Hebrews and the

---

[33] George Kennedy, *New Testament Interpretation through Rhetorical Criticism* (Chapel Hill and London: University of North Carolina Press, 1984) 10.

[34] Aune, *The New Testament*, 160.

[35] For example, F.W. Hughes (*Early Christian Rhetoric and 2 Thessalonians* [JSNTSup 30; Sheffield: Sheffield Academic Press, 1989] 47-50) has shown that the letters of Demosthenes were written according to rhetorical rules.

[36] For a discussion of Demetrius, see George A. Kennedy, *A New History of Classical Rhetoric* (Princeton: Princeton University Press, 1994) 88-90.

[37] Demetrius, *Eloc.* 227 (LCL; trans. W. Rhys Roberts; London: Heinemann; Cambridge, MA: Harvard University Press, 1927).

[38] Kennedy, *A New History*, 90.

[39] Jeffrey T. Reed, *A Discourse Analysis of Philippians. Method and Rhetoric in the Debate over Literary Integrity* (JSNTSup 136; Sheffield: Sheffield Academic Press, 1997) 454.

[40] For example, Stanley E. Porter, ("The Theoretical Justification for Application of Rhetorical Categories to Pauline Epistolary Literature," *Rhetoric and the New Testament. Essays from the 1992 Heidelberg Conference* [ed. Stanley E. Porter & Thomas H. Olbricht; JSNTSup 90; Sheffield: JSOT Press, 1993] 100-22) argues that studies of Paul's letters should limit themselves to the rhetorical style of Paul's letters, as the rhetorical handbooks only discuss style when it comes to letters. In his view, there is not enough warrant in the handbooks for applying basic rhetorical categories to letters. In contrast, see Betz (*Gala-

Catholic Epistles, there is little debate about the applicability of ancient rhetorical practices. They are seen as highly literary speeches that were intended to be read aloud, and thus scholars assume that the authors incorporated rhetorical conventions into their texts.[41] Moreover, there is general agreement that the authors of these ancient texts did not simply absorb and subsequently reflect rhetorical practices from the world around them, but that they consciously and skillfully applied rhetorical conventions to their texts in a "studied" manner, which suggests that at least some of the authors may have been schooled in ancient rhetoric.[42]

Several early critics had used rhetoric in their analyses of James during the 19th century.[43] But studies incorporating rhetoric into the examination of James did not reappear until relatively recently, with the publication of Wilhelm Wuellner's "Der Jakobusbrief im Licht der Rhetorik und Textpragmatik," followed by Ernst Baasland, who proposed that James consisted of deliberative rhetoric and was essentially a wisdom speech (*weisheitliche Rede*).[44] John H. Elliott also develops his analysis of James based upon Wuellner's work, but he focuses on the insights that the social sciences can bring to the letter. Elliott explores James in light of contrasts between purity and pollution, which figured importantly in Second Temple Judaism and early Christianity, and shows how purity and pollution "serve as an important means for conceptualizing, distinguishing, and evaluating appropriate and inappropriate attitudes, actions, and alliances with regard to the community, its members, and their relation to God and society."[45]

The most recent rhetorical study of the entire letter of James is that of Lauri Thurén, who argues that James is primarily epideictic rhetoric in that it attempts to reinforce ideas and values that the recipients already possess.[46] Thurén suggests that the seeming obscurity of the rhetorical structure is actually the subtlety of an author who knows that

tians), who performs a full-fledged application of ancient rhetorical practices to Paul's letter to the Galatians.

[41] Duane F. Watson, "Rhetorical Criticism of Hebrews and the Catholic Epistles Since 1978," *CR:BS* 5 (1997) 178.

[42] Watson, "Rhetorical Criticism," 179.

[43] This is mentioned by Wachob (*Voice of Jesus*, 54), who refers to Baasland ("Literarische Form," 3648) who, in turn, refers to the work of J.D. Schulze, C.G. Küchler, C.G. Wilke, and J.A. Bengel, all of whom applied insights from rhetoric to their analyses of James before the beginning of the 20th century.

[44] Baasland, "Literarische Form," 3654.

[45] Elliott, "The Epistle of James," 78-79.

[46] Lauri Thurén, "Risky Rhetoric," 276-77. Thurén also grants that there are aspects of judicial and deliberative rhetoric within the letter as well.

his audience is rhetorically knowledgeable, and thus resists making his rhetorical shifts too obvious.[47]

Other authors have offered more focused work on sections of James. J.D.N. van der Westhuizen performed a close analysis of Jas 2:14-26, which he classifies as deliberative rhetoric in that it exhorts the audience to action.[48] Duane F. Watson has published two rhetorical studies, on James 2 and 3:1-12 respectively. He understands ch. 2 and 3:1-12 as deliberative rhetoric, for these sections exhort the audience to a particular type of action and dissuade them from other kinds of behavior. Watson shows how there are three complete arguments created in these pericopae, each of which includes a *propositio*, *ratio*, *confirmatio*, *exornatio*, and *conplexio*. He also explains how James uses diatribe and paraenetic materials in these sections to amplify the arguments.[49] Wachob's work concentrates upon the use of a saying of Jesus in 2:5 within the rhetorical structure of 2:1-13. He also considers James to be deliberative rhetoric, and, applying Vernon K. Robbins's method of socio-rhetorical criticism, he explores how 2:5 contributes to the social, cultural and ideological understanding of James as a whole.[50] Finally, Patrick J. Hartin's most recent book on the letter of James finds rhetorical patterns throughout the letter, arguing that 2:1-13, 2:14-26, 3:1-12, and 3:13-4:10 each conform to the pattern of a perfect argument.[51]

The work of the scholars mentioned above, as well as others whom we will engage presently, suggests that there is an emerging agreement that this text is informed by Graeco-Roman rhetorical practices insofar as these practices pervade the culture and society of the day, although considerable disagreement remains regarding how exactly these conventions figure in James. This lack of consensus does not mean that a rhetorical investigation is not warranted, for in rhetorical speeches and especially so in letters, the precise starting and ending points of rhetorical units are not always obvious nor do they plainly conform to the instructions provided in handbooks and instruction manuals.[52] Moreover, early Christian rhetoric, insofar as it served a new social

---

[47] Thurén, "Risky Rhetoric," 283.

[48] J.D.N. van der Westhuizen, "Stylistic Techniques and Their Functions in James 2:14-26," *Neot* 25 (1991) 89-107.

[49] Watson, "James 2;" "The Rhetoric of James 3:1-12."

[50] For a brief summary of Wachob's thesis, see Watson, "Rhetorical Criticism," 189.

[51] Patrick J. Hartin, *James* (Sacra Pagina 14; Collegeville: Liturgical Press, 2003).

[52] Mack (*Rhetoric and the New Testament*, 49) points out that the rhetorical handbooks were simply guides; they "were never understood in antiquity as rigid templates, nor has it been assumed ... that every rhetorical composition must follow these patterns."

experiment, was imaginative and inventive in its reference to new language and figures, and did not draw upon all of the stock phrases and heroic examples of its non-Christian contemporaries.[53] Therefore, the aim of this study is not to offer a comprehensive rhetorical outline of James, but insofar as sections of James use the language of friendship and the related concepts of patronage and benefaction, it will analyze the rhetorical form and function of the unit under question.

James 1:2-18

A. Common Features of the Exordium

Before arguing that Jas 1:2-18 serves as the exordium of the letter, attention must be paid to the nature and function of an exordium within ancient rhetoric. Subsequently the chapter will delineate how 1:2-18 forms an exordium and how friendship language and related concepts function within the unit.

Most ancient writers concur that the exordium is a requirement for an argumentative speech,[54] although Aristotle indicates that it is "only admissible when there is a conflict of opinion."[55] The purpose of the exordium is to establish an *ethos* of authority for the speaker and a climate of *pathos* that will engage the audience and predispose it to listen. The exordium is always adjusted to suit the circumstances of the discourse, speaker, audience (including potential opponents), and the particular subject under discussion. Cicero says that the exordium should be serious and must

> contain everything which contributes to dignity, because the best thing to do is that which especially commends the speaker to his audience. It should contain very little brilliance, vivacity, or finish of style, because these give rise to a suspicion of preparation and excessive ingenuity (*Inv.* 1.25 [LCL]).[56]

Although the entire narrative should induce the audience to be well disposed, attentive and receptive to the speaker, the *Rhetorica ad Herennium*

---

[53] See Mack, *Rhetoric and the New Testament*, 94-97.

[54] See C. Perelman and L. Olbrechts-Tyteca, *The New Rhetoric. A Treatise on Argumentation* (trans. John Wilkinson and Purcell Weaver; Notre Dame, London: University of Notre Dame Press, 1969) 495.

[55] Aristotle, *Rhet* 3.13.3 (LCL; trans. John Henry Freese; London, Cambridge, MA: Harvard University Press, 1926).

[56] Translated by H.M. Hubbell (Cambridge, MA: Harvard University Press; London: Heinemann, 1949).

says that this stance "must in the main be won by the Introduction to the cause."[57]

In any speech, the exordium is the crucial place for establishing the authority of the speaker, for if the speaker is believed to be a good person at the beginning, the audience will be more inclined to listen.[58] Ancient rhetoricians agree that the character of the speaker has a central role in the effectiveness of the speech; in fact, Aristotle says that this *ethos*, or moral character, "constitutes the most effective means of proof" (*Rhet.* 1.2.4). Thus the exordium must carefully establish the credibility of the speaker, especially if the speaker knows that the audience is not sympathetic.

One may begin a speech with either a direct or a subtle opening, the latter reserved for situations in which the speaker's cause is discreditable, the hearer has already been persuaded by the opposition, or the hearer is tired from listening to previous speakers.[59] If one uses the direct approach, an effective method of beginning is to address the situation of the hearers and praise them for their "courage, wisdom, humanity and nobility of past judgments they have rendered ..." (*Rhet. ad Her.* 1.8). One also attracts the audience's attention if it is made clear that the matter under discussion is important, and that it concerns all of humanity or the hearers themselves.[60] The speaker may refer to the good relationship between himself and the audience, or he will address the situation of the audience, which in turn, can be understood as giving rise to the speech.[61]

The exordium may also be used to introduce some main points which will be developed later in the argument. The *Rhetoric to Alexander* states that one of the tasks of the exordium is to provide a "summary explanation of the business to persons who are not acquainted with it, in order to inform them what the speech is about and to enable them to follow the line of argument ..."[62] According to Quintilian, such an introduction is not a requirement and should not enumerate every issue to be discussed, but it may be prudent to include a few references to the main questions as they "will exercise a valuable influence in winning the judge

---

[57] Pseudo-Cicero, *Rhet. Her.* 1.11 (LCL; trans. Harry Caplan; Cambridge, MA, London: Harvard University Press, 1954).

[58] Quintilian, *Inst.* 4.1.7 (LCL; trans. H.E. Butler; London: Heinemann; Cambridge, MA: Harvard University Press, 1960).

[59] *Rhet. ad Her.* 1.9.

[60] Cicero, *De Inv.* 1.23.

[61] Perelman and Olbrechts-Tyteca, *The New Rhetoric*, 497.

[62] Pseudo-Aristotle, *Rhet. Alex.* 29 (LCL; trans. H. Rackham; London: Heinemann; Cambridge, MA: Harvard University Press, 1957).

to regard us with favour" (4.1.26). Likewise, Cicero says that a faulty exordium is one which neglects to find connections with the rest of the speech.[63] Thus one expects to find ideas and themes within the exordium that will be developed later on. Such an introduction aids in preparing the audience for what is to come.

B. James 1:2-18 as an Exordium

The transition markers between the exordium, narratio and other parts commonly referred to in the rhetorical handbooks are not always obvious in rhetorical speeches, even less so in letters,[64] and as Watson points out, "it is more likely that James simply does not conform to Greco-Roman standards in its overall argumentation."[65] Moreover, James uses many obvious division markers, such as the appeal to "my brothers" or "my beloved brothers" to indicate small units, but thereby making it difficult to determine the exact outline of larger rhetorical sections. Therefore, one cannot rely solely upon clear syntactic shifts but on how the sections function on a rhetorical level.

Nearly all studies of James agree that 1:1 is an epistolary prescript, the format of which is actually typical of ancient non-literary letters.[66] Certainly the prescript contributes to the authority of the speaker, for it wants to be heard as coming from James of Jerusalem, or James the Just, clearly an important figure within early Christianity. Other than to call himself a "slave of God and of the Lord Jesus Christ," this speaker has no need to qualify himself, indicating that he knew that the recipients would recognize the name. Moreover, Thurén argues that the prescript must be considered as part of the exordium, because it establishes the *ethos* of the speaker as authoritative, its use of the epithet δοῦλος "emphasizes his solidarity with the addressees," and the identification of the audience with the true Israel would be pleasing, for despite their *diaspora* situation, they really have high status. Moreover,

---

[63] Cicero (*De Inv.* 1.26): "The unconnected [exordium] is one which is not derived from the circumstances of the case nor closely knit with the rest of the speech, such as a limb to the body."

[64] Especially when, as discussed earlier, the rhetorical handbooks do not address the use of rhetoric in letters.

[65] Watson, "Rhetorical Criticism," 190.

[66] See John L. White, *Light from Ancient Letters* (Philadelphia: Fortress, 1986) 194-95. As noted earlier, Llewelyn ("The Prescript of James") argues that the prescript was only added later to give James the appearance of a letter, which enabled its survival. Unfortunately, however, Llewelyn does not engage the important essay by Francis ("Form and Function") who, as discussed previously, explores the ways in which different ancient letter forms can deviate from standard practices, such as a lack of a final farewell.

the use of χαίρειν would create an amiable atmosphere and connects the verse to the next one, which refers to joy (χαράν).[67] However, it is just as likely that the author may have written a prescript which would nicely cohere with the rest of the letter, for 1:2-18 is able to develop an *ethos* and *pathos* quite well apart from the prescript.

When we turn to the rest of the exordium, most rhetorical analyses of James have argued that 1:2-18 forms either part or all of the exordium and even Dibelius grants that this is a seemingly unified section of the letter.[68] Apart from his inclusion of Jas 1:1, Thurén's arguments regarding the outlines of the exordium are the most convincing.[69] For Thurén, 1:1-4 forms the exordium proper, with its emphasis upon perseverance and perfection, 1:5-11 then amplifies these themes with relation to wisdom and money, while 1:12-18 forms an inclusio by returning to the themes of perseverance and perfection. Wuellner, however, argues that the exordium is found in 1:2-4, followed by a *narratio* (1:5-11), a *propositio* in 1:12, and an *argumentatio* in 1:13–5:6. Thurén rightly points out that such an arrangement is awkward, for there are no signs of a transition between 1:12 and 1:13, and 1:19, which begins with "Know this, my beloved brothers," is much more likely the beginning of a new section.[70] Other studies of James have divided the opening of the letter differently, such as Fred O. Francis, who argues that 1:13-18, 1:19-21 and 1:22-25 have restated the three opening themes of testing, wisdom/speech, and money,[71] but he has not addressed how such a structure would function rhetorically. If we examine the unit of 1:2-18, however, we will see that it performs the typical functions of an exordium.

There are several ways in which a speaker can establish an *ethos* of authority and integrity.[72] One is the use of direct address, which, as mentioned earlier, is often used within the exordium in rhetorical speeches. Many ancient writers confirm that forthright, frank speech (παρρησία or *licentia*), which offers criticism but criticism for the bet-

---

[67] Thurén, "Risky Rhetoric," 270-71.

[68] Dibelius, *James*, 69.

[69] Baasland ("Literarische Form," 3658-59) also considers Jas 1:2-18 to be the exordium, although he thinks that 1:16-18 functions as a *transitus* to the *propositio* in 1:19-27.

[70] Thurén, "Risky Rhetoric," 270.

[71] Francis, "Form and Function," 118.

[72] I am following the approach of Shawn Carruth here ("Strategies of Authority. A Rhetorical Study of the Character of the Speaker in Q 6:20-49," *Conflict and Invention. Literary, Rhetorical, and Social Studies on the Sayings Gospel Q*, ed. John S. Kloppenborg [Valley Forge, PA: Trinity, 1995] 98-115), who applies the principles of rhetorical theory to the character of the speaker in the Q inaugural sermon.

terment of the hearers, reveals the fine character of the speaker. Dio Chrysostom insists that to find a man who speaks frankly and out of concern for the good of others, even to the point of risking alienation and rejection from the mob, is not easy, "so great is the dearth of noble, independent souls and such the abundance of toadies, mountebanks, and sophists."[73] Rhetoricians thought highly of frankness. Isocrates, for example, wrote that one ought to commend those who admonish others for their betterment, "for such a man can soonest bring you to abhor what you should abhor and to set your hearts on better things."[74] This frankness must not descend to the level of a humiliating invective, we recall, for such disparagement would ultimately not aid or improve the recipients, but only depress or demoralize them. Thus frankness must always keep the good of the listeners in view, and must be done sensitively and with moderation.[75]

The beginning of James does not admonish the audience, but it does directly warn them about their behaviour. The author speaks confidently and with authority when he cautions them to ask God for wisdom (if they lack it) with faith, unlike the double-minded man who is unstable and as a result will receive nothing from God (1:5-7). Although we have not established who the recipients of the letter were, nor what their economic status was, James asserts squarely that the rich man will fade away (1:10-11). If the recipients of the letter consisted of both rich and poor, James does not resist the possibility of offending the wealthy, at least if they intend upon remaining wealthy.

Signs of a speaker's *ethos* are also evident in the use of imperatives. Ancient rhetoricians do not discuss the use of imperatives in creating an *ethos*, but some modern theorists point out that the force of the imperative lies in the authority of the speaker.[76] Thus, if a speaker knew that she lacked authority, she would likely resist using the imperative mood, as the audience would immediately begin ignoring her. James, however, does not hesitate to use the imperative throughout his letter, as it appears 31 times,[77] eight of which are in Jas 1:2-18. Even from the very beginning of the letter, then, the author seems to be aware of his au-

---

[73] Dio Chrysostom, *Alex.* 32.11 (LCL; trans. J.W. Cohoon & H. Lamar Crosby; London: Heinemann; Cambridge, MA: Harvard University Press, 1961).

[74] Isocrates, *De pace* 72-73 (LCL; trans. George Norlin; London: Heinemann; New York: Putnam, 1929).

[75] See Plutarch, *Adul. amic.* 74D-E.

[76] See Carruth, "Strategies of Authority," 103 and Perelman and Olbrechts-Tyteca, *The New Rhetoric*, 158.

[77] See Joseph B. Mayor, *The Epistle of St. James* (London: Macmillan, 1913) ccxxx.

thoritative hold on the audience, for otherwise he would likely avoid so many direct instructions.

The use of maxims can enhance the authority of the speaker, for by using a known saying or phrase which is understood to be generally true, the speaker reveals a good character.[78] However, indiscriminately flinging maxims about in a speech will not impress an audience; the maxims must be used sparingly and appropriately. Quintilian makes it clear that the application of well-known sayings is "useless, unless the pleader has the wit to apply them in such a manner as to support the points which he is trying to make" (5.11.42). Thus proverbs or sayings with which the audience may be quite familiar are not effective unless they are placed carefully within an appropriate context.

James 1:12 is commonly understood to be a macarism or beatitude, a type of maxim which often appears in the LXX with the formula μακάριος ἀνήρ,[79] and is a characteristic feature of wisdom literature.[80] George Kennedy discusses the beatitudes in Matthew's Sermon on the Mount, explaining that Jesus makes the minor premises ("the poor in spirit will enter the kingdom of heaven" and so forth) acceptable to his listeners "by avoiding any attempt to justify them, thus relying on the ethos of his authority, and also by the way he puts the verbs into the future tense."[81] Similarly, Shawn Carruth has shown how the beatitudes in Q 6:20-21 derive their claim to truth from the authority of the speaker. In fact, the speaker must have significant authority as the Q beatitudes are generally thought to run counter to conventional wisdom.[82] The content of Jas 1:12 is not necessarily counter to accepted wisdom, given the emphasis upon testing within Jewish wisdom literature,[83] but it does offer the future promise of an eschatological reward, the "crown of life." Therefore, it seems that the speaker in James again asserts his authority by making a firm statement about the future, with no need to justify himself. Secondly, the reference to a trial (πειρασμός) recalls 1:2 and prepares the way for the discussion of temptation in 1:13-18, a section in which the verb πειράζειν occurs three times and the adjective ἀπείραστος appears once in v. 13. While maintaining the *ethos* of the speaker, therefore, the beatitude also fits well within the

---

[78] Aristotle (*Rhet.* 2.21.16) says that "he who employs [maxims] in a general manner declares his moral preferences; if then the maxims are good, they show the speaker also to be a man of good character."

[79] Dibelius, *James*, 88.

[80] Patrick J. Hartin, *A Spirituality of Perfection*, 43.

[81] Kennedy, *New Testament Interpretation*, 50.

[82] Carruth, "Strategies of Authority," 108.

[83] Ralph P. Martin, *James* (WBC 48; Waco: Word Books, 1988) 33.

opening section of James, connecting themes introduced at the very beginning of the letter with those that immediately follow v. 12.

James 1:13-18 then continues the theme of temptation/testing with a series of statements about God and temptation. 1:13 is particularly notable as it conforms somewhat to the characteristics of a rhetorical syllogism or *enthymeme* whereby a statement is made, which is an imperative in this case ("Let no one say when he is tempted, 'I am tempted by God'"), followed by a reason for the statement with the connective γάρ ("for God cannot be tempted with evil and he himself tempts no one"). Although there are biblical passages such as Gen 22 which suggest that God does indeed test, here James is likely expressing the view found in wisdom literature that rather than taking responsibility for their choices, humans are quick to blame God when they experience difficulties.[84] It could be, moreover, that God does not "tempt to evil" but does "test" for virtue, for surely the author would admit that God tested Abraham in Jas 2:21?[85] Verses 14 and 15 then place the blame for temptation to evil upon one's own desire, ἐπιθυμία, which eventually leads to sin and death, while vv. 16-18 affirm that only goodness and perfection come from God, in direct contrast to ἐπιθυμία.[86]

Such a series of strong statements about the source of temptation and the nature of God would not emerge from a speaker who lacks respect from his audience. Quintilian states that "reflexions of universal application" are "best suited to those speakers whose authority is such that their character itself will lend weight to their words" (8.5.7-8). James 1:13-18 makes firm assertions about human desire and the nature of the divine, which suggests that this author possesses an *ethos* of self-assuredness and respect, for he requires such authority to affirm these opinions.

Yet the beginning of James does not focus upon *ethos* at the expense of *pathos*, for the text attempts to arouse emotion from the audience. Although the author speaks with authority, he expresses concern for the recipients. 1:2, for example, makes emotional appeals to the audience with a reference to the trials (πειρασμοί) that they, the author's "brothers" (ἀδελφοί) meet, and the assurance that the testing

---

[84] See Prov 19:3; Sir 15:11-20; Martin, *James*, 34.

[85] See Johnson, *The Letter of James*, 192.

[86] The contrast between desire and God is most pronounced in v. 18, whereby God "gives birth" to humans "by the word of truth" as opposed to desire which conceived sin, which in turn "gave birth" to death. See Johnson, *The Letter of James*, 205; Martin, *James*, 39.

(δοκίμιον) of faith will lead to a virtue, namely steadfastness or endurance (ὑπομονή). Of note here is the fact that James describes the audience as "knowing" that testing will produce endurance, a positive statement which would make the addressees more inclined to listen.[87] Such endurance, in turn, leads to an even greater end, that of perfection, for 1:4 states that ὑπομονή should have a "full effect" or "perfect work" (ἔργον τέλειον) such that the audience may be "perfect and complete, lacking in nothing." Thus the end of testing is not steadfastness but ultimately perfection or wholeness; something which James presents as an attainable goal.

Moreover, at the close of the exordium, James refers to his "beloved brothers" (1:16) and assures them that all good things come from God, that "we" were brought forth by the word of truth that "we" should be a kind of "first fruits" of God's creatures (1:18). This verse is often interpreted as a reference to the salvific actions of God, whereby the believer becomes one of the "first fruits" or one of the reborn.[88] Rhetorically, it could not help but have a positive effect upon the audience, for it assures them that they are indeed the first fruits of God's creatures.

Thus far, 1:2-18 has fulfilled the duties of the exordium in that it has presented the speaker as authoritative, direct, and concerned for the well-being of the audience, but it has done so with a certain sensitivity for their situation and assurance of God's reliability. But an exordium will also often refer to the subject(s) of the entire speech[89] and thus it is not unusual that the main themes of James be introduced in this section. Many analysts agree that an overall thrust of James is to seek perfection or wholeness,[90] for we observe this theme to be taken up throughout the rest of the letter, with τέλειος occurring five times, as well as other instances of the verb τελεῖν and related words such as ὅλος and ὁλόκληρος.[91] By perfection, James does not mean the unat-

---

[87] See Thurén, "Risky Rhetoric," 271.

[88] See Dibelius, *James*, 104-107.

[89] Perelman and Olbrechts-Tyceca, *The New Rhetoric*, 497.

[90] See, for example, Elliott, "The Epistle of James in Rhetorical and Social Scientific Perspective," 71; Hubert Frankemölle, "Das semantische Netz des Jakobusbriefes. Zur Einheit eines umstrittenen Briefes,"*BZ* 34 (1990) 193; Patrick J. Hartin, "Call to be Perfect through Suffering (James 1,2-4). The Concept of Perfection in the Epistle of James and the Sermon on the Mount," *Bib* 77 (1996) 477-92; and *A Spirituality of Perfection*; Martin, *James*, lxxix-lxxxiv; Josef Zmijewski, "Christliche 'Vollkommenheit.' Erwägungen zur Theologie des Jakobusbriefes," *Studien zum Neuen Testament und seiner Umwelt* (ed. Albert Fuchs; ser. A, vol. 5; Linz: A. Fuchs, 1980) 50-78.

[91] The use of τέλειος and related words has been analysed by Zmijewski, "Christliche 'Vollkommenheit,'" 52-53.

tainable thing for which moderns sometimes aspire, but the notion of complete or total allegiance to God.[92] To be perfect is to withstand the trials of faith which seek to divide one from God, as well as to live out one's life in dedication to God, whether it be through bridling one's tongue (3:2) or through consistency between hearing and doing (1:25).

Perfection is gained, at least in part, not through one's own merits, but through the gift of wisdom from God, which is the focus of Jas 1:5-8. Thurén, Elliott and Wuellner argue that this section is an expansion or *amplificatio* of the proper exordium in 1:2-4, which firmly lays out the need for perseverance in the quest for perfection. 1:9-11, which refers to the rich and poor, a theme taken up later on throughout the letter, is also an amplification of perfection, for part of being perfect is to resist the desire for riches.[93] 1:12-18 then invokes a theme of the exordium, endurance leading to perfection, by stating that μακάριος ἀνὴρ ὃς ὑπομένει πειρασμόν, ὅτι δόκιμος γενόμενος λήμψεται τὸν στέφανον τῆς ζωῆς, ὃν ἐπηγγείλατο τοῖς ἀγαπῶσιν αὐτόν ("Blessed is the man who endures trial, for when he has stood the test he will receive the crown of life which God has promised him"), and by furnishing another meaning of πειρασμός: "steadfastness in tribulation is rewarded by God [1:2-4], but the trial can also be a temptation which leads to death [1:13-15]."[94] The section then closes with 1:16-18, which provides a contrast to 1:13-15 by emphasizing that "every perfect gift" comes from God who "brought us forth," unlike sin which "brings forth" death. God, who provides "every perfect gift" is the source of perfection, it seems, echoing 1:5-8. Thus, it is clear that 1:2-18 performs another of its duties as an exordium, and that is to introduce a main subject of the letter.

C. Friendship and Benefaction within the Exordium

Having made a case for Jas 1:2-18 as the exordium of the letter, to what extent do notions of friendship, benefaction and/or patronage play a role in this unit? The subsequent section will attend to this question at three levels: author to audience; the attributes of community members; and the character of God and God's relationship to the community. Here we see that the author speaks to the audience authoritatively, but invokes aspects of the tradition of friendship, he

---

[92] Hartin ("Called to Be Perfect through Suffering," 483-84) discusses this concept of perfection in Jewish literature.

[93] Thurén, "Risky Rhetoric," 272; Elliott, "The Epistle of James in Rhetorical and Social Scientific Perspective," 72; Wuellner, "Der Jakobusbrief," 41. Baasland ("Literarische Form," 3655) includes Jas 1:5-15 within the exordium.

[94] Thurén, "Risky Rhetoric," 272.

introduces some of the virtues of friendship as important for the audience to uphold, especially the ability to withstand testing and faithfulness, and he introduces God as a benefactor and the tie between the community members and God as one of friendship and benefaction.

1. Author to Hearers/Readers

The epistle cannot be categorized as a "friendly letter" type, but one of moral exhortation and advice.[95] The speaker, as we have seen, is a figure of respect; in fact, in claiming to be James the Just, the brother of Jesus,[96] he is speaking as one who was close to Jesus. Robert Wall has also suggested that in supplying the credentials of "servant of God and of the Lord Jesus Christ," the author is drawing upon the image of Jacob, who is identified as God's servant by Isaiah (Isa 49:5-6) and called to draw together the scattered sheep of Israel. For Wall, the servanthood of James is comparable to that of Jacob, and thus James writes as "a tradent of an authoritative revelation tradition, but also as an agent of God's salvation, whose vocation is to teach the word of the Lord for salvation."[97] Whoever actually wrote James, and whether or not Wall's point is correct, the implied author speaks with a voice of authority.

In antiquity, wise men, teachers and friends had particular responsibilities to speak with frankness, as Philodemus's essay on frank criticism makes clear.[98] The notion that the speaker is self-consciously speaking as a teacher becomes evident in Jas 3:1-2, when he refers to teachers, himself included, in the context of a discussion of the role and power of the tongue. Given the author's self-understanding as a teacher, his knowledge of the responsibilities of teachers, his warnings about the dangers of the tongue (3:1-12) as well as the frank tone that pervades the letter, I think that he is aware of the value of frank speech and values it, even though he never explicitly mentions the word παρρησία. And as discussed in the previous chapter, frank speech was closely associated with friendship. Plutarch emphasizes the fact that true friends will speak directly to one another, out of concern for each one's well-being and betterment.[99] Παρρησία was the focus, as we saw, of

---

[95] See Stowers, *Letter Writing*, 91-151.

[96] Scholarship on James is virtually unanimous that the James whom the author purports to be is James the Just, or James of Jerusalem. This was the most famous James in the early church, and claiming to be this James with little qualification presumes that the audience knew who he was.

[97] Wall, *Community of the Wise*, 41.

[98] Philodemus, *Lib.* 1; 10.

[99] *Amic.adul.* 71B.

Philodemus's treatise on how members of the Epicurean school, friends and fellow disciples, should treat one another. In this same tradition, James does not make emotional appeals; rather he firmly exhorts the audience to patience and perfection, and warns his listeners not to fall prey to temptation. James is blunt, with no trace of flattery.

But consistently with advice about frank speech from Philodemus and Plutarch, James does not demolish the hearers. Plutarch says that friends should not speak with anger and resort to fault-finding for "frankness is friendly and noble, but fault-finding is selfish and mean".[100] There are no insults in James; rather, the letter offers reassurances that those who withstand testing and trial will receive "the crown of life" (1:12). The exhortations are for the good of the audience, not for their humiliation. Indeed, harsh warnings and apocalyptic images are applied to the rich, but these rich are outside the community, as we will discuss below. In speaking to his intended audience, and beginning in the exordium, James provides strong instruction intertwined with references to God's reliability and promises of God's gifts (1:5, 12, 17).

Moreover, the author addresses the audience as ἀδελφοί μου (1:2) and as ἀδελφοί μου ἀγαπητοί (1:16), an address which he continues to use throughout the rest of the letter.[101] As discussed in Chapter 2, Arzt-Grabner and Harland have shown that the use of "brothers" could, among other things, be used to designate friends in a variety of contexts, including many Greek documentary papyri, as well as in inscriptions from associations.[102] By consistently referring to the audience as ἀδελφοί μου, James tempers his firm exhortation with fictive family language that evokes, as it does in other ancient contexts, belonging and friendship. Moreover by calling the audience "my" brothers (and presumably women were included, as indicated by 2:15), James stresses his relationship with the audience. Even though he speaks with authority, he places himself alongside the community, as a brother, perhaps even as an equal, as Hartin suggests.[103] The references to the first person plural in 1:18 further underscore this identification with the recipients. Therefore, although the voice is strong, it also bears aspects of intimacy and stresses a common identity between the author and the audience. James clearly wants to offer directives to his readers/hearers, but he also accentuates his relationship to them. He speaks as a wise, respected and

---

[100] Plutarch, *Adul. amic.* 66E. Philodemus (*Lib.* 26) makes a distinction between "caring admonishment and an irony that pleases but also stings everyone".
[101] See Jas 1:19; 2:1, 5, 14; 3:1, 10; 4:11; 5:7, 9, 12, 19.
[102] See Chapter 2, nn. 202-207.
[103] Hartin, *James*, 56.

honest friend, and rhetorically such language and tone would inspire a receptive and genial disposition in the audience, which is one of the goals of an exordium.

2. Community Members

In addition to speaking with the voice of a friend, James encourages qualities in his audience consistent with the friendship tradition. In 1:2-18, these qualities focus primarily on the audience's relationship to God, although later in the letter, as we will see, qualities associated with how the members of the audience should treat one another are stressed.

In an earlier chapter we observed that often friends were required to prove their friendship through testing. In the classical and Hellenistic periods, the true test of friendship was whether one friend would help another during difficult times,[104] even to the point of death, as Plutarch reports.[105] Cicero, we recall, insists upon putting friends through trials rather than naively accepting preliminary expressions and acts of goodwill.[106] Most explicit in his references to testing is Ben Sira, who uses the same word, πειρασμός, as James to describe what a new φίλος should endure before earning the trust of another (6:7). Like the other writers, Ben Sira concurs that the best test of friendship is how the friend behaves in the face of affliction or adversity of some kind (6:8; 12:8-9).

The focus of testing in James is the testing of faith (1:3). The object of faith is God, for directly after telling the audience to ask God for wisdom, the author exhorts them to ask in faith (ἐν πίστει). James says that the testing of the audience's faith will produce steadfastness, and that steadfastness will have its full effect, such that the audience will be perfect and complete, lacking in nothing (1:2-4). It is worth observing here that this notion of perfection, or having integrity, is consistent with the characterization of a friend who does what he says. Moreover, the man who endures testing will receive the crown of life which God has promised to those who love God (1:12). Thus for James, a key component of authentic faith is a faith that has withstood testing and trials. Central to the audience's loyalty to or faith in God is the ability to maintain such faith in the face of tribulation. As we saw in the first chapter, loyalty is a key characteristic that emerges again and again in the history of friendship. Philo's view, as we saw, is that only God and

---

[104] *Orest.* 655-57.
[105] *Adv. Col.* 8.1111b.
[106] *Lael.* 63.

those who are friends of God are faithful.[107] Often such faithfulness is authenticated through a period of trial. James, in referring explicitly to the testing of faith, reflects this tradition.

In the history of friendship, we saw that friends could test one another, or that testing could come from another source. On this issue James clearly allies his teaching with the latter situation. The letter goes out of its way to make it clear that although testing is very important, God is not the source of testing (1:13-14). Some commentators point out that the use of the noun πειρασμός in 1:2 and 1:12 refers to external testing and trials, while the verb πειράζω in 1:13-14 "refers to internal, subjective temptation"[108] and thus "tempted" is more appropriate than "tested" in the latter verses. James's point here, in any case, is that the notion that God tests or tempts is incorrect. James thus differs from the LXX interpretation of Genesis 22:1, which reads Καὶ ἐγένετο μετὰ τὰ ῥήματα ταῦτα ὁ θεος ἐπείραζεν τὸν Αβρααμ, and thereby acknowledges God as a source of testing. Despite the fact that he refers to the story of the binding of Isaac as a great manifestation of faith and works in 2:21-24, James would presumably reject the LXX reading, for testing does not come from God, but from desire. Testing, whatever its form, can be viewed as a positive thing that promotes endurance and perfection in Jas 1:2-4, but it is not evident that James shares wisdom literature's view that testing is educative, wherein "the whole life of the righteous is a test, since God educates His own throughout their lives."[109] The elimination of God as the source of testing therefore distances James from various biblical texts comfortable with this idea, such as Deut 8:2, but it likens the letter, as Johnson points out, to other texts such as Sir 15:11 and Philo (*Opif.* 24; *Leg.* 2.19) which roundly reject the notion that God can be blamed for one's defects.[110] God may be a true friend in James, but God is not the sort of friend who tests or tempts another.

Reading James through the lenses of the *topos* of friendship also offers a perspective on a rather mysterious word found twice in the letter (1:8; 4:8), namely δίψυχος. This word is translated variously as "double-

---

[107] *Leg.* 2.204.

[108] Hartin, *James*, 90.

[109] Heinrich Seesemann, "πεῖρα, πειράω, πειρασμός, ἀπείραστος, ἐκπειράζω," *TDNT* VI (1968) 26.

[110] See Johnson, *James*, 192. Dibelius (*James*, 90-91) explains how some Jewish writers resisted the idea that God could test, for they were concerned to maintain the connection between sin and human responsibility. Various texts were corrected, such as Gen 22:1, which in *Jub.* 17:16 is changed to state that God did not test Abraham, but the devil, Mastema.

souled," "double-minded," or "double-spirited."¹¹¹ James identifies the person who wavers to and fro as a person who lacks stability and will not receive anything from God because of a lack of faith. Δίψυχος is intriguing, as this appears to be its first instance in Greek literature. Stanley Porter has traced the history of the word and found no antecedents to its appearance in James, although it is picked up by other early Christian writers.¹¹² Porter concludes with the suggestion that this is a Christian word, and possibly one that the author of James invented.¹¹³

The notion of being divided, however, did not originate with James, for we find various words in different texts which are prefixed by δι to designate "two" or division of some sort. The *Testament of Asher* 3.2, for example, describes the "double-faced" (διπρόσωπος) person who follows his own desire (ἐπιθυμία).¹¹⁴ Joel Marcus, who compares the Jewish concept of *yēṣer*, or evil inclination, to James's reference to following one's own ἐπιθυμία, considers διπρόσωπος and the word δίψυχος in James to "correspond to a condition of 'double-heartedness' which means being ruled by both the good and the evil inclination, in rabbinic traditions."¹¹⁵ Susan R. Garrett discusses this psychological feature of "doubleness" in her analysis of Luke's use of "sound eye" (ὅταν ὁ ὀφθαλμός σου ἁπλοῦς ᾖ) imagery in Luke 11:34-36.

> Such authors referred "singleness" and its opposite, "doubleness" or "duplicity," not only to the eye but also to the face (hence one can be "two-faced"), to the soul ("double-souled," in Greek *dipsychos*), and especially to the heart ("double-hearted" or having a "divided heart"). The "single" person was viewed as entirely devoted to God, with no fraction of the self wavering or holding back in its commitment.¹¹⁶

James is undoubtedly tapping into this "doubleness" imagery with his references to the δίψυχος but it is intriguing to consider why he

---

¹¹¹ Stanley Porter, "Is *dipsuchos* (James 1,8; 4,8) a 'Christian' Word?" *Bib* 71 (1991) 474.

¹¹² Porter ("Is *dipsuchos*," 475-76) points out the verbal and conceptual parallels between *1* and *2 Clement* and James which suggest that the former were influenced by the latter.

¹¹³ As Porter ("Is *dipsuchos*," 498) writes: "In this instance, however, the evidence as a whole does at this stage of investigation point to δίψυχος being a Christian word, and probably one originating with the book of James as well.

¹¹⁴ *The Testaments of the Twelve Patriarchs. A Critical Edition of the Greek Text* (PVTG; ed. M. de Jonge; Leiden: Brill, 1978) 138.

¹¹⁵ Joel Marcus, "The Evil Inclination in the Epistle of James," *CBQ* 44 (1982) 617 n. 37.

¹¹⁶ Susan R. Garrett, "Beloved Physician of the Soul? Luke as Advocate for Ascetic Practice," *Asceticism and the New Testament* (ed. Leif E. Vaage & Vincent L. Wimbush; New York: Routledge, 1999) 77.

chose, or perhaps invented, this word when he could have used "double-hearted" or "double-faced" as others do.

One possibility is that again, James is thinking of friendship. We recall from an earlier chapter that friends were often described as being of "one soul" or "one mind" (μία ψυχή). This goes as far back as the tragic poets and Aristotle,[117] and is carried on in the works of Plutarch and Cicero,[118] New Testament authors such as Paul (Phil 1:27) and Luke (Acts 4:32), and early Christians such as Gregory Nazianzus[119] among others. Some writers simply talk about friends loving one another as they love their own soul, including those who authored the LXX (1 Sam 18:1), and others used variations, such as ὁμόψυχος, to describe friends.[120] Ben Sira (6:1), moreover, contrasts the friend with the enemy who is characterized as a "double-tongued sinner" (ὁ ἁμαρτωλὸς δίγλωσσος).

For James, the δίψυχος person is also διακρινόμενος. Usually the latter word is translated as "one who doubts," but recently, Peter Spitaler has shown that the word in James as well as elsewhere in the New Testament has experienced a shift in interpretation from patristic and medieval authors to the modern day.[121] Modern scholars usually interpret and translate this word to refer to "one who doubts." However, Classical and Hellenistic writers understand it to mean "to be separate from or "to contend with." Spitaler demonstrates that despite the fact that many post-Reformation authors have argued for the New Testament meaning of the word to be "special" in the sense that it refers to "doubting" in opposition to faith, the notion of "doubt" actually crept into New Testament understandings of the word when the Greek was translated into Latin. Rather than a "semantic shift," the word came to be associated with doubt as a result of interpretive moves that came with a move "from *eastern* anthropology with its concern for the person insofar as he or she is embedded within a larger social unit and socio-cultural context, to *western* preoccupation with the individual and the individual's intrapersonal well being. Doubt does not need "the other; dispute does."[122] There is no need to assume that James is talking

---

[117] Euripides, *Orest.* 1046; Aristotle, *Eth. Eud.* 7.6.8-13.
[118] Plutarch, *Amic. mult.* 96E. Cicero, *Lael.* 80; 92 describes friends as *unus animus*.
[119] *Or.* 43.20.
[120] John Chrysostom, *Hom 1 Thess.* 2. See White, *Christian Friendship in the Fourth Century*, 91.
[121] Peter Spitaler, "Διακρίνεσθαι in Mt. 21:21, Mk. 11:23, Acts 10:20, Rom. 4:20, 14:23, Jas 1:6, and Jude 22 – the `Semantic Shift' That Went Unnoticed by Patristic Authors," *NovT* 49 (2007) 1-39.
[122] Spitaler, "Διακρίνεσθαι,"39.

about doubt here. He is more likely thinking of someone who tries to argue with God.

Spitaler's insights about διακρινόμενος are also relevant to understanding how James uses δίψυχος. As Spitaler has shown, early commentators on James have interpreted the δίψυχος and διακρινόμενος person not as a doubter but as an insolent person who attempts to argue with God or who sets himself apart from God.[123] Unlike God, who as we will see, behaves as a true friend and benefactor should, the δίψυχος and διακρινόμενος human acts in opposition to and separate from God. The letter is not interested in the audience's interior faith, but in the faith manifested in the interaction between humanity and God. This person is so divided between God and another pole that he cannot be μία ψυχή with another being. He is the complete opposite of a friend in seeking either to distance himself from God or argue with God.

James 1:6-8 therefore provides an illustration of what characteristics the audience members need to avoid. The insolent δίψυχος person will not receive wisdom nor achieve perfection for he is not steadfast. Furthermore, Oscar Seitz, who has compared the use of δίψυχος to its use in other early Christian texts, such as *1* and *2 Clement*, the *Shepherd of Hermas*, and the *Epistle of Barnabas*, has found that such a character is consistently portrayed as an unstable person who cannot endure trials and who cannot withstand temptation.[124] James 1:6-8 is not describing someone whose faith is in doubt, so much as a fair weather friend, who will distance himself from or object to God, ultimately indicating how unstable (1:8) and unreliable he truly is. This person, this non-friend, will not receive anything from God (1:8), whereas the loyal person who withstands testing will ultimately receive the crown of life (1:12) which God promises to those who love God.

Lastly, James's exordium introduces the contrast between rich and poor (1:9-11), a theme which is taken up several times throughout the letter. Here an allusion to LXX Isa 40:6-8 appears,[125] with parallel im-

---

[123] Spitaler ("Διακρίνεσθαι," 18) cites a number of early writers on James, including Cyril of Alexandria (*Commentarii in Lucam* 848.32-33 = PG 72, 476-949) who indicates that he understands Jas 1:6 as describing someone who wants to argue with God. Spitaler (36) also shows how Theophylact (*Expositio in Epistulam Sancti Jacobi* 1137.23 = PG 125, 1134-1190) concurs with Cyril that Jas 1:6 refers to an insolent person who, for Theophylact, wants to set himself apart.

[124] Oscar J. F. Seitz, "Antecedents and Signification of the Term ΔΙΨΥΧΟΣ," *JBL* 63 (1944) 212-13.

[125] Dibelius, *James*, 85-86; Johnson, *The Letter of James*, 190-91; D.J. Verseput, "Genre and Story: The Community Setting of the Epistle of James," *CBQ* 62 (2000) 102-103.

ages such as the passing of flowers in the grass and the withering of the grass. Commentators agree that the words ταπεινός and πλούσιος refer to a lack or excess of material wealth (although it is important to add that honour and status should be included here too),[126] but there is disagreement as to whether or not the rich person is considered to be a member of the community (commentators agree that these two individuals are not specific people but representative of the rich and poor). Ropes, for example, thinks that ἀδελφός should be supplied with ὁ πλούσιος as it is with ὁ πλούσιος, therefore making the rich man a member.[127] However, it could be that James did not refer to the rich person as a brother in a deliberate attempt to describe the wealthy man's outsider status. Moreover, the parallelism between the outcomes between the rich and poor is odd. The poor brother is offered hope for the future, for he will be exalted, while the rich person will be humiliated with no sense of hope.[128] James is not holding out any possibility for salvation for the affluent here; indeed, the rich will "pass away" and "wither away,"[129] thereby turning the verses into a clear threat to the rich. Interestingly, Donald Verseput has found a comparison in the way that 4Q185 uses the imagery from Isa 40:6-8 to provide "an oracle of doom spoken against the adversaries of God's people."[130] Here, woe is pronounced upon the "sons of man," then the poem continues with language similar to Jas 1:9-11:

> For see, (man) sprouts like grass
> and his loveliness blooms like a flower.
> His grace makes the wind blow over him
> and his root shrivels,
> and his leaves: the wind scatters them,
> until hardly anything remains in his place,
> and nothing but wind is found. [...]
> They will look for him and not find him,
> and no hope remains;

---

[126] On the terms "rich" and "poor" in antiquity, see Bruce J. Malina, "Wealth and Poverty in the New Testament and Its World," *Int* 41 (1986) 354-67; Paul Hollenbach, "Defining Rich and Poor Using Social Sciences," *SBLSP* 26 (1987) 50-63.
[127] Ropes, *Epistle of James*, 146.
[128] See Laws, *The Epistle of James*, 63.
[129] Ropes (*Epistle of James*, 148-49) thinks that it is not the person who will pass away and wither away, but his riches, but he does not given a solid argument for this position.
[130] Donald J. Verseput, "Wisdom, 4Q185, and the Epistle of James," *JBL* 117 (1998) 704.

their days are like a shadow on the earth.[131]

Moreover, there is considerable agreement that the rich who are condemned in Jas 5:1-6 are understood to be "powerful outsiders and enemies of the 'elect poor'."[132] Again, they may not be real people, insofar as this letter likely circulated among a variety of communities, but they represent the type of lifestyle and behaviour that is not acceptable to God. In light of the letter overall, their condemnation could function as a stern warning to members of the community who are tempted to pursue relations with wealthy patrons and even to call them "friends," for it prohibits such people from God's salvation. It does not even offer them the possibility of repentance! Such harsh invective against the rich, which only intensifies later on in the letter (see 2:6-7; 5:1-6) may indicate the degree to which the author thinks their influence could threaten the integrity of the community. Moreover, in referring to the exaltation of the lowly brother, James may be preparing his audience for the kind care for the poor he subsequently exhorts the community members to practise (see 1:26-27; 2:14-16).

Thus, while Jas 1:9-11 does not contain explicit references to the friendship tradition, it does offer hope to the "lowly" brother while it expresses antipathy for the rich man. Later on in the letter, as we will see, James continues this negative portrayal of the wealthy, making it clear that the audience should identify with the poor. This stress on caring for the poor and *identifying with* the poor is consistent with the practice of mutual aid and the sharing of possessions in common that we saw advocated by other writers, including the author of Luke–Acts. It would also discourage the audience from initiating or agreeing to alliances with the rich.

3. God as Benefactor

In Jas 1:5 the audience is exhorted to ask God for wisdom, who gives to all and without reproaching (μὴ ὀνειδίζοντος). The word ἁπλῶς can mean "simply," "without ulterior motive," "wholeheartedly" or "generously," and is sometimes, as we saw, used to describe a true friend. Plutarch compares this type of person to the flatterer, the antithesis of the friend, when he writes,

---

[131] Translation by Wilfred G.E. Watson in Florentino García Martínez, ed., *The Dead Sea Scrolls Translated. The Qumran Texts in English* (2nd ed., Leiden, New York, Cologne: Brill; Grand Rapids: Eerdmans, 1999) 380.

[132] Wachob, *The Voice of Jesus*, 153.

4. *The Exordium: James 1:2-18*

> For the character of a friend, like the "language of truth," is, as Euripides puts it, "simple (ἁπλοῦς)", plain, and unaffected ... but the flatterer's activity shows no sign of honesty, truth, straightforwardness (ἁπλοῦν), or generosity ...[133]

The friend possesses this virtue of simplicity[134] as opposed to the flatterer who may say one thing but mean another. Moreover, Plutarch goes on to describe the flatterer's favours, in which there is reproach (ἐπονείδιστον) and mortification (*Amic. adul.* 64B). The φίλος, in contrast, reports his actions modestly, "and says nothing about himself" (*Amic. adul.* 64B). The friend is gracious, and does not complain about being put out in order to grant a favour. Plutarch also compares the generous act of a true friend to the acts of the gods in whose nature it is "to take pleasure in the mere act of being gracious and doing good" in contrast to the flatterer who does not speak ἁπλῶς.[135] Similarly, Sir 20:15 describes the fool "who has no friends" (Sir 20:16) who "gives little and upbraids (ὀνειδίσι) much" while Sir 41:25 warns against the use of abusive words (λόγων ὀνειδισμοῦ) before friends and of insults after giving a gift. For James, God is anything but a flatterer or a fool. God is characterized as a friend who possesses the virtue of straightforwardness, generosity and lack of reproach, and thus those who ask for wisdom will receive it without any complaints or hesitation from God. The author goes out of his way to make this clear.

God also appears in the exordium as a clear contrast to the δίψυχος person. Other texts, such as *The Testament of Benjamin* 6.7, place the terms for "double" (διπλοῦς) and "single" (ἁπλοῦς), side by side,[136] just as the *Testament of Asher* 4.1 juxtaposes διπρόσωπος with μονοπρόσωπος.[137] As H.W. Hollander and M. de Jonge point out:

> The use of the words μονοπρόσωπος and διπρόσωπος runs parallel to that of ἁπλοῦς and διπλοῦς ... a man who is 'double' has 'double sight' and 'doublehearing', 'two tongues', of blessing and cursing, of contumely and honour, of sorrow and joy, of quietness and confusion,

---

[133] *Adul. amic.* 62C; 63F.

[134] The central theme of *The Testament of Issachar* is the virtue of ἁπλότης, which reveals to what an extent this notion of simplicity had become a virtue in Hellenistic Jewish thought. In *The Testament of Issachar*, however, the focus is upon leading a simple life, as Issachar is depicted as a farmer. For some discussion of this theme in *The Testament of Issachar*, see Hollander and De Jonge, *The Testaments of the Twelve Patriarchs*, 233-34.

[135] Plutarch, *Adul. amic.* 62C.

[136] *The Testaments of the Twelve Patriarchs*, 173.

[137] *The Testaments of the Twelve Patriarchs*, 138.

of hypocrisy and truth, of poverty and wealth. All Beliar's work [*Testament of Benjamin* 6:7] is διπλοῦς, not having any 'simplicity'.[138]

James is playing upon the phrase μία ψυχή with its opposite in order to accentuate the contrast between God, the gracious friend, and the vacillating person who is δίψυχος and so divided that he or she cannot "share a soul" with another. *1 Clement*, especially, contrasts δίψυχος with ἁπλῶς.[139] Although he does not discuss friendship language, Porter comes to a similar conclusion:

> If one lacks knowledge of how to pray in such circumstances [tests], one is to turn to God, who gives to all ἁπλῶς, either generously or more likely "straightforwardly", and not reproachfully. Thus the command for the believer to pray in faith ... is set against the character of God, who is willing to give. Therefore it is true that this section is constructed around a practical dualism regarding the believer ... but this practical dualism is set within the context of theology, which counts on a God who is unlike the doubting man.[140]

God does not waver nor argue with one who is faithful to God. Moreover, God is reliable and will provide the crown of life (Jas 1:12) to those who love God. God is loyal to those who return such loyalty.

James 1:16-18 emphasizes the need to rely upon God as a generous benefactor. These verses remind the audience that God is the source of all good things and that God is constant. Although there is a complex text critical problem here as to the precise wording,[141] all the variant readings mean the same thing: "the text opposes the steadfastness of God to the changeableness of creation."[142] God is a loyal and unchanging provider, just as friends and ideal benefactors were expected to be, for no friendship could survive without constancy.[143]

---

[138] *The Testaments of the Twelve Patriarchs*, 340.

[139] See Jean Daniélou, *Théologie du Judéo-Christianisme* (Bibliothèque de Théologie; Histoire des Doctrines Chrétiennes avant Nicée; Paris: Desclée, 1957) 420.

[140] Porter, "Is *dipsuchos*," 482.

[141] The best attested text for Jas 1:17b (παραλλαγὴ ἢ τροπῆς ἀποσκίασμα) is supported by the corrector of ℵ, A, C, K, P, Ψ, most minuscules, many lectionaries, the Vulgate, the Peshitta and Harklean and Armenian versions, and Jerome. A second reading (παραλλαγὴ [or ἡ] τροπῆς ἀποσκιάσματος) is supported by the original author of ℵ, and B. A third reading (παραλλαγὴ ἢ τροπὴ ἀποσκιάσματος) appears in several minuscules, a fourth (παρραλλαγῆς ἢ τροπῆς ἀποσκιάσματος) only in 𝔓²³, a fifth (ἀποσκίασμα ἢ τροπὴ ἢ παραλλαγή) only in the Sahidic Coptic manuscript, a sixth (παραλλαγὴ ἢ ῥοπῆς ἀποσκίασμα) only in Augustine, and a seventh (παραλλαγὴ ἢ ῥοπὴ ἀποσκιάσμαστος) in the Old Latin version Corbeiensis I and possibly the Bohairic Coptic manuscript.

[142] Johnson, *The Letter of James*, 197.

[143] Cicero, *Lael.* 92.

God's character as a benevolent provider, in contrast to the changeable and "double-minded" person, thus emerges clearly in the exordium. Small details, such as the fact that God gives "simply" and "without reproach" bear similarities to the ideal images of friends and benefactors that were explored in an earlier chapter of this book. This image of God seems "unprovoked," as Kloppenborg Verbin has noticed,[144] but it could be perceived as preparation for further development of the presentation of God as a benefactor and friend, who does not manipulate the recipients of God's gifts. God is clearly depicted as the opposite of a human patron, for God will continue to provide without reproach, and not disappear when calamity strikes.[145]

Despite the fact that James does not present God as an equal to the audience, it is striking that attributes of friends, such as "simplicity" and constancy are stressed in these opening verses. God will be reliable to those who persevere through testing, just as a true friend is expected to remain faithful to others. Moreover, God provides generously to those who ask for wisdom from God. One recalls the Wisdom of Solomon (7:14) here for it states that those who receive wisdom become friends of God. The author of James presents God as a friend but also as a transcendent benefactor reminiscent of Jewish wisdom literature, but also recalling that Greek inscriptional and literary evidence that was comfortable merging the imagery of benefactor and friend together. Moreover, God is a clear contrast to the δίψυχος person, who wavers and who will ultimately not receive anything from God.

Conclusion

The exordium of James draws upon some characteristics of friendship that were present in the first century. The author speaks authoritatively, directly and with frankness, as a friend should, but he also deliberately uses fictive kinship language, as many friends did, which indicates an intimacy with the audience. Moreover, by using the first person plural, the author allies himself with the audience and indicates that he shares a common identity with them.

The exordium also stresses loyalty, testing and steadfastness as important attributes of the audience. In contrast, the "double-minded" vacillating person is portrayed as unreliable and unstable. This combination of characteristics both to uphold and avoid recalls the *topos* of friendship and indicates that the author wants the members of the audi-

---

[144] Kloppenborg Verbin, "Patronage Avoidance," 768.
[145] See Kloppenborg Verbin, "Patronage Avoidance," 770.

ence to act as friends do, just as he is a friend to them. However, the speaker is particularly concerned in the exordium that the listeners focus upon their relationship with God, who, as I have argued, is introduced in the letter as a reliable friend and benefactor – the complete opposite of a δίψυχος person. The audience can ask for wisdom from this great benefactor, God, who will supply it bountifully, with no reproach.

Certainly a discussion of the later expressions of friendship in James is required, but it is significant that some allusions to it appear in the exordium, as one of its purposes is to introduce themes and ideas which will be developed in the argument of the speech. As friendship was such a noble bond in the ancient world, these allusions to it would have aided the exordium in performing its function of developing a sense of *pathos*, stressing the authority and reliability of the speaker, and introducing important themes that are then taken up throughout the remainder of the letter. Noteworthy is the fact that the exordium introduces the audience to the author's understanding of God, in this case as a benefactor and friend.

What type of social and cultural textures might the author of James be attempting to address with such an introduction?[146] This question is impossible to answer on the basis of the exordium alone, for other than the issue of rich and poor, James does not refer to concrete problems within the community, but focuses upon the audience's relationship to God and the necessity of loyalty, on God's reliability and generosity and on the importance of enduring testing. Classifying James within the subgenre of a "covenantal letter to the Diaspora," Verseput has observed that an emphasis upon withstanding hardship is appropriate after an opening that addresses the recipients as the "twelve tribes in the diaspora" (Jas 1:1), if we take this opening as a geographical reference to their whereabouts, for references to Israel's exile (in the diaspora) were painful and evoked the idea that Israel must endure until God's salvific intervention.[147] He then reads Jas 1:2-4 as a reference to the "afflictions of life in the Diaspora [that] have a purifying effect by concentrating the attentions of suffering Israel upon the anticipated deliverance of God."[148] Given the eschatological reward linked to endurance through trial in 1:12, and the emphasis upon patient suffering until the coming of the Lord in 5:7-12, it is important to bear in mind that salvation and deliverance are important themes for James, and in

---

[146] See Robbins, *Exploring the Texture of Texts*, 71-94.
[147] Verseput, "Genre and Story," 100, 102.
[148] Verseput, "Genre and Story," 102.

4. The Exordium: James 1:2-18 121

no way do I wish to dismiss the eschatological dimension of the letter. However, this promise of salvation is part of James's rhetorical aim, which is, as I see it, to promote mutual aid in the community and trust in God. James may be beginning his letter with references to testing and endurance because he wants to prepare his audience for the type of social life that he anticipates can or will produce trials or even "afflictions." The promise of salvation, as well as the doom that the rich will face, are there in the background, but they are not central themes. In the exordium James is getting the audience ready for the type of positive activity that he is going to exhort. He says, for example, that testing produces steadfastness, which produces a positive outcome, perfection, an important theme of the letter. Perfection, it appears, refers to wholeness, or the notion of faith in action, or belief and ethics, joined inextricably to one another,[149] but there is no clear link to salvation in this passage.

James 1:2-4 makes no reference to patronage per se, but it could be that the suffering and trials James has in mind relate to what will happen if members of the community resist the support and influence of wealthy patrons, especially when one considers the condemnation of the rich in 1:9-11. In his study of patronage as the social setting for the letter of James, Thomas Coleman points out how this "matter of trials, broached as it is at the outset of the letter, shows that James's primary concern is not propounding new doctrines but addressing troublesome issues."[150] Given the fact that the system of patronage was a "troublesome issue," at least for the poor, in various parts of the Roman Empire in the first centuries of the Common Era, we cannot dismiss it as one of the problems with which James and his audience had to contend. In pointing out to his audience in the exordium that God is the ultimate benefactor, James sets the stage to critique human patrons and the havoc that patron–client relations could wreak.

---

[149] Hartin, *A Spirituality of Perfection*, 129-47.
[150] Thomas M. Coleman, *Patronage and the Epistle of James: A New Social Setting for the Epistle of James* (Master of Theology dissertation; University of Aberdeen, 1996), 65.

5

A Challenge to Patronage: James 2:1-13, 14-26

Introduction

All rhetorical analysts agree that James 2 forms part of the *argumentatio* and main body of the letter.¹ Many also understand this passage to be a self-contained unit,² within which are two subunits, 2:1-13 and 2:14-26, each introduced by the phrase, ἀδελφοί μου.³ Each unit is similar, as evidenced by the examples set forth in 2:2-3 and 2:15-16, which indicate that the "needs of the poor are not being met. Faith is not being demonstrated by good works toward the poor (cf. 1.22-7)."⁴ The two sections address the same problem of neglect of the destitute, for both seek to persuade the audience not to show partiality to the rich but to care for the poor.⁵

The purpose of the *argumentatio* is to present evidence, using different methods, which will support one's case. The stylistic and argumentative features of James 2 have been studied closely by van der Westhuizen and Watson and I will not rehearse them in great detail here. Rather, I will provide a brief overview of the rhetorical structure of the chapter, following Watson and others, then focus on the speaker and community attributes in each section, followed by the portrayal of God in 2:1-13 and of Abraham and Rahab respectively in 2:14-26. I

---

¹ For example, Baasland, "Literarische Form," 3656; Wuellner, "Der Jakobusbrief," 36; Thurén, "Risky Rhetoric," 278.

² See, for example, Dibelius, *James*, 1; Peter H. Davids, *The Epistle of James. A Commentary on the Greek Text* (NIGTC; Grand Rapids: Eerdmans, 1982) 105; Patrick J. Hartin, *James*, 149-62; van der Westhuizen, "Stylistic Techniques," 90; Wuellner, "Der Jakobusbrief," 48-51.

³ Watson, "James 2," 98.

⁴ Watson, "James 2," 100.

⁵ Hartin (*James*, 124) thinks that James 2 uses such strong and vivid language that it suggests an "actual context whereby the rich and powerful exploit their positions and oppress the powerless."

will mention at the outset, however, that it is this portion of James that provides the clearest evidence that one of the problems James seeks to resolve among those who receive his letter is their temptation to cede to the influence and strength of the wealthy. Here we find evidence that patronage is one of the serious issues that James is attempting to confront in this letter. Although James made negative comments about the rich in the exordium, the rich again come under scrutiny in ch. 2. The aim of ch. 2, however, is to exhort the audience to care for the poor, which itself is an example of how faith and works can never be separated.

James 2:1-13

A. Rhetorical Structure

Watson has examined James 2 in light of ancient rhetorical handbooks and found that 2:1-13 and 2:14-26 each conform to a complete argument, as outlined in texts such as Pseudo-Cicero's *Rhetorica ad Herrenium*. Briefly, this pattern consists of a proposition (*propositio*) which sets forth what the speaker wants to prove; the reason (*ratio*) obviously provides a cause or reason for the proposition; the proof of the reason (*confirmatio*) offers additional support for the reason; the embellishment (*exornatio*) beautifies the argument while the résumé (*conplexio*) consists of a conclusion that draws the sections of the argument together.[6] These are the elements of a perfect argument. Watson, and more recently, Hartin,[7] see them all in Jas 2:1-13.

The proposition of this section lies in 2:1 with its exhortation not to show partiality, but before explaining this proposition, we must make some observations about the text. The verse instructs the audience not to show partiality as "you hold to the faith of our Lord Jesus Christ, the Lord of glory." There are several issues with this latter section. Is it "faith in Jesus Christ" or a reference to Jesus' faith? Current debates about the Greek phrase τὴν πίστιν τοῦ κυρίου ἡμῶν Ἰησοῦ Χριστοῦ τῆς δόξης are relevant here. Is this an objective genitive and therefore a reference to faith *in* Jesus Christ, or a subjective genitive and thus a reference to the faith of Jesus Christ? Given the theocentric nature of James and the fact that there is only one other explicit reference to Jesus in the letter (1:1) and that nowhere in James does it stress believing in Jesus, only believing in God, the subjective genitive makes more

---

[6] *Ad Her.* 2.18.28 cited by Watson, "James 2," 95.
[7] Hartin, *James*, 128-38.

sense for some current scholars.⁸ However, there is also disagreement about whether or not the reference to Jesus is original to the letter. At least since the late 19th century, scholars have questioned whether "our Lord Jesus Christ" is original to 2:1.⁹ There is no text critical issue here, but the phrase is very awkward,¹⁰ especially the τῆς δόξης, which is hard to fit grammatically within the sentence.¹¹ This awkwardness would disappear, however, if "our Lord Jesus Christ" was not present and the verse would refer to holding faith in "the Lord of glory."¹² As Dale Allison points out, early Christian scribes were prone to adding "Christ", "Jesus", and "Jesus Christ" to manuscripts, and adding "our Lord Jesus Christ" would have been "natural" for a scribe who was familiar with the phrase. Moreover many concur that there are interpolations in early Christian texts, such as 2 Cor 6:14–7:1, which lack textual support – textual support need not be the only factor for deciding the issue.¹³ Finally, the idea of God being the object of faith is consistent with other references to faith such as Jas 1:2-4 and 2:18-26 in which the object of faith or faithfulness is God – Jesus is nowhere to be found. In the James 2 text, references to Abraham's faith and friendship with God appear. Clearly Abraham's faith is not for Jesus, but for God. I would therefore concur with those who argue that the reference to "our Lord Jesus Christ" is a later addition to the letter.

Thus the proposition consists of the claim that discrimination or showing partiality is inconsistent with faith in God. James puts his claim in an exhortative mode, typical of deliberative rhetoric.¹⁴ The reason follows in Jas 2:2-4 beginning with γάρ, which shows that it is supporting a rationale for the proposition. It consists of a scenario, which could be real or imagined, in which a rich man and a poor man enter the gathering, and the affluent figure is offered a nice seat while

---

⁸ For further discussion of arguments in favour of the subjective genitive, see Wachob, *The Voice of Jesus*, 64-66 and Hartin, *James*, 117.

⁹ Both L. Massebieau ("L'épître de Jacques: est-elle l'oeuvre d'un chrétien?" *RHR* 31-32 [1895] 249-83) and F. Spitta (*Zur Geschichte und Literatur des Urchristentums 2: Der Brief des Jakobus* [Göttingen: Vandenhoeck & Ruprecht, 1896]) argued that the references to Jesus in Jas 1:1 and 2:1 were later interpolations inserted by Christians into what was originally a Jewish document.

¹⁰ Laws, *Epistle of James*, 94.

¹¹ On the difficulties in understanding the function of τῆς δόξης while including the reference to "our Lord Jesus Christ," see Davids, *James*, 106-107.

¹² Dale Allison, "The Fiction of James and its *Sitz im Leben*,"*RB* 118 (2001) 543. Given that other references to faith in James refer to the faith of the audience, I take the view that Jas 2:1 refers to faith in God as opposed to God's faith.

¹³ Allison, "The Fiction," 543.

¹⁴ Watson, "James 2," 102.

the pauper is ordered around. In v. 4 James asks the rhetorical questions: "Have you not made distinctions (διεκρίθητε) among yourselves and become judges with evil thoughts?" Of course the audience must admit "yes," for the scene describes exactly the kind of partiality that is inconsistent with faithfulness to God. It also echoes Lev 19:15 with its admonition not to give unjust judgments nor to be partial to the poor and defer to the rich but to judge one's neighbour justly.[15] This illustration from community life thus serves as a clear example of how the actions of the audience, were they to give the best seat to the rich man and squawk at the poor man, clearly violates the whole notion of being faithful to God and hence it provides a clear cause for stating the proposition in the first place.

James 2:5-7 forms the proof of the reason or corroboration for the reason.[16] It begins with ἀδελφοί μου and consists of three rhetorical questions which "emphasize the point"[17] that discriminating against the destitute dishonours him and only supports the rich who are oppressive, drag people into court and blaspheme the honourable name invoked over the audience. Significantly, the first question reminds the audience of an important teaching in the Jewish tradition, namely that God chooses the downtrodden (Deut 4:37; 7:7).[18] Moreover, there is wide consensus that v. 5 finds its antecedent in the first beatitude, "Blessed are the poor, for theirs is the kingdom of God." This use of a teaching attributed to Jesus is the focus of Wesley Wachob's monograph on James, in which he argues that the letter uses Q 6:20b (or a form of it) but recasts it to suit its own purposes.[19] John S. Kloppenborg has further developed Wachob's idea, showing how James engages in the rhetorical practice of *aemulatio* when he refashions these earlier sayings to serve his purposes. Kloppenborg points out that James must have known the Q version of "Blessed are the poor ..." because James and Q are the only sources that place "the poor" and "the kingdom" together, and Jas 2:6 shows familiarity with Q 6:29 and Q 12:58-59 while 2:7 seems to recall Q 6:22.[20] For Wachob, Jas 2:5 uses a saying of Jesus as a deliberative teaching to illustrate the exigence not to show partiality to the rich man. Part of the argument lies in the fact that Jas 2:8 refers to the law of Lev 19:18 and thus shoving around the

---

[15] See Hartin, *James*, 132..
[16] See Watson, "James 2," 104 who refers to *Ad Her.* 2.18.28.
[17] Watson, "James 2," 104 referring to Quintillian *Inst.* 9.2.7.
[18] See Hartin, *James*, 119.
[19] See Wachob, *The Voice of Jesus*, 138-51.
[20] John S. Kloppenborg, "The Reception of Jesus Traditions in James," in *The Catholic Epistles and the Tradition* (ed. J. Schlosser; BETL 176; Leuven: Peeters, 2004) 136-40.

poor would be a violation of the Torah. Wachob also thinks that the reference to Jesus Christ in Jas 2:1 is original to the letter and thus for him, to discriminate against the "poor in the world" who are "rich in faith" violates the faith of Jesus Christ. For Wachob, James wants his audience to identify as the "poor" of Jesus' teaching.[21] Kloppenborg takes this point further to underline the fact that if the audience gives the best seat to the rich man they are not only disobeying Torah, they are working against their own interests insofar as they *are* the poor.[22]

James 2:8-11 embodies the *exornatio* or embellishment which further entrenches an already established argument. Orators could draw upon judgments by nations, gods, oracles or respected men to support their case.[23] Here, James draws upon Lev 19:18, the use of which, as indicated above, makes plain the fact that mistreatment of the poor is a bald violation of Torah. What follows in Jas 2:9-10 and 2:11 is a pair of enthymemes, or incomplete syllogisms that contain an unstated premise.[24] The unstated premise of the first enthymeme is that "showing partiality is a failure to obey the law" while that of the second is: "if you disobey any commandment of the law, you have transgressed the whole law."[25] Moreover, James chooses the laws against adultery and murder to emphasize that harsh treatment of the poor *is as bad as killing or committing adultery.*[26]

The conclusion of the pattern is found in Jas 2:12-13, which contains what may be a proverb: "For judgment is without mercy to one who has shown no mercy"[27] and the traditional teaching that "mercy triumphs over judgment."[28] The overall conclusion to the unit is supplied by v. 12 with its emphasis upon speaking and acting as those who are judged under the law of liberty. What the "law of liberty" means exactly is debated,[29] but what is important for our purposes is that James has concluded his argument with an exhortation to action, a fitting way for orators to conclude their arguments.[30]

---

[21] Wachob, *The Voice of Jesus*, 21. See also, Batten, "Ideological Strategies in James," 26.
[22] Kloppenborg, "The Reception," 141.
[23] Watson, "James 2," 105, who refers to Quintilian, *Inst.* 5.11.36 on this point.
[24] Watson, "James 2," 106.
[25] Watson, "James 2," 107.
[26] Hartin, *James*, 137.
[27] See Hartin, *James*, 138.
[28] See Watson, "James 2," 107.
[29] On the possibility that James's perception of the law is that it is the written form of Stoic understandings, see Matt A. Jackson-McCabe, *Logos and Law in the Letter of James. The Law of Nature, the Law of Moses, and the Law of Freedom* (NovTSupp 100; Leiden, Boston, Cologne: Brill, 2001).
[30] See Watson, "James 2," 108, who refers to Anaximenes, *Rhet. Alex.* 20.1433b.30ff.

The above summary of Jas 2:1-13 as a discrete argument is precisely that: a summary, and a brief one at that. There is considerable agreement among scholars that this unit centres upon the theme of not favouring the rich at the expense of the poor. What I want to focus on now is how the unit reflects the three phenomena of friendship, patronage and benefaction.

B. Friendship, Patronage and Benefaction in James 2:1-13

1. Author to Hearers/Readers

As in the exordium, the author speaks to the audience with authority, but tempered with intimate language. The voice of a wise teacher is upheld through his careful argument, use of proverbial wisdom and appeals to common Jewish tradition. The fact that he knows how to develop a persuasive argument is evidence, in itself, that he is familiar with the school and thus the roles of teachers and students.[31]

James is therefore teaching people a firm lesson about discrimination in this passage but he weaves his care for the community throughout the unit. Twice he refers to the audience as "my brothers" (Jas 2:1, 5), the second time calling them ἀδελφοί μου ἀγαπητοί, maintaining the use of fictive kinship language that we saw in the exordium. This type of language, as discussed, belongs to the *topos* of friendship, for "companionship, intimacy, kinship, and similar relations are the species of friendship."[32] James also talks to the audience directly, using the 2nd person plural consistently throughout the section. The author does not shy away from sternly exposing the audience's discrimination against the poor as an act contrary to being faithful both to God and to the law – a tough message indeed for the audience to receive – and his use of rhetorical questions that expose the error of the audience's ways would presumably leave his listeners or readers feeling somewhat sheepish. He speaks bluntly, in the tradition of frank speech that was so admired by Philodemus and Plutarch. Yet the writer effectively pushes forward his argument with "friendliness for the persons under examination, with the intention that if they understand what they are doing they may not do it any longer."[33] This is not to suggest that James simply takes on the guise of friendliness; indeed I think he truly cares for his audience. However, he needs to use all the rhetorical skills he can in order to help them behave in a manner that he understands to be in their best interests because it is consistent with what he thinks God wants of

---

[31] See Wachob, *The Voice of Jesus*, 137.
[32] Aristotle, *Rhet.* 2.4.28.
[33] Anaximenes, *Rhet. Alex.*37.1445b.1ff.; quoted by Watson, "James 2," 104.

them. Perhaps some audience members found it alienating, but as παρρησία demanded, one must be willing to "risk one's own standing with another for the good of the other," and this "is why frank speech can only be understood in the context of genuine friendship."[34]

2. Community Members
First, several authors have identified patronage as an "exigence," or problem requiring solution,[35] that the author of James is attempting to address,[36] with Jas 2:1-13 providing the most explicit support for such an exigence. As we know, the pericope begins with an exhortation to show no partiality (2:1), followed by a scenario in which a rich man with fine clothing and gold rings and a poor man in shabby clothes enter the assembly; the rich man is treated well, while the impoverished one is ordered around (2:2-3). Of note here is the fact that the πτωχός person was someone who had no guarantee of the minimum required for survival.[37] The author concludes the specific scene with the rhetorical question: "have you not made distinctions among yourselves, and become judges with evil thoughts?" (2:4), reminds them that God has chosen the "poor in the world" – surely a reference to the shabbily dressed man – to be rich in faith and heirs of the kingdom which God has promised to those who love God, then scolds the audience for dishonouring the poor man despite the fact that it is the rich who oppress them, drag them into court, and blaspheme the honourable name invoked over them (2:6-7).

---

[34] J. Paul Sampley, "Paul's Frank Speech with the Galatians and the Corinthians," *Philodemus and the New Testament World* (ed. John T. Fitzgerald, Dirk Obbrink, & Glenn S. Holland; NovTSupp 111; Leiden, Boston: Brill, 2004) 296.

[35] "Exigence" is Lloyd Bitzer's term, which he defines as "an imperfection marked by an urgency; it is a defect, an obstacle, something waiting to be done, a thing which is other than it should be" ("Rhetorical Situation," *Philosophy and Rhetoric* 1 [1968] 6).

[36] Alicia Batten, "An Asceticism of Resistance in James," *Asceticism and the New Testament*, 355-70; Coleman, *Patronage and the Epistle of James*; John S. Kloppenborg Verbin, "Status und Wohltätigkeit bei Paulus und Jakobus," *Von Jesus zum Christus: Christologische Studien. Festgabe für Paul Hoffmann zum 65. Geburtstag* (BZNW 93; ed. Rudolf Hoppe & Ulrich Busse; Berlin, New York: de Gruyter, 1998) 127-54; "Patronage Avoidance in James," *HTS* 55 (1999) 755-94; Stephen J. Patterson, "Who are the 'Poor to the World' in James?" (unpublished paper delivered at the Society of Biblical Literature Annual Meeting, Boston, November, 1999). I am grateful to Dr. Patterson for allowing me to cite his paper. Donald J. Verseput, "Genre and Story: The Community Setting of the Epistle of James," *CBQ* 62 (2000) 96-110; Nancy J. Vhymeister, "The Rich Man in James 2: Does Ancient Patronage Illumine the Text?" *AUSS* 33 (1995) 265-83; Wachob, *The Voice of Jesus*, 181-85.

[37] See Stegemann and Stegemann, *The Jesus Movement*, 84.

5. A Challenge to Patronage: James 2:1-13, 14-26

As Kloppenborg has observed, such a scene of an affluent figure entering a room or gathering is reminiscent of Lucian's criticism of wealthy people who flaunt their trappings, expecting grand recognition (*Nigr.* 21).[38] We have seen that flattery was often associated with patronage during the Hellenistic and Roman periods, and one form of expressing it was to offer the best seat or the platform to the wealthy patron; what Plutarch refers to as "silent flattery" (*Adul. amic.* 58B). Considering how pervasive patronage was in the early centuries of the Common Era, there is no reason to believe that the author of this text would not be familiar with the system, nor that he would not be critical of it, as some other Hellenistic writers were.

Moreover, given the general bitterness that James displays towards the rich in this text (e.g. Jas 1:10; 5:1-6), a denunciation of patronage and the behaviour that it could produce, namely flattery from clients and ill treatment of the poor, would not be surprising. In 5:1-6, the author directly attacks the rich, using prophetic and apocalyptic language. Aspects of this assault find parallels within Jewish literature,[39] as the notion that those who exploit the poor (5:4) should be condemned was a common idea, especially among the great social prophets.[40] This section is also comparable with Jas 4:13-17,[41] as they both sharply denounce specific attitudes and behaviours associated with gaining wealth, and both begin with "come now, you" (4:13; 5:1), but they are quite different in content. What is specifically noteworthy for our purposes is some of the detail that James provides. For example, there is reference to the rusting of gold and silver, indicating that these are people who let their riches pile up, putting their faith in wealth instead of God. Moreover, they exploit their workers, the equivalent of murder (Sir 24:37) and as such, have lived out the life of envy and fighting that, as we will see, is contrasted with friendship with God in Jas 3:13–4:10.[42] If these rich people represent potential patrons for the audience, here they are categorically scorned and exposed in the worst possible terms. It is hard to imagine that an author would simply craft such a polemic, despite the fact that it draws upon prophetic ideas and imagery, unless he or she had been provoked by some sort of social problem related to wealth, or perhaps seen the problem emerging on the horizon.

---

[38] Kloppenborg Verbin, "Patronage Avoidance," 765.
[39] See Kloppenborg Verbin, "Patronage Avoidance," 773 nn. 63 and 64. In particular, see *1 Enoch* 97, which refers to the unjust accumulation of gold and silver.
[40] See, for example, LXX Mal 3:5.
[41] Dibelius, *James*, 230.
[42] See Johnson, *The Letter of James*, 309.

One of the purposes of Jas 2:1-13 is to discourage the audience from participating in patron–client relationships and to avoid relying on the wealthy to support the community. Even though the scene may be a stock illustration, the care James has taken to present a vivid image that was likely familiar to the audience and to give a subsequent elaboration, indicates James has nothing but scorn for such favouritism. Showing partiality to the rich over against the poor is so wrong, in James's view, that he develops a sophisticated and vivid argument against it, claiming that it flatly contradicts the whole idea of being faithful to God and of upholding the law. The community is not to act like clients, who busy themselves over the interests and needs of rich patrons, but to care for the poor, for, as already observed, they *are* the poor. If they are "rich in faith" then they are the poor for God has chosen the "poor in the world" to be "rich in faith and heirs of the kingdom" (2:5). Patronage is "of the world" for James. We have seen in an earlier chapter that patronage forces clients to remain in dependent and vulnerable roles, never able to fully repay their patrons. I am not suggesting that patronage creates poverty, and indeed in various examples it enables people to stay alive. However, James does not care for the kind of behaviour it generally breeds, and thus advocates different models of behaviour that he understands to be consistent with faithfulness to God.

The values of honour and shame factor importantly into this argument. As many studies have demonstrated, honour and shame were and continue to be pivotal values in the regions that formed a rim around the Mediterranean Sea.[43] Such characteristics have not only been confirmed by anthropologists and by biblical scholars using social scientific criticism,[44] but also by classicists. J.E. Lendon, for example, understands honour to have been so fundamental in the Roman empire that the ancients were not even conscious of it. Nonetheless, he examines various aspects of that world in order to bring honour and the manner in which it could function for these people into sharper relief. As he writes,

> an attempt to schematize perceptions so natural to ancient man that he needed no such explicit ordering is at once artificially tidy and incom-

---

[43] See Peregrine Horden and Nicholas Purcell, *The Corrupting Sea. A Study of Mediterranean History* (Oxford: Blackwell, 2000) 485-523.

[44] Much of the groundbreaking work in social scientific criticism has been done by members of the Context Group. See, for example, Bruce J. Malina, *The New Testament World. Insights from Cultural Anthropology* (Louisville: John Knox Press, 1981) 25-50.

plete, but perhaps adequate to offer an inkling of how men and entities to which honour was ascribed could exert power in their world.[45]

Honour stands for a person's sense of worth and place in society.[46] Men, in particular, are expected to defend and uphold their honour and the honour of their family and community. Words such as "rich" (πλούσιος – see Jas 1:10, 11; 2:5, 6; 5:1) and "poor" (πτωχός – see 2:2, 3, 5, 6) refer to the capacity to maintain and gain honour in the case of the rich, and the loss of honour, in the case of the poor. Thus "rich" and "poor" were not solely economic terms, although they certainly included important economic dimensions, but pertained to the gain or loss of honour.[47] Wealthy benefactors were often praised for their "love of honour" or φιλοτιμία,[48] and described with a variety of positive moral attributes such as "good" or "beautiful" (καλόν), while the πτωχός person was associated with bad characteristics.[49] However, since all goods, including honour, were understood to be limited – the ancient Mediterranean had no concept of a "growth economy" but rather perceived everything to be in limited supply[50] – and thus one person's gain was another person's loss, the ruthless pursuit of riches for the sake of wealth alone was not admired, for it meant that one was greedy, depriving others often of their basic needs. Therefore, even though the affluent were deemed honourable, if they did not share their wealth with the association or village, or if they exploited others for their own gain, they would not receive such admiration.[51]

---

[45] J.E. Lendon, *Empire of Honour*, 31.

[46] Malina, *New Testament World*, 47.

[47] Malina, "Wealth and Poverty in the New Testament and Its World"; Hollenbach, "Defining Rich and Poor Using Social Sciences"; Batten, "Ideological Strategies," 14; Alicia Batten, "The Degraded Poor and the Greedy Rich: Exploring the Language of Poverty and Wealth in the Letter of James," *The Social Sciences and Biblical Translation* (ed. Dietmar Neufeld; Symposium Series 41; Atlanta: Society of Biblical Literature; Leiden: Brill, 2008) 65-77.

[48] See, for example, *IG* II² 1292 (Athens; c. 250 BCE); *IG* II² 1314 (Athens; 36/35 BCE). This inscription features a priestess, Glaukon, who is praised for her φιλοτιμία), indicating that sometimes women could be associated with a love of honour. See also, Alicia Batten, "The Moral World of Greco-Roman Associations," *SR* 36 (2007) 138-39.

[49] See G.E.M. de Ste. Croix, *The Class Struggle in the Ancient Greek World* (Ithaca: Cornell University Press, 1981) 423-24.

[50] See Malina, *The New Testament World*, 71-93.

[51] Many if not most of our literary sources come from elite and wealthy persons, and thus it is practically impossible to get at what poor peoples' attitudes towards these issues were. However, even among wealthy writers, such as Plutarch (*Am. prol.*), there is disdain for those who are preoccupied with money. Ben Sira makes many positive comments about wealth, but if seeking wealth gets out of control, it causes blindness. See Victor

What is unusual about the letter of James is that those who are not usually associated with honour, namely the poor, are indeed worthy of honour. James castigates the audience for showing partiality to the rich because it "dishonours" the poor man (2:6), and the "poor in the world" (2:5) are those whom God has chosen to be rich in faith and heirs of the kingdom. James does not come out and say that the rich are without honour, but he never portrays the wealthy in a positive light, and in ch. 5 the rich are condemned to apocalyptic miseries for their exploitation of others (5:1-6). For James, the poor are honoured by God and to treat them badly is "evil" (see 2:4).[52] The letter may be said to be countercultural in this regard, for it goes against the custom of the day which was to show high regard for those who had wealth; a convention that supported patron/client relations. Thus not only does James challenge patronage and the practices that it demanded, he inverts the value system of honour and shame, at least with regard to the wealthy, that supports it.[53]

This section of the letter also upholds some of the community attributes that were introduced in the exordium. Faithfulness to God is again emphasized in the opening statement (2:1) and in 2:5, in which it is clear that God has chosen the "poor in the world" (πτωχοὺς τῷ κόσμῳ) to be "rich in faith" (πλουσίους ἐν πίστει). We observe another instance of the verb διακρίνω, although in the passive form, in 2:4. Here, the verb is never translated as having anything to do with "doubt" but usually as "have you not made distinctions among yourselves" (NRSV) and thus more consistent with the Hellenistic Greek understanding of the word. James does not apply the term to the relationship between the person and God here though, but to relationships among community members. They should not order the poor person around for it leads to the type of division within the community that recalls the δίψυχος person in the exordium – the latter being the exact the opposite of a friend. In light of the subsequent section, 2:14-26, one also might argue that hospitality is in view here, given that Abraham (2:21) and Rahab (2:25), both known for their hospitality, are presented as examples. James wants the audience to identify with and offer hospitality to the poor. Such behaviour was consistent with the

---

Morla Asensio, "Poverty and Wealth: Ben Sira's View of Possessions," in *Der Einzelne und seine Gemeinschaft bei Ben Sira* (ed. Renate Egger-Wenzel & Ingrid Krammer; BZAW 270; Berlin and New York: Walter de Gruyter, 1998) 151-78.

[52] See Hartin, *James*, 147.

[53] Wachob (*The Voice of Jesus*, 178-93) also takes this view, arguing that James's challenge to the honour/shame dynamics is informed by Jewish culture.

tradition of friendship in which hospitality was understood to be the beginning of friendship.[54]

Other obvious community attributes appear in this segment including the theme of integrity or the pairing of speaking and acting (Jas 2:12), the importance of upholding the law, especially the commandment to love your neighbour as yourself (2:8) which is certainly compatible with friendship. The importance of mercy is also stressed in 2:13 which recalls Matt 5:7 and Tob 4:10, both of which refer to showing mercy (ἔλεος) and in Tobit is connected to almsgiving or showing mercy to the poor. It is also interesting to note that according to Aristotle, ἔλεος was not simply a response to the suffering of another, but a response that acknowledged that that suffering was undeserved.[55] Moreover, for Aristotle one pities others whom one knows, but not those who are too closely connected, for then the one who feels pity will feel that he or she will likely suffer. Aristotle explains that this is why

> Amasis is said not to have wept when his son was led to execution, but did weep when his friend (φίλος) was reduced to beggary, for the latter excited pity (ἔλεος), the former terror (*Rhet.* 2.8.12).

If this is what James understood ἔλεος to mean here, then it suggests not only that the audience should show pity for the πτωχός person, but that the poor person clearly did not deserve to be suffering. Moreover, Aristotle's example is intriguing in that it refers to Amasis showing pity for a friend who has become a beggar. Is it possible that the author of James has friendship in the back of his mind when he advocates caring for the poor, who have lost their honour in the world's eyes, and been reduced to penury?

3. God

The description of God in Jas 2:1-13 is also consistent with what we found in the exordium. For example, God's reliability is stressed in 2:5 with a reference to God's promises to those who love God. God's care for the poor is especially brought out here, with an emphasis upon how God "chooses" the poor in the world to be rich in faith, probably recalling the tradition in Judaism of God choosing God's people (Num 16:5; Deut 4:37; 7:7; Isa 14:1).[56] God is a benefactor who cares for the

---

[54] Dio Chrysostom, *1 Regn.* 41.
[55] Aristotle, *Rhet.* 2.8.2. See Aaron Ben-Ze'ev, "Aristotle on Emotions towards the Fortune of Others," in *Envy, Spite and Jealousy*, 112-14.
[56] See Hartin, *James*, 119.

poor unlike the rich, such as the man with the gold rings, who oppress the poor and drag them into court (Jas 2:6). The rich, including rich patrons, are the opposite of God.

These rich, moreover, "blaspheme the honourable name (καλὸν ὄνομα) which was invoked over" the audience (2:7). Some commentators understand this "name" to be that of Jesus, especially if they think that the reference to Jesus Christ in 2:1 is original to the letter,[57] while others, even if they think that 2:1 is original to the letter, think it could be Jesus or God.[58] Although the phrase does appear in early Christian literature with reference to Jesus' name (Herm. Sim. 8.6.4), this need not mean that James is using the phrase in the same manner, for some Christians, building upon a biblical tradition that condemned the blasphemy of God (see Lev 24:10-23), simply replaced the name of God with that of Jesus. James is also drawing from this same tradition, but there is nothing in the text to suggest that the same type of substitution is occurring, especially as I do not think that the earliest text of James included a reference to Jesus in 2:1. The phrase applies to God's name, especially with the qualification of the name as καλόν (see LXX Ps 134:3). For James, it is the rich who blaspheme this good and honourable name. Obviously this is not the sort of behaviour that James desires of his audience. James wants his audience to love God (2:5) and to hold faith in God (2:1), and implicitly, to honour God, and for this, as we will see in the next section, God provides gifts of friendship, as Philo also makes clear.[59]

James 2:14-26

A. Rhetorical Structure

James 2:14-26, as stated above, is understood to be a further development of the argument about partiality set out in 2:1-13, but elaborated to the broader topic of faith and works.[60] Watson has worked out the following structure again according to patterns described in rhetorical texts such as the *Rhetorica ad Herennium* and others, and Hartin's most recent work on James generally follows this pattern but with some differences.[61]

---

[57] For example, Davids, *The Epistle of James*, 113.
[58] For example, Johnson, *James*, 226.
[59] See Philo, *Abr.* 129.
[60] Watson, "James 2," 108; Wachob, *The Voice of Jesus*, 111.
[61] Hartin, *James*, 156-62.

The proposition (2:14), which states the theme that faith must be accompanied by works, uses two rhetorical questions, both of which expect a negative response. This theme of the impossibility of the separation of faith and works is at the "heart of Jewish faith and piety,"[62] and would presumably be self-evident to the audience. James backs the proposition with a reason, however, in 2:15-16, which invokes the example of how to treat a badly clothed and hungry brother or sister – obviously not simply with words, but with practical aid. As Watson says, the example is ironic, for the response of "go in peace, get warm and get something to eat" to the shivering, famished person without actually providing food and shelter is ridiculous.[63]

Directly following the reason, James provides further proof for the reason which restates the proposition (2:17), a repetition which amplifies the initial proposition.[64] Then we encounter an engagement with an imaginary interlocutor which includes anticipation or the strategy for delaying the objection to the argument, and personification – the representation of an absent person – in 2:18a,[65] and the author's posing of a dilemma to the opposition of this interlocutor in 2:18b. 2:19 anticipates another objection by the opponent; that is, that one must simply confess that God is one, which is the *Shema Israel* (Deut 6:4). James refutes this by saying even the demons believe, and thus *believing* by itself is clearly not sufficient. The opponent's argument is shown to have no weight whatsoever. As many scholars, including Dibelius,[66] have shown, the section exhibits many aspects of the ancient diatribe form, including the use of an imaginary opponent in 2:18-23 who makes objections (2:18) and forms false conclusions (2:19).[67]

The embellishment (2:20-25) of the argument again amplifies in 2:20 with a reiteration of the proposition and a tone of surprise or *exclamatio*.[68] It then offers a proof from example in 2:21-22 with the story of the binding of Isaac, a *iudicatio* (judgment) in the form of a supernatural oracle in 2:23, another amplification which repeats the proposition in 2:24, and another proof from example in 2:25 with the story of Rahab. The brief summary conclusion appears in 2:26, recalling v. 17 and using a figure of thought that forms "a one-to-one

---

[62] Hartin, *James*, 157.
[63] Watson, "James 2," 108.
[64] Cicero, *Part. or.*15.54; cited in Watson, "James 2,"109.
[65] Watson, "James 2," 112.
[66] Dibelius, *James*, 149-51.
[67] Watson, "James 2," 119. Hartin (*James*, 156-62) follows roughly the same pattern
[68] See *Rhet. Her.* 4.15.22; cited in Watson, "James 2," 114.

correspondence between body-faith and spirit-works."[69] Thus we see that Jas 2:14-26 conforms to the structure of a perfect argument, just as did the unit directly preceding it.

B. Friendship and Benefaction in James 2:14-26

This section of James fully develops the necessity for faith to be completed or perfected by works (ἐκ τῶν ἔργων ἡ πίστις ἐτελειώθη) as it says in 2:22. 2:14-26 therefore picks up one of the opening themes of the letter: the necessity of perfection, or wholeness (τέλειος) as introduced in the exordium (1:4). It is also in these verses that the notion of friendship with God appears explicitly as Abraham is called a "friend of God." God is not a central figure here, but Abraham and Rahab emerge as examples or models of human beings who demonstrate how neither faith nor works are sufficient on their own, but are inseparable. In the following we will explore friendship in the communication between author and hearers/readers as we have been doing thus far, then focus on community attributes and finally, the specific roles of Abraham and Rahab.

1. Author to Hearers/Readers

As in Jas 2:1, the author begins this section with ἀδελφοί μου and the audience members are referred to with fictive kinship language as "brother" and "sister" (2:15), just as members of ancient associations would often refer to one another. The author therefore begins on an intimate and "friendly" note with the audience, and he remains direct with them, consistently using the second person (2:16, 18-20, 22, 24).

However, the author also continues to use rhetorical questions in this section, such as in Jas 2:14, and provides an example in 2:15-16 that may well have taken place among the recipients of the letter. If so, presumably the hypocrisy of giving advice to a poor person, who is a member of the community, without offering concrete aid would embarrass some members of the audience, and clearly James is willing to risk this reaction. He also forcefully uses the diatribe form including engagement with a hypothetical opponent in 2:18-20. Diatribes were often used within ancient philosophical schools as effective modes of teaching in order to move people to action.[70] The imaginary interlocutor would sometimes be addressed with the vocative such as "O

---

[69] Watson, "James 2," 116.
[70] See Stanley K. Stowers, "The Diatribe," *Greco-Roman Literature and the New Testament* (ed. David E. Aune; SBLSBS 21; Atlanta: Scholars, 1988) 71-83.

man."[71] We see this happening in James as the author addresses the man who says "You have faith and I have works" (2:18) with the exclamatory "you empty person" in 2:20. By using these techniques, James maintains his *ethos* as an authoritative, direct and skilled teacher, and indicates how strongly he feels about the issue of faith and works, and especially the need to live out faith by offering hospitality and care to the poor.

The combination of firm, authoritative teaching and friendly address continues throughout Jas 2:14-26, consistent with the other portions of the letter examined thus far. James wants to maintain a warm tone with the audience but he also continually reasons assertively using tools from Greek educational traditions. Using the diatribe is effective in this section because it allows James to speak forcefully without directly attacking the audience and risking the alienation of its members. He wants to be firm, but not nasty. This prudence in offering correction and advice is often commented upon by those who wrote about frank speech and friendship. Plutarch, for example, warns against being too heavy handed:

> But the man who has been hard hit and scored by frankness, if he be left rough and tumid and uneven, will, owing to the effect of anger, not readily respond to an appeal the next time, or put up with attempts to soothe him. Therefore those who employ admonition should be particularly on their guard in this respect ... (*Adul. amic.* 74E).

Given the facility with writing and rhetoric that we have seen so far in James, the author must be aware that speaking too directly will defeat his overall purpose to guide the audience in altering their behaviour, especially towards one another. He has thus continued his address, using a strong but measured tone, and tempered with "my brothers," such that upon hearing or reading the document, his audience will not snort with anger and discard the letter.

2. Community Members

This unit, as mentioned above, focuses upon the need to embody both faith and works, or the theme of wholeness or integrity. This theme further elaborates the need to care for the poor, which as Jas 2:14-17 makes clear, would be a manifestation of faith accompanied by works. It follows the previous argument in which attitudes towards the wealthy and poor men who enter the assembly are criticized sharply, and which presumes a background of patronage.

---

[71] Stowers, "Diatribe," 76.

James 2:14-26 contains the reference to Abraham as a "friend of God" (2:23), a phrase earned in this case, and as we will discuss below, from both Abraham's works of hospitality as well as his willingness to undergo a great test and nearly sacrifice his son. Thus the theme of testing is maintained; one must endure tests in order to achieve friendship with God, but also an emphasis upon providing hospitality, further substantiated by the reference to Rahab (2:25). James exhorts the audience to practise hospitality and in order to encourage such charity the writer supplies a human example, Abraham, who possessed friendship with God, and another example, Rahab, who is justified by works. To be a friend of God not only involves trials, but works of hospitality and care for those in need. We recall Dio Chrysostom's comment here that hospitality is the beginning of friendship,[72] and the general feature of friendship, discussed in Chapter 2, that friends share all in common. The community members' relationship with God is intimately dependent not only upon their ability to withstand testing, as developed in the exordium, but also on how they treat each other, especially the more vulnerable in their midst.

As many scholars have determined, there were people from different social strata within early Christian groups.[73] Such complex groups experienced inner conflicts and problems similar to other associations of people in the ancient world.[74] James's audience is unlikely to be any exception. These people are probably in urban areas, given the reference to the "crown" (στέφανος) of life in 1:12 and the man with gold rings in 2:2, regardless of whether or not the man is a real figure.[75] Some members of the community have more serious needs than others, and this section of the letter suggests that these people were not always assisted. For example, Jas 2:15-17 explicitly addresses the plight of a "brother or sister" in shabby clothes, without enough food, who requires things "needed for the body." Rather than aiding these poor in their own community, it is likely that some members were seeking advantages through alliances with the leisure class, as is explicit in Jas 2:1-13, and neglecting their own. The author adamantly rejects such

---

[72] *I Regn.* 1.41.

[73] On the Pauline churches, for example, see Wayne A. Meeks, *The First Urban Christians. The Social World of the Apostle Paul* (New Haven and London: Yale University Press, 1983).

[74] Verseput ("Genre and Story," 107-108) provides some helpful comparisons with some ancient associations, but the inscriptions for these groups generally do not provide moral and theological grounds for their moral codes in the manner that James does.

[75] See Batten, "Ideological Strategies,"12.

liaisons with the rich, imploring the audience to offer hospitality to those who truly need it.[76]

Given the strong possibility that the audience is not of identical social status, therefore, how is it possible to imagine these people as being "friends" to one another, when true friendship could only exist within the context of balanced reciprocity, as we saw in Chapter 3? This is where I think that the overlap between friendship and benefaction is especially important. Like others in the ancient world, James sees a certain commonality between friendship and benefaction.[77] He does not state that the audience is to be a community of φίλοι, yet he emphasizes characteristics of friendship, such as testing, faith, integrity and hospitality, that distinguish that ideal. I therefore think that his appeals to characteristics of friendship are rhetorical in that they aid in persuading a mixed audience to manifest the qualities inherent in friendship without necessarily advocating that it be a community of equals. The line between friendship and benefaction is blurred, just as it is in some of the inscriptional evidence that refers to an individual as both a benefactor *and* as a friend, or the Hellenistic Jewish evidence that will speak of God as a friend and benefactor.[78] Epicurus, as we saw, associates friendship with practical aid although help should not be the foundation of friendship.[79] Friends were expected to be supportive of one another, even to the point of suffering and dying for the well-being of their φίλοι. Proverbs 14:21 contrasts the sinfulness of hating a friend with the blessedness of caring for the poor, thereby suggesting that to love friends is also to have compassion for the needy. An emphasis upon aid within the community is consistent with the ethos of friendship as well as the ethos of benefaction. James is able to draw upon the tradition of friendship, therefore, effectively to encourage more benefaction for the needy. In contrast to the frantic jostling for attention

---

[76] Patterson ("Who are the 'Poor' in the World," 6-7, 10) thinks that this emphasis upon hospitality in Jas 2:14-26 may reflect problems in the community related to hospitality towards itinerant prophets, whom the author of the letter supports. These wandering radicals may be the τέλειοι comparable to those of the *Didache* (6:2) and those in Matt 19:21 "who embrace a more radical form of discipleship." In James, they may be those who have the true authority to teach (Jas 3:2). This argument is also presented in Patterson's monograph, *The Gospel of Thomas and Jesus* (FFRS; Sonoma, CA: Polebridge, 1993) 178-88.

[77] Jerome H. Neyrey, SJ ("God, Benefactor and Patron: The Major Cultural Model for Interpreting the Deity in Greco-Roman Antiquity," *JSNT* 27 [2005] 465-92) has recently explored the benefactor/patron image (he makes no distinction between the two) and further reveals the degree to which benefactors were associated with friendship.

[78] See Chapters 2 and 3.

[79] *Sent. Vat.* xxxix.

and favours from the affluent combined with an indifference to the truly destitute, it is precisely this sort of ethos that James promotes.

3. Abraham and Rahab

The references to Abraham and Rahab appear within the *exornatio*, the latter being used to embellish, or "adorn and enrich the argument, after the proof has been established" (*Rhet. Her.* 2.18.28). Both Abraham and Rahab are referred to as specific historical examples of people who were justified by works and not by faith alone (2:24). The use of either historical or invented examples, as we saw, was a common practice within rhetorical speeches for they provide concrete proof in support of the argument.[80] In the New Testament, examples used in rhetorical arguments were often taken from Jewish history,[81] and the examples of Abraham and Rahab were well known within Jewish and Christian circles.[82] Sometimes they were cited together, as they were famous for their hospitality and faith, among other things.[83]

It is therefore not unusual for Abraham and Rahab to be referred to together; however, the identification of Abraham's works (ἔργα) (Jas 2:21, 22) has puzzled scholars. James explains the meaning of Rahab's works (ἔργα): she practised hospitality by sheltering, hiding and helping two strangers to escape from Jericho (Josh 2:1-21), and this story fits well with the theme of showing mercy to the poor as referred to in Jas 2:15-16 and the larger argument about partiality as introduced in 2:1-13. However, the works which justified Abraham are not so clear. Is it because he was willing to offer Isaac upon the altar, as Jas 2:21 seems to say? Why, then, is ἔργα in the plural and not the singular? Roy Bowen Ward suggests that the author presupposes his audience's knowledge of Abraham's works of hospitality (Gen 18), as this was well known

---

[80] Aristotle, *Rhet.* 2.20.

[81] Kennedy, *New Testament Interpretation*, 16.

[82] For a list of references to Rahab in Jewish and Christian literature, see Anthony Hanson, "Seminar Report on 'The Use of the Old Testament in the Epistle of James,'" *NTS* 25 (1979) 527. The list of references to Abraham in Jewish and early Christian literature is, as one could imagine, rather lengthy. For references to Abraham within the earliest Christian literature, at least, see Roy Bowen Ward, "Abraham Traditions in Early Christianity," *Studies in the Testament of Abraham* (ed. George W.E. Nickelsburg; SBLSCS 6; Missoula: Scholars, 1976) 173-84.

[83] For example, *1 Clement* 10-12 admires Abraham, Lot and Rahab for their hospitality, and in the case of Abraham and Rahab, for their faith. For a discussion of these examples in *1 Clement*, see H. Chadwick, "Justification by Faith and Hospitality," *Studia Patristica* 4 (1961) 281-85. Dibelius, (*James*, 167) points out that there were lists of pious persons which were well known within ancient Judaism and apparently to some New Testament writers as well.

within Jewish and Christian literature. Moreover, the title "friend of God" was a reasonably common epithet for Abraham, and could be associated with a variety of Abraham's good deeds, including hospitality. For example, in his treatise, *On Sobriety*, Philo cites Gen 18:17 as "'shall I hide anything from Abraham my friend (φίλου μου)'" even though the LXX uses παιδός μου.[84] Ward argues that Jas 2:15-16 prepares the audience for the story of Abraham's hospitality because it refers to caring for those in need, then sending them on their way (2:16) which is exactly what Abraham did in Gen 18:16.[85] He thus concludes that Abraham's "works" should be understood with reference to his hospitality rather than to his willingness to sacrifice his son.

Ward's argument would be persuasive were it not for the fact that Jas 2:23, which links a citation from Gen 15:6 to a description of Abraham as a "friend of God," has a precedent in Jewish literature.[86] Irving Jacobs has pointed out that within Midrash, the association of the binding of Isaac story in Gen 22:1-19, or the *Akedah*, and the citation of Gen 15:6 had occurred prior to the emergence of James.[87] Thus, the notion of being a "friend of God" is probably related to the *Akedah*. In keeping with Jewish tradition, James associates Abraham's friendship with God with the endurance of a great test.[88] However, Ward is correct to point out that Abraham's hospitality was well known and it would not be surprising if the letter's author presumed that the audience knew about it. It could be, then, that the letter writer refers to the binding of Isaac because "it was at this point in his life that Abraham was declared righteous for this and his many previous acts of hospitality and charity (cf. Heb. 11.17-19)."[89] This would explain the reference to Abraham's works in the plural and it also maintains the connection between the actions of Abraham and Rahab, as well as the coherence between Abraham's works and the focus of ch. 2, which is to act mercifully toward those in need.

---

[84] Philo (*de. Sob.* 56 [LCL III; trans. F.H. Colson; Cambridge, MA: Harvard University Press; London: Heinemann, 1960]). R.B. Ward ("The Works of Abraham," *HTR* 61 [1968] 286) notes that the "title 'friend of God' was related to various characteristics of Abraham, e.g. his humility (*1 Clem.* 17:2), his faithfulness (*Jub.* 19:9), his obedience to God's commandments (CD 3.2) – as well as his hospitality."

[85] Ward, "The Works," 288.

[86] See Davids, *The Epistle of James*, 130.

[87] Irving Jacobs, "The Midrashic Background for James II, 21-3," *NTS* 22 (1975-76) 457-64. See 1 Macc 2:52; Sir 44:20-21.

[88] Again, one needs to remember that this is not the only reason why Abraham was called a friend of God.

[89] Watson, "James 2," 114-15.

Returning to the question of rhetoric, Watson states that Jas 2:23 is a *iudicatio* or judgment (in this case, from the past) which, within the *exornatio*, serves to embellish the argument once the proof has been set forth. 2:23 is a supernatural oracle of a god, which can function as a type of judgment, and in turn, "confirms" the ideas set forth in the unit, that faith should be accompanied by works, especially the "works" of caring for the needy. The example of Abraham is the "clincher" with which none of James's listeners could argue. It is a compelling elaboration upon the theme that faith must be accompanied by works.

As we have seen, this section finds continuity with ch. 1, in that endurance through "testing" is admired, the reference to "perfection" (Jas 2:22) is repeated, but also in that the importance of doing (1:22-25) and caring for the needy (1:27) is stressed. Although James is undoubtedly describing Abraham in terms which were well known within Judaism, he has maintained the association between perfection, testing and being a friend of God, and he has added the notion of providing hospitality, both because Abraham was associated with hospitality in tradition, and because the overall chapter focuses upon faith and works, particularly works of caring for others. Johnson comments that the title "friend of God" is the most distinctive element in the description of Abraham, for it is "the most revealing aspect of James's understanding of Abraham within the dualistic framework of his own composition."[90] Abraham, as friend of God, is the opposite of the δίψυχος person. He is unwavering in his faith even to the point of withstanding the ultimate test: the binding of his own son, which is one of his works. "Abraham's willingness to give back to God what God had given demonstrated and perfected his faith and revealed what 'friendship with God' might mean."[91] Abraham is a perfect example of one who avoids friendship with the world in favour of friendship with God, an opposition which emerges clearly in ch. 4.

Abraham functions, therefore, not only as a proof in the form of an example, but as a model of how a human being can be a friend of God. It is through testing and caring for others that the audience can become friends with God, not through buttering up the rich. James does not imagine that humans are on the same level as God, but clearly, given the precedents within Jewish sources particularly, friendship between humans and God was entirely possible. Friendship, as we have seen, was partly embodied through sharing with others. Abraham engaged in

---

[90] Johnson, *The Letter of James*, 248.
[91] Johnson, *The Letter of James*, 248.

such sharing, and given that James adamantly insists that the audience members care for one another, especially for the poor in their midst, Abraham does not behave like a patron, demanding honour from others, but freely provides hospitality to strangers. Abraham is a model for how the community members should treat one another, particularly how those who had more should support the most vulnerable. As Abraham's activities were connected to his relationship with God, so the community's actions are integral to their rapport with the divine. To be a friend of God the benefactor is to be a friend to one another and to provide aid to those who need it, just as Abraham not only demonstrated his faith and loyalty to God, but his care for other human beings.

The notion that Abraham's hospitality is in mind here is underscored by the reference to Rahab and her care for strangers. The inclusion of Rahab in the unit further supports the point that faith must be accompanied by works and underlines the type of morality that James advocates within the community. Moreover, perhaps James included a reference to Rahab not only because she was often associated with Abraham, but because James emphasizes care for both a brother *and a sister* in Jas 2:15, as Johnson has suggested.[92] If this is the case, then Rahab functions as another example of how community members should treat one another. Rather than succumb to the influence and power of wealthy patrons, the audience should care for the impoverished among them – they should act as friends, and those who have more should provide benefits to the poor.

Conclusion

This chapter has explored the two discrete units of James 2 keeping in mind the traditions of friendship, patronage and benefaction. The author continues to speak as a friend, but again with the authoritative voice of one who is not afraid to teach. Overall the section stresses the need to care for the needy, which relates to James's insistent point that faith without works is dead. I join other scholars who argue that the scene of the rich and poor men entering the assembly and the resultant behaviour are typical in a world in which patronage pervaded many aspects of social life. James rejects this system of patron–client relations, and argues passionately that the needy must be cared for, and not left abandoned without sufficient food and clothing. The rich, after all, are not reliable for they simply oppress people, and drag them into court.

---

[92] Johnson, *The Letter of James*, 245.

Friendship lies in the background here, for the themes associated with friendship that were introduced in the exordium, such as faith, integrity, and testing, are maintained in James 2. The use of the examples of Abraham and Rahab especially emphasizes the need to practice hospitality, which again is a characteristic of friendship and also of benefaction. James, I think, draws upon the noble tradition of friendship in this chapter in order to push his hearers/readers to practise more benefaction towards those who have less. The explicit reference to Abraham as a friend of God is an effective reminder, as well, that how the members of the community treat one another is related to their relationship with God. Abraham practised hospitality, among other things, and Abraham is called a friend of God. It is this beneficent God upon whom the audience must rely, and not wealthy patrons. The unit holds out the attractive possibility that perhaps, like their great ancestor Abraham, the audience can be friends with God, an idea that receives further attention in James 4.

6

Friendship with God: James 3:13–4:10

Introduction

The final section that evinces the theme of friendship clearly is Jas 3:13–4:10. The present chapter will focus on this unit, which I also think conforms to the "elaboration of a theme" exercise comparable to what we have witnessed in 2:1-13 and 2:14-26. We will begin with a discussion of how 3:13–4:10 manifests this exercise, then proceed to analyze how friendship, benefaction and patronage figure within the voice of the author to the hearers/readers, within the guidelines for the community, and in the portrayal of God. As in James 2, I think that the author advocates a manner of life among the audience members that conforms to the tradition of friendship in many ways, and draws upon friendship and benefaction in speaking of the relationship between the audience and God. Again, as in James 2, the way in which the community members treat one another is integral to how they are to understand their relationship to God, who is their benefactor and friend.

James 3:13–4:10

A. Rhetorical Structure

First, a few remarks must be made about the issue of the unity of Jas 3:13–4:10. This section is part of the *argumentatio*, as all rhetorical analysts of James would agree, although they disagree over the question of whether it is unified. Dibelius considered 3:1-12 to be a cohesive treatise on the tongue,[1] and Watson has shown how 3:1-12 displays a classical pattern of argumentation,[2] and both support the notion that 3:13 is the beginning of a new section of the letter. Dibelius, however,

---
[1] Dibelius, *James*, 181-206.
[2] Watson, "The Rhetoric of James 3:1-12," 48-64.

does not consider 3:13–4:10 to be a smooth unity, but a sequence of two admonitions in 3:13-17 and 4:1-6 broken up by an isolated saying in 3:18 and containing a series of imperatives in 4:7-12.³ He also thinks that 4:11-13 can be included with the rest of 3:13–4:10 because it consists of imperatives which conform in form to the previous imperatives although he admits that 4:11 introduces "something new, as is indicated also by the change in tone: instead of 'sinners' (ἁμαρτωλοί) or 'double-minded' (δίψυχοι) the address in v 11 is 'brothers and sisters' (ἀδελφοί)."⁴ Thurén considers 3:1–4:12 to be a unity based upon the themes of speech and wisdom, and notices that there is a break between 3:12 and 3:13, but he thinks that there is no clear change of audience after 3:13 until 4:13, although he does not provide any explanation for this position.⁵ Davids admits that 4:11-12 may be a free-floating admonition, but he then suggests that they fit well with the previous section in that they address community conflict.⁶ However, one could argue that a good proportion of James addresses the issue of community conflict and, moreover, Davids grants that 4:10 "clearly rounds off a section."⁷ James Hardy Ropes claims that 4:11-12 is an appendix to 4:1-10 in that the "thought of the writer reverts ... to those facts of life which had given him the text for his far reaching discussion and exhortation (4:1-10)."⁸ Ropes's scenario is certainly possible but as with the other positions mentioned above, hardly final proof.

In contrast to the above authors, some scholars view 3:13–4:10 as a logical unit. Although Davids includes 4:11-12 with 4:1-10, he does see the relationship between 3:13-18 and 4:1-10. He challenges Dibelius's view that 3:18 is a free-floating saying by pointing out how the "εἰρήνην at the end of 3:18 forms a contrast with the πόλεμοι of 4:1. The latter section makes the more general accusation of 3:13-18 pointed and specific."⁹ Ralph P. Martin states that "the text from 3:13 to 4:10 is indeed a coherent and self-consistent unit, with some telltale markers to indicate the closely woven texture."¹⁰ He then goes on to

---

³ Dibelius, *James*, 208.
⁴ Dibelius, *James*, 228.
⁵ Thurén, "Risky Rhetoric," 280.
⁶ Davids, *The Epistle of James*, 169.
⁷ Davids, *The Epistle of James*, 168.
⁸ Ropes, *A Critical and Exegetical Commentary*, 273.
⁹ Davids, *The Epistle of James*, 149.
¹⁰ Ralph P. Martin, *James*, 142. Note that in his earlier work, Hartin (*James and the Q Sayings of Jesus*, 31) treats 3:13-18 and 4:1-10 as discrete units which parallel each other

describe several ways in which 3:13-18 is connected to 4:1-10, including the fact that 4:1-10 picks up on the consequences (for example, wars and strife) of following the wisdom from below, which is contrasted to the wisdom from above in 3:13-18. Moreover, he points out how Jas 3:17 describes the wisdom from above to be "impartial" (ἀδιάκριτος), which contrasts with the person who follows the wisdom from below (3:15-16) and who is not impartial but "double-minded" (δίψυχος).[11]

Johnson also refers to this latter point in his analysis of Jas 3:13–4:10 as a unified section.[12] However, he understands the unit to consist of an indictment in 3:13–4:6 followed by a call to conversion in 4:7-10. The thematic focus of the indictment is envy, which reaches a climax in 4:5-6, with the citation of Prov 3:34. "The whole exposition comes down to the validity of the scriptural witness to the way God works in the world. Is all that Scripture says in vain? Is envy really the proper sort of longing for the spirit God placed in humans?"[13] Following the indictment is thus a series of exhortations to submit to God and be humble, or said otherwise, a call to conversion from a life of envy and enmity to a life of friendship with God (4:4).[14]

Johnson's study of this section of James is compelling, and envy certainly figures importantly in the unit, but he has not performed a full-fledged rhetorical analysis. However, even though we have not proven that Jas 3:13–4:10 is clearly a coherent whole, the evidence presented by scholars, as well as the fact that James is clearly familiar with rhetorical arguments as indicated by the previous chapters, provides sufficient warrant to attempt a rhetorical study of 3:13–4:10. In the following section we will therefore examine the section particularly to determine whether the instructions provided by various rhetorical guides in antiquity are followed here. The interest is thus the "inner texture" of this part of James: "its form, structure, and argumentative pattern."[15]

As we saw in the previous chapter, a complete argument is composed of five parts. To quote the *Rhetorica ad Herennium*:

---

and "form the very heart of the epistle," although in his more recent commentary, as we will see, he treats 3:13–4:10 as a unified whole.

[11] Martin, *James*, 142.
[12] Johnson, *The Letter of James*, 268.
[13] Johnson, *The Letter of James*, 269.
[14] See also, Luke Timothy Johnson, "James 3:13-4-10 and the *Topos* ΠΕΡΙ ΦΘΟΝΟΥ," *NovT* 25 (1983) 327-47, which discusses the *topos* of envy more thoroughly.
[15] Wachob, *The Voice of Jesus*, 59.

a perfect argument ... is that which is comprised of five parts: the Proposition, the Reason, the Proof of the Reason, the Embellishment, and the Résumé. Through the Proposition we set forth summarily what we intend to prove. The Reason, by means of a brief explanation subjoined, sets forth the causal basis for the Proposition, establishing the truth of what we are urging. The Proof of the Reason corroborates, by means of additional arguments, the briefly presented Reason. Embellishment we use in order to adorn and enrich the argument, after the Proof has been established. The Résumé is a brief conclusion, drawing together the parts of the argument (*Rhet. Her.* 2.18.28).

Such an outline may not have been true for all rhetors, but rhetorical speeches did have a standard, or skeletal, format consisting of the introduction (προοίμιον, *exordium*) which was discussed in Chapter 3, a statement of the case (διήγησις, *narratio*), supporting arguments (πίστις, *confirmatio* or *argumentatio*), and a conclusion (ἐπίλογος, *peroratio* or *conclusio*).[16] This pattern was characteristic of judicial speeches but subsequently became common for deliberative speeches. Burton Mack points out that during the second century BCE, a general outline for a complete argument, or "thesis," emerged which was more accessible to most people in that it enabled them to bypass deciphering the complex instructions within the rhetorical handbooks. This outline consisted of the four major elements described above as well as a few other pieces and is structured as follows: (1) an introduction; (2) a proposition; (3) a reason (rationale); (4) an opposite (contrary); (5) an analogy (comparison); (6) an example; (7) a citation (authority); and (8) a conclusion.[17] As Mack and Wachob explain, this pattern was flexible. For example, Hermogenes's elaboration of a chreia exercise consisted of eight stages (praise, paraphrase, rationale, statement from the opposite point of view, statement from analogy, statement from example, statement from authority, exhortation).[18] Similar to this is the elaboration of a theme, or *tractatio*, which is outlined in the *Rhetorica ad Herennium* and consisted of seven stages: (1) statement of the theme (*res* or *propositio*); (2) the reason (*ratio*); (3) the expression of the theme in another form (*pronuntiatum*) with or without the reasons; (4) a statement of the contrary (*contrarium*); (5) a comparison (*similie*); (6) an example (*exemplum*); and

---

[16] Mack, *Rhetoric and the New Testament*, 41.
[17] See Mack, *Rhetoric and the New Testament*, 42; and Wachob, *The Voice of Jesus*, 62.
[18] Mack, *Rhetoric and the New Testament*, 44-47; Wachob, *The Voice of Jesus*, 62-63; see Burton Mack and Edward O'Neil, "The Chreia Discussion of Hermogenes of Tarsus," *The Chreia in Ancient Rhetoric*, 155-71.

6. *Friendship with God: James 3:13–4:10* 149

(7) a conclusion (*conclusio*).[19] Again, this pattern may vary, but at least some of these elements are essential to a complete argument.[20]

A close analysis of Jas 3:13–4:10 reveals that this particular section follows the elaboration exercise with some adaptations. Before describing the structure in detail, however, it is important to note that in his 2003 commentary on James, Patrick Hartin explored 3:13–4:10 and concluded that it conforms to the rhetorical structure of a "perfect argument,"[21] a structure which he finds in 2:1-13, 2:14-26 and 3:1-12 as well. Hartin analyses these sections of James according to the patterns explained in the *Rhetorica ad Herennium* and while I am in agreement with many aspects of his approach, I differ on the precise pattern that I see in this section of the letter. I will thus refer to his work occasionally while working through the structure, but in general I will follow the analysis of the section that I developed independently in my 2000 dissertation.[22] In my view, 3:13–4:10 contains the following pattern:

1. Statement of Theme – 3:13-14
2. Reason – 3:15-18
3. Argument Proper
   a. Opposite – 4:1-3
   b. Maxim – 4:4
   c. Citation (Authority) – 4:5-6
4. Conclusion – 4:7-10

1. Statement of Theme: Jas 3:13-14

The opening verse introduces part of the theme of this section, namely, the importance of leading a life of wisdom. James asks who is "wise and understanding" among his listeners, and then exhorts the one who might respond, "I am," to live a good life and "show his works in the meekness of wisdom." The verse begins with a reference to σόφος and ends with the word σοφία, the theme of wisdom giving direction to the whole section, and, as we will see, "to what follows in 4:1-10 as well."[23]

---

[19] See *Rhet. Her.* 4.43.56; Wachob, *The Voice of Jesus*, 62.

[20] Wachob (*The Voice of Jesus*, 63) writes: "Rhetoricians and texts, both ancient and modern, agree and demonstrate that, while the sequence of those figures may vary and one or several of them may be absent in a given case, one or more of them are the necessary ingredients for a complete argument."

[21] Hartin, *James*, 206-16.

[22] Alicia Batten, "Unworldly Friendship: The 'Epistle of Straw' Reconsidered" (doctoral diss.; Toronto: University of St. Michael's College, 2000) 173-201.

[23] Hartin, *James and the Q Sayings of Jesus*, 99.

James associates two things with this life of wisdom: works (ἔργα) and meekness (πραΰτης). Neither association is new or surprising, either in this letter or in early Christian literature. In James the relationship between works and wisdom is similar to that between works and faith, discussed in James 2. Wisdom, like faith, is not simply an intellectual possession, but must be manifested in a good life of works.[24] Other early Christian texts also made this association between works and wisdom such as *1 Clem.* 38:2, 1 Pet 2:12; 3:2, and Heb 13:7.[25] James's emphasis upon how one lives and acts is continued throughout the entire section with the discussion of wars and divisions between people (3:16; 4:1-13), underscoring the fact that he is dealing with concrete behaviour here, as he does throughout most of the letter.

The second connection, meekness, or calmness, is no less important, for James spends a good deal of this section warning against the opposite of meekness, namely pride, and selfish ambition (3:14, 16; 4:2, 6). In ch. 1 James refers to πραΰτης (1:21) as that which is required in order to receive the word from God and likewise here he reminds his audience that they need wisdom but wisdom received with meekness. Again, meekness was a virtue within early Christianity (Gal 6:1; Eph 4:2; 2 Tim 2:25; Tit 3:2; 1 Pet 3:15), and in Graeco-Roman culture was associated with "friendliness" and "gentleness" as opposed to roughness or anger.[26]

The second part of the opening theme is an exhortation to those who have "bitter jealousy" (ζῆλος) and "selfish ambition" (ἐριθεία) in their hearts not to boast (κατακαυχάομαι) and be false to the truth. This latter phrase (ψεύδεσθε κατὰ τῆς ἀληθείας) is awkward but most commentators understand it as "lying against the truth."[27] The overall meaning of the verse, however, seems reasonably explicit: if you are jealous and full of your own pride and ambition (the opposite of receiving wisdom meekly), you should not boast of your wisdom for then you are lying. You cannot be wise and be selfishly ambitious or boastful simultaneously for the truly wise person is meek and shows his wisdom through a good life of works, as the previous verse explained.

---

[24] Hartin, *James and the Q Sayings of Jesus*, 100.

[25] Hartin, *James and the Q Sayings of Jesus*, 100.

[26] Aristotle (*Rhet.* 1.9.5) considers πραΰτης to be one of the components of virtue, and he places it as the median between anger (ὀργιλότης) and "spineless incompetence" (ἀοργησία). See F. Hauck and S. Schulz, "πραΰς, πραΰτης," *TDNT* VI (1968) 645-51.

[27] Davids, *The Epistle of James*, 151; Laws, *The Epistle of James*, 160; Joseph B. Mayor, *The Epistle of St. James* (London: MacMillan, 1913) 127-28; Ropes, *A Critical and Exegetical Commentary*, 246.

The central message of this section of James, therefore, is that the truly wise are those who are humble and show their wisdom through works, as opposed to those who are jealous, selfish and full of words of pride. This contrast, positive and negative, truly wise vs. jealous and selfish, is conveyed throughout the rest of the section. As the rhetorical instructor wrote, this opening statement sets forth "summarily what we intend to prove" (*Rhet. Her.* 2.18.28) and thus the audience can anticipate a series of arguments which will support the call to live a life of wisdom and to avoid a life of jealousy and selfishness.[28]

2. Reason: James 3:15-18
The next section of the argument is the reason why one should humbly accept and follow God's wisdom and not be selfish and envious.[29] Within the *ratio*, rhetors would provide examples that would not only demonstrate the correctness of the proposition,[30] but supply proof of why the audience should follow their advice. As Wachob states, the *ratio* includes an example which provides a "compelling social basis for what [James] says."[31] There are different types of examples which rhetors could draw upon, notably the historical example (παράδειγμα), the comparison or analogy (παραβολή), and the fable (μῦθος). The historical example was a well-known case taken from history such as we saw with the figures of Abraham and Rahab in the previous chapter, while a comparison was usually an example from everyday social life and a fable was from an imaginary world or story.[32]

In this particular pericope, James builds an antithetical comparison of two lifestyles, one without wisdom and one wise. His comparison here is not as concrete as the reasons he provides in other sections of his letter, for example, the contrast in treatment of the wealthy and poor men who enter the assembly in Jas 2:2-4, but nonetheless, it functions in a similar manner. James describes the characteristics of each life, and subsequently illustrates their concrete effects for society. He begins by stating clearly that this "anti-wisdom"[33] is not from above, then provides a list of negative adjectives to describe it: it is "earthly"

---

[28] Hartin (*James*, 208-209) argues that 3:14 introduces the reason or ratio why one should live a life of works in wisdom's meekness, but this fails to account for the dual nature of the statement which is both to live a life of works in the meekness of wisdom and to resist living selfishly and being boastful.

[29] Hartin (*James*, 209-11) also thinks that Jas 3:15-18 forms a *ratio*.

[30] *Rhet. Her.* 2.23.35.

[31] Wachob, *The Voice of Jesus*, 77. See also Mack, *Rhetoric and the New Testament*, 40.

[32] Mack, *Rhetoric and the New Testament*, 40.

[33] Hartin, *A Spirituality of Perfection*, 73.

(ἐπίγειος), "unspiritual" (ψυχική) and "devilish" (δαιμονιώδης). The most plausible explanation of this list is that James wants to emphasize the negative features of this anti-wisdom in increasingly worsening increments.[34] First, it is ἐπίγειος; it is from the world, as opposed to being from God.[35]

The term ἐπίγειος can mean simply "existing on earth" with no negative connotation, but in contexts in which there is a clear distinction between earth and heaven ἐπίγειος does come to mean "what is earthly in the sense of what is completely opposed to the heavenly."[36] The next word, ψυχική, is a little more puzzling, as it simply means "of the soul,"[37] but within the New Testament it becomes one pole of the contrast between "the earthly, human, and non-spiritual and the heavenly, divine and spiritual,"[38] the opposite pole being πνευματικός. The third adjective, δαιμονιώδης, represents the worst characteristic of anti-wisdom, as it baldly states that it is from the devil. This word is unattested prior to its appearance in James and is a *hapax* in the New Testament but

> James also refers to τὰ δαιμόνια in 2:19 who believe but shudder, and other New Testament texts present demons as the opposite of God (1 Cor 10:20-21; 1 Tim 4:1).[39]

Thus James is not granting that there is another type of wisdom, from below, so to speak, but that no one can claim to hold true wisdom when they engage in selfish, false and arrogant behaviour. As Sophie Laws puts it, James's "point is not that there is a different wisdom in opposition to the true one, but that a claim to true wisdom cannot be upheld in the context of an inconsistent style of life."[40] In other words, a life of envy and dishonesty does not originate in another type of wisdom but comes from the devil.[41]

In v. 16, James then describes the concrete effects of the manifestation of ζῆλος, which we saw could be understood as envy, and ἐριθεία (selfish ambition). This might best be translated as "social unrest" or

---

[34] Hartin, *A Spirituality of Perfection*, 73.

[35] This theme of "earthliness" or "worldliness" is again picked up in Jas 4:4 (see below).

[36] Hermann Sasse, "ἐπίγειος," *TDNT* I (1964) 680-81. Another text which makes this comparison between heaven and earth is 2 Cor 5:1.

[37] Albert Dihle, "ψυχικός," *TDNT* IX (1974) 661.

[38] Dihle, "ψυχικός," 661.

[39] Johnson, *The Letter of James*, 272.

[40] Sophie Laws, *The Epistle of James*, 162.

[41] Hartin, *A Spirituality of Perfection*, 73.

even, "anarchy."⁴² Πρᾶγμα refers to concrete acts or practices, thus underscoring that James is talking about behaviour within the community and not simply thoughts or dispositions. He may even be referring to problems in court as mentioned in 2:6, for πρᾶγμα can refer to lawsuits.⁴³ Thus the reason why the audience should not be envious and ambitious, but meek and humble is very clear, for envy finds its source in the devil and produces strife; indeed it produces every evil action.

James 3:17 presents a balanced contrast to a jealous life by specifying the attributes of wisdom and illustrating the effects of such a lifestyle.⁴⁴ This wisdom from above (ἄνωθεν σοφία) is pure (ἁγνή); in other words she is free of all things bad, such as ζῆλος and ἐριθεία.⁴⁵ Next, James provides a list of the virtues of wisdom which are related by their alliteration (the first three adjectives each begin with an ε) but also by the fact that "they amount in combination to a definition of 'meekness' enjoined by 3:13."⁴⁶ Wisdom from above is peaceable (εἰρηνική), which is in contrast to the disorder produced by envy and ambition; it is gentle (ἐπιεικής), a word which is paralleled by "meekness" (πραΰτητος) in 2 Cor 10:1,⁴⁷ and trusting (εὐπειθής), another *hapax* "which does not indicate a person without convictions who agrees with everyone and sways in the wind (cf. 1:5-18), but the person who gladly submits to true teaching and listens carefully to the other instead of attacking him."⁴⁸ This wisdom is also "full of mercy and good fruits" (μεστὴ ἐλέους καὶ καρπῶν ἀγαθῶν) the latter which anticipates the "fruit of righteousness in 3:18,"⁴⁹ "impartial" or "simple" (ἀδιάκριτος),⁵⁰ and "without hypocrisy" or "sincere" (ἀνυπόκριτος). These descriptive expressions recall the characterization of God in ch. 1 and are the antithesis of the doubting, wavering δίψυχος person whom we encountered earlier and who returns in 4:8.

The rationale concludes with Jas 3:18, which may have been well known to the audience, and thus may be a maxim: "And the fruit of righteousness is sown in peace by [for] those who make peace [peace-

---

⁴² Ropes, *A Critical and Exegetical Commentary*, 248.

⁴³ Johnson, *The Letter of James*, 273.

⁴⁴ Many authors agree that Jas 3:15-16 and 3:17-18 form a balanced contrast. See, for example, Hartin, *James and the Q Sayings of Jesus*, 98.

⁴⁵ Compare with Wis 7:25. See Ropes, *A Critical and Exegetical Commentary*, 249.

⁴⁶ Johnson, *The Letter of James*, 274.

⁴⁷ See Davids, *The Epistle of James*, 154.

⁴⁸ Davids, *The Epistle of James*, 154.

⁴⁹ Johnson, *The Letter of James*, 274.

⁵⁰ Scholars debate about the precise meaning of ἀδιάκριτος. It could mean "simple" as opposed to δίψυχος, or "not given to party spirit." See Davids, *The Epistle of James*, 154.

makers]."⁵¹ In particular, it bears a resemblance to Matt 5:9: "Blessed are the peacemakers," a saying probably familiar to James's readers given the overall density of Jesus sayings in James.⁵² Jas 3:18 and Matt 5:9 are in fact the only two New Testament texts to address peacemaking and they are similar in their thinking.⁵³ In both sayings, the ability to make peace emerges from a relationship with God. In Matt 5:9 the peacemakers are referred to as "the sons of God" while in Jas 3:18, the peacemaker receives the gift of righteousness from God.⁵⁴ The possibility that James is refashioning the beatitude, or a form of the beatitude, is increased given the fact that the description of the wisdom from above in 3:17 uses adjectives which correspond strikingly to the words used in Matthew's beatitudes.⁵⁵

James 3:18 could be an example of *aemulatio*, or a restatement of an idea from another text or famous teacher using new words. As Kloppenborg has observed, "what we might call plagiarism and intellectual theft is what rhetoricians called *aemulatio* – the restating of predecessors' ideas in one's own words."⁵⁶ Rhetors such as Theon describe multiple ways in which one can paraphrase an expression, including the practice of substitution, whereby "we replace the original word with another; for example, *pais* or *andrapodon* for *doulos* (slave), or the proper word instead of a metaphor or a metaphor instead of the proper word, or several words instead of one or one instead of several."⁵⁷

When an author refashions a statement using this method, and applies the new form of the expression to a new situation, some of the audience members likely recognize the original statement and can now admire how the author has adapted it to a new situation.⁵⁸

Although the author and audience of James may be aware of "Blessed are the peacemakers," the writer may have deliberately paraphrased the statement to fit the particular context. Such a practice

---

⁵¹ The dative can be read as "by those who make peace" or "for those who make peace." Douglas J. Moo (*The Letter of James* [PNTC; Grand Rapids: Eerdmans, 2000] 177) points out that the verse "has a simple proverbial style ... which suggest[s] that James may here be quoting a saying current in the early church."

⁵² See Hartin, *James and the Q Sayings of Jesus*, in particular, 112.

⁵³ Hartin, *James and the Q Sayings of Jesus*, 155.

⁵⁴ Hartin, *James and the Q Sayings of Jesus*, 155.

⁵⁵ Compare Jas 3:17, with its references to wisdom from above as pure, peaceable, gentle and merciful to Matt 5:5, 7, 8, 9. See Hartin, *James and the Q Sayings of Jesus*, 214.

⁵⁶ Kloppenborg, "The Reception of Jesus Traditions in James," 121.

⁵⁷ Theon, *Progymnasmata* 109 in *Progymnasmata. Greek Textbooks of Prose Composition and Rhetoric* (trans., ed. George A. Kennedy; Writings from the Greco-Roman World 10; Atlanta: Society of Biblical Literature, 2003) 70.

⁵⁸ Kloppenborg, "The Reception of Jesus Traditions," 122.

would have the rhetorical effect of assuring the audience that the speaker's teaching corresponds to Jesus' teaching, which in turn, increases the credibility of the speaker.

This verse is also striking in that it associates peacemaking with righteousness (δικαιοσύνη). Within the inscriptional evidence, the epithet of δικαιοσύνη was often awarded to the secretaries of Greek associations when they had done an exemplary job of managing their association's finances. This does not mean that δικαιοσύνη was devoid of a moral dimension, for in the context of the inscriptions it could suggest that the secretary was fair and honest in how he distributed the monies.[59] However, sometimes individuals were praised for both δικαιοσύνη and φιλοτιμία, the latter of which could refer to having a competitive spirit, and to possessing zeal and great ambition.[60] Again, this word could have a positive moral connotation, in the sense that it could refer to "generous zeal,"[61] but often it was sharply criticized for it could "shade into aggression, pride and boastfulness,"[62] precisely the sorts of things that James criticizes. Thus the linkage between peacemaking and δικαιοσύνη would not necessarily have been self-evident to ancient society in general, which may have normally associated financial skills, or perhaps competition, with δικαιοσύνη. James turns the latter linkage upside down by associating peacemaking, not competition, with righteousness. Again, James is attempting to demonstrate that living according to the wisdom from above, the wisdom from God, is diametrically opposed to the "normal" workings of the world. In addition, Jas 3:18 is an apt way to end this section, for it resembles the form of Jas 3:16 in that it refers to actions;[63] just as Jas 3:16 specified negative behaviour associated with jealousy, Jas 3:18 refers to positive behaviour (peacemaking) which is born of an acceptance of the wisdom of God. It also lifts up peacemaking, mentioned in Jas 3:17 as a characteristic of wisdom from above, as a "prime quality of all the characteristics of wisdom."[64] Finally, it anticipates its opposite, strife and fighting, which follow in ch. 4.

The rationale within this rhetorical unit not only reemphasizes the theme of pursuing wisdom meekly and not succumbing to selfish am-

---

[59] Frederick W. Danker, *Benefactor: Epigraphic Study of a Graeco-Roman and New Testament Semantic Field* (St. Louis: Clayton, 1982) 345.

[60] Danker, *Benefactor*, 328.

[61] Danker, *Benefactor*, 328.

[62] K.J. Dover, *Greek Popular Morality in the Time of Plato and Aristotle* (Oxford: Basil Blackwell, 1974) 232.

[63] Johnson, *The Letter of James*, 275.

[64] Hartin, *A Spirituality of Perfection*, 75.

bitions and envy, but it offers a comparison, taken from the social sphere, as to why one should choose the wisdom path. A lack of wisdom will lead to disorder and bad practice whereas those who accept wisdom will seek justice/righteousness peacefully. James has reasoned inductively, for he has used examples from the social sphere (conflict vs. peace) and probably a version of a Jesus saying (3:18) to introduce reasons for his argument, but he has also used a deductive proof (commonly called an enthymeme), in that he makes a statement (3:15) and subsequently provides a supporting statement for it beginning with γάρ in 3:16.[65]

Both techniques were common within rhetorical speeches,[66] and the type of enthymeme which James uses in 3:15-16, which is "derived from opposites"[67] (in this case, the opposite of true wisdom), was a common topic of demonstrative enthymemes. Moreover, James has introduced the issue of peace versus conflict which will figure importantly in his subsequent main argument.

3. Argument Proper (Jas 4:1-6)
a. Opposite: James 4:1-3

In Jas 4:1-3, the letter writer commences his argument proper with a series of impassioned questions and statements focusing upon conduct that is in dramatic opposition to the type of demeanor which James exhorts. Again, opposites remind us that rhetoric is debate, for they keep the other side in view.[68] Opposites could be used in a variety of ways, and in this particular case, it appears that James employs the opposite in order to "censure the opposite proposition, showing that the opposite would not make any sense ..."[69] In this instance, the opposite proposition would be to ignore the author's plea to seek the wisdom from above, but rather, to live according to one's own ambitions, one's own inclinations. In this section, then, James builds an argument against such behaviour.[70]

James begins this "oppositional" segment with two questions, both of them rhetorical, which address conflict within the community. Most commentators understand James's use of the terms "wars" (πόλεμοι) and "fightings" (μάχα) as metaphors for disputes among the audience,

---

[65] See Kennedy, *New Testament Interpretation*, 16. For a comparable analysis of ch. 2 of James, see Wachob, *The Voice of Jesus*, 77.

[66] Aristotle, *Rhet.* 1.2.8-9.

[67] Aristotle, *Rhet.* 2.23.1.

[68] Mack, *Rhetoric and the New Testament*, 42.

[69] Mack, *Rhetoric and the New Testament*, 43.

[70] Hartin (James, 212-15) takes Jas 4:1-6 as an *exornatio* or embellishment of 3:13.

as these words are used as "synonyms for strife and quarreling."[71] The second question refers to passions (ἡδοναί) at war "in your members," which makes it clear that the source of all of these conflicts is human passion, whether it is for physical pleasure, or for wealth, fame, authority etc. The term ἡδονή, moreover, is linked to social disorder within Hellenistic and Hellenistic-Jewish literature.[72] The next verse is grammatically difficult. Does it say that you desire and do not have *and so you kill*, as some commentators would punctuate it;[73] or is it that the addressees desire and do not have, kill out of jealousy, and cannot obtain, fight and wage war?[74] Several authors have puzzled over James's reference to killing (φόνος) and emended the text to refer to envy (φθόνος), which would certainly make sense, although there is little basis for the emendation. Johnson shows that murder is often linked to the topic of envy and untrammeled desire within Hellenistic literature[75] and in Jas 1:14-15, the author did make it clear that desire (ἐπιθυμία) could lead to death. With regard to the grammatical structure of the verse, Mayor's reading (following Hofmann) seems the most logical. He explains:

> The easiest way of seeing how the words naturally group themselves is to put them side by side without any stopping: ἐπιθυμεῖτε καὶ οὐκ ἔχετε φονεύετε καὶ ζηλοῦτε καὶ οὐ δύνασθε ἐπιτυχεῖν μάχεσθε καὶ πολεμεῖτε. Can anyone doubt that the abrupt collocations of φονεύετε and μάχεσθε are employed to express results of what precedes, and that in the second series ζηλοῦτε καὶ οὐ δύνασθε ἐπιτυχεῖν correspond to ἐπιθυμεῖτε καὶ οὐκ ἔχετε in the first series? Unsatisfied desire leads to murder; disappointed ambition leads to quarrelling and fighting.[76]

---

[71] Dibelius, *James*, 216; Martin, *James*, 144.

[72] See, for example, 4 Macc 1:25-27.

[73] For example, Johnson, *The Letter of James*, 277.

[74] Martin, *James*, 146.

[75] For example, Wis 2:24. *1 Clem* 4:9–5:2 (LCL; trans. Kirsopp Lake; London, Cambridge, MA: Harvard University Press, 1912) refers to various stories of jealousy in the Hebrew Bible, such as the story of Cain and Abel, which illustrates that "jealousy and envy wrought fratricide." See Johnson, *The Letter of James*, 277. *Didache* 3:2 also states that anger (ὀργή) leads to murder (φόνον). See John S. Kloppenborg, "The Transformation of Moral Exhortation in *Didache* 1-5," *The Didache in Context. Essays on Its Text, History and Transmission* (ed. Clayton N. Jefford; Leiden, New York, Cologne: Brill, 1995) 107. Huub van de Sandt ("James 4,1-4 in the Light of the Jewish Two Ways Tradition 3:1-6," *Biblica* 88 [2007] 38-63) has recently argued that Jas 4:1-4 should be understood as a development of the admonitions in *Did.* 3:1-6.

[76] Mayor, *The Epistle of St. James*, 136. Johnson (*The Letter of James*, 277) also takes this reading.

If one allows one's desires and envy to reign, one only encounters fighting and death, rather than peace, which is the result of following God's wisdom. Using a series of questions, which function rhetorically to hold the audience's attention,[77] and indictments, the author boldly makes plain the folly of clinging to one's own desires. His audience has not learned that they must ask for wisdom from God (Jas 1:5), rather they covet and they do not have, because they do not ask (4:2b). James 4:3 indicates, moreover, that some are asking things of God, but they are asking wrongly or "evilly," to spend it on their passions. By this the writer likely means that some are approaching God with the wrong motives;[78] their petitions are born out of selfishness.[79]

Through the depiction of the type of conduct which the author wishes his audience would avoid, then, James exposes the futility of leading a life without wisdom, for it is ruled by voracious desires which, ever unsatisfied, lead to fighting and killing. The language is very strong, but for James, the importance of the subject appears to demand such a vivid depiction.

b. Maxim: James 4:4

This verse, I will suggest, is a Jacobean version of a Jesus saying, but for our immediate purposes we will address its role as a maxim within the argument proper of Jas 3:13–4:10.[80] This is not the only place where a maxim occurs in James, as we have seen from the discussion of the exordium, where the maxim served to enhance the authority of the speaker. There are different forms of maxims, and some are more complex than others in that they provide a reason for the saying.[81] They should be used only rarely, but when they are used, they "will add much distinction."[82] Moreover, they should be related to the matter under discussion, "in order that what you say may not seem clumsy and irrelevant."[83] Maxims are proofs drawn from words, persons or actions.[84] As Aristotle explains, they are statements of the general,[85] and

---

[77] *Rhet. Her.* 4.16.24.

[78] Johnson, *The Letter of James*, 278.

[79] Mayor, *The Epistle of St. James*, 138.

[80] Although Hartin (*James*, 198-99) does think that Jas 4:4 corresponds to Jesus' wisdom from Matt 6:24; Luke 16:13, he does not explicitly address its rhetorical role as a maxim.

[81] *Rhet. Her.* 4.17.24-25.

[82] *Rhet. Her.* 4.17.25.

[83] *Rhet. Alex.* 9.

[84] *Rhet. Alex.* 7.

they are advantageous for more than one reason. First, if they are familiar to the audience, they will be much more acceptable and likely to be put into action, and second, if they are good, they will make the speech ethical, which will in turn render the character of the speaker to be "a man of good character" (*Rhet.* 2.21). Certainly, a maxim could be rejected by the audience, "but so great is its force, so great the presumption of agreement attaching to it, that one must have weighty reasons for rejecting it."[86] If the maxim does run contrary to the desires and expectations of the audience, however, one must "specify the reasons briefly, so as to avoid hostility and not arouse incredulity."[87]

James 4:4 begins with a caustic condemnation of the audience members as "adulteresses," an expression that disturbed some scribes who amended it to μοιχοὶ καὶ μοιχαλίδες,[88] but which refers to the covenant relationship between God and Israel which, in the author's view, the audience has sundered. In so doing, they have effectively committed adultery,[89] and indeed idolatry, for they have put other things before God.[90] The phrase anticipates the rest of the verse as it focuses upon choosing between loyalty to God and loyalty to something else. It is followed by the phrase "do you not know," which indicates that the audience are aware of what they should do but refuse to do so; it is "the clearest example in James of the diatribal rebuke for not acting upon an assumed store of shared knowledge."[91] This question/rebuke is then followed by a repetition of what the question asked, but in statement form, beginning with ὃς ἐάν. This is the maxim proper, for it states clearly that if one is a friend of the world then one is an enemy of God. Despite the fact that the audience is conscious that they cannot be friends with both the world and God at the same time, the letter writer bluntly reminds them of this fact.

---

[85] The author of the *Rhetorica ad Herennium* (4.17) explains, as well, that a maxim is a "saying drawn from life, which shows concisely either what happens or ought to happen in life ..."

[86] Perelman and Olbrechts-Tyteca, *The New Rhetoric*, 166.

[87] *Rhet. Alex.* 11.

[88] As we have seen, James usually refers to his audience as "brothers" or "beloved brothers" and thus the gender-inverted address would likely have been surprising to some scribes.

[89] See LXX Ps 72:27; Jer 3:6-10; 13:27; Isa 57:3; Hos 3:1; 9:1; Ezek 16:38; 23:45. See Johnson, *The Letter of James*, 278.

[90] James 4:1-13 is using what the author of the *Rhetorica ad Herennium* (4.15.22) calls an "Apostrophe" which expresses grief or indignation: "If we use Apostrophe in its proper place, sparingly, and when the importance of the subject seems to demand it, we shall instill in the hearer as much indignation as we desire."

[91] Johnson, *The Letter of James*, 278.

This maxim thus introduces friendship into this particular unit of James, but it is also connected to the previous sections. In the opening statement and rationale the writer has made it clear that his readers should seek wisdom and live by it with humility. He then delineates the nature of this wisdom and its effects in contrast to those who live without it, and who are thus selfish and envious. True wisdom comes from God, who gives simply and without reproach (Jas 1:5), and from whom every perfect gift comes (1:17). These gifts come from above (ἄνωθέν) as does this wisdom (ἄνωθέν 3:17) whereas the opposite to this wisdom is "earthly" (ἐπίγειος 3:15). With Jas 4:4 the author has maintained the contrast between above and below, between God's desires and the world's desires; between God's wisdom, which brings peace, and the lack of wisdom in the world, wherein envy and ambition reign, producing fighting and death. As Johnson writes, to be "'friends of the world,' then, means to live by the logic of envy ἄνωθέν, rivalry, competition, and murder."[92]

Although it introduces a new idea (friendship with the world/enmity with God) to the section, Jas 4:4 states the main theme of the section, albeit in another way.[93] 3:13-14 expresses the notion that one must make a choice between living according to God's wisdom and according to one's own envious desires. In the *ratio*, a clear contrast between the wisdom from God "from above" and all which is from below – "earthly" – is drawn such that no compromise can be made between them; one cannot live according to both. 4:4 re-emphasizes this choice, but using the language of friendship with the world and enmity with God[94] and with an even stronger emphasis upon the fact that one must make a choice between God and the world. This is a vivid example of how absolutely no compromises can be made; to be a friend of the world, in effect, will cause one to hate God! How could anyone argue that friendship with the world would be desirable?! And to attempt to live in allegiance to both would make one a δίψυχος person (Jas 1:8; 4:8) who wavers in the wind. This verse, therefore, functions as a dramatic, powerful, and vivid proof of the type of choice that James's listeners must make. Moreover, it holds out the attractive possibility of becoming friends with God if one is willing to resist the world. If one lives in the meekness of God's wisdom, one could presumably be called a friend of God, as Abraham and others

---

[92] Johnson, *The Letter of James*, 288.

[93] See *Rhet. Her.* 4.43.56.

[94] Johnson (*The Letter of James*, 279) points out that ἔχθρα and φιλία are opposites; see LXX Sir 6:19; 37:2; Luke 23:12.

were. This verse would thus have been an especially cogent means of convincing the audience that they should only follow God's wisdom in humility, and resist their own selfish ambitions.

The maxim, as discussed above, was one type of proof used in constructing a rhetorical speech. Briefly, I want to suggest that this particular maxim of Jas 4:4 is a form of recitation of a Jesus saying, albeit recast in the letter writer's words, using language amenable to the writer's intents and interests. As such, the audience, or at least some of the audience, would have recognized the main emphasis of this saying as being something which Jesus himself taught.

It is well known that the letter of James shares many things in common with the sayings of Jesus, especially those sayings found in the shared material between Matthew and Luke, namely Q. Patrick J. Hartin has explored these comparisons thoroughly in his monograph, *James and the Q Sayings of Jesus*, in which he argues that James stands in an intermediary position between Q and the Gospel of Matthew. Indeed, most authors have noticed these similarities between James and the sayings of Jesus,[95] even though James never credits Jesus with the material. Moreover, the common view is that James did not have access to the canonical Gospels, but drew from the sources which the Gospel writers used, such as Q, or at least, a version of Q. As some studies of James have shown, the author freely and regularly recasts pre-existing texts in order to suit his own purposes.[96] Thus, James may be using a variety of Jesus sayings, as well as LXX texts, and other traditions, but shows no sign of feeling compelled to preserve them with accuracy. Rather, they are shaped and edited according to the style and content of his message.

James 4:4 is comparable, at least in meaning, to the saying about serving two masters, found in Matt 6:24/Luke 16:13, both of which also include the saying about the impossibility of serving God and mammon at the same time, and *Gos. Thom.* 47:2. It is possible, as Hartin argues, that James's source for these materials was a pre-Matthean version of the Sermon on the Mount, for James preserves materials more common to Matthew than to Luke.[97]

---

[95] See Dean B. Deppe, *The Sayings of Jesus in the Epistle of James* (diss. Amsterdam; Chelsea, MI: Bookcrafters, 1989); Dibelius, *James*, 28-29. Mayor (*The Epistle of James*, 139) states, for example, that Jas 4:4 is a reference to "our Lord's words Matt vi 24." Wachob's work focuses upon Jas 2:5 as an allusion to Matt 5:3; Luke 6:20b; *Gos. Thom.* 54; Phol. Phil. 2:3.

[96] Wachob, *The Voice of Jesus*, 151.

[97] Hartin (*James and the Q Sayings of Jesus*, 243) writes that "because of its common use of the Jesus tradition, it would be logical to presume that James took it over from the

There are few verbal similarities between Jas 4:4 and the Jesus saying, apart from the reference to God as one pole of commitment. However, the sense of the two sets of materials is very similar. Both forms of the maxim emphasize that there can be no compromise between love of the "world," as is the case in James, or love of "mammon," as is the case with the Jesus saying, and love of God. "Mammon" was commonly thought to be a Semitic reference to money or riches, and although James is not talking explicitly about wealth in this section of the letter (as he does in other sections) he is focusing upon the evils of selfish ambition and covetousness which lead to fighting. Moreover, as Kloppenborg has observed, the "world" for James, represents a place of pride, ambition, and values opposed to God; it is a place where the pursuit of mammon runs rampant. In fact, the "poor in the world" are those who are rich in faith and heirs of the kingdom (2:5). The Jesus saying does not use friendship language, but James must have thought it appropriate to recast the saying in friendship terms as such a refashioning would be suitable given the earlier characterization of God as a friend, and the example of Abraham as a friend of God.

Moreover, it makes sense for James not to use the verb "to serve" or "to be a slave to" (δουλεύω) as found in the saying attributed to Jesus, for James is stressing friendship with God here and not servitude to God.[98]

The notion that this is a revision of a Jesus saying is further substantiated by *2 Clem.* 6:1-5. This early Christian document is another illustration of the connection between the Jesus saying (in this case, Jesus is credited with the saying) and the notion of friendship with the world:

> 1. And the Lord says: – "No servant can serve two masters." If we desire to serve both God and Mammon it is unprofitable to us, 2. "For what is the advantage if a man gain the whole world but lose his soul?" 3. Now the world that is, and the world to come are two enemies. 4. This world speaks of adultery, and corruption, and love of money, and deceit, but that world bids these things farewell. 5. We cannot then be friends (φίλοι) of both; but we must bid farewell to this world, to consort with that which is to come.

---

tradition being handed on within the Matthean community. This description does not come to James via Q, but rather from his connection with the Matthean community."

[98] Even though the author does refer to himself as a δοῦλος of God in Jas 1:1. On the removal of δουλεύω in Jas 4:4, see John S. Kloppenborg, "The Emulation of Jesus Tradition in the Letter of James," *Reading James with New Eyes*, 135.

2 *Clement* thus makes a clear link between the Jesus saying, and the fact that one cannot be friends (φίλοι) with the world, but instead of contrasting the world with God, it contrasts this world with the world to come. The letter of James has a strong eschatological dimension, but unlike 2 *Clement*, the letter does not *focus* upon the world to come but on the audience's relationship to God. James is profoundly theocentric, and thus rather than focusing upon the next world, James centres this maxim upon the exclusive commitment to God required for all believers. This commitment, as we have seen, will abide no concessions to the world, nor, in the Jesus saying, to wealth and riches. In maintaining the contrast between God and this world, James has therefore preserved the sense of the Jesus saying better than 2 *Clement*, which has taken a much more eschatological turn.

Although it has offered another interpretation of the Jesus saying, 2 *Clement* reveals that other early Christian writers recognized the similarities between Jesus' saying about God and Mammon and James's saying about competing friendships. I have not found any other early Christian text which makes as close an association between these two ideas as 2 *Clement* does, and indeed, whether there is a direct relationship between James and 2 *Clement* is not clear.[99] But even so, 2 *Clement*'s linkage supports the possibility that when the author of James wrote this verse, he had Jesus' teaching in mind.

The next question is, Why does James refer to Jesus' teaching without crediting Jesus with his own instruction? Wachob has dealt with this issue in grappling with Jas 2:5 as a version of "Blessed are the poor" and concluded that James did this in order to say something about God's attitude toward the poor as well as about the author's own view. By avoiding the attribution to Jesus (in attributing a chreia to a speaker, one was obviously making a comment about the character and moral stance of the speaker), James shifts the focus away from Jesus and

---

[99] 2 *Clement* never quotes James directly, although the unusual word διψυχία (2 *Clem.* 19.2) appears in this letter. However, as we saw earlier, this word is found in 1 *Clement*, which contrasts "simplicity" (ἀπλότη) with "duplicity" (διψυχία) (1 *Clem.* 23.1). These two ideas are also opposed in the *Epistle of Barnabas*'s contrast between the "two ways" (*Barn.* 18-20) and the *Shepherd of Hermas* provides considerable reflection upon διψυχία. Debates continue as to the relationship between this collection of early Christian literature and the letter of James, but 1 *Clement* and the *Shepherd of Hermas* bear more lexical and thematic similarities to James than 2 *Clement* does. For a list of indirect parallels between early non-canonical Christian literature and James, see Mayor, *The Epistle of James*, lxvi-lxxxiv, and for a discussion of the relationship between James and 1 *Clement*, see D.A. Hagner, *The Use of the Old and New Testaments in Clement of Rome* (NovTSup 34; Leiden: Brill, 1973) 248-56. Hagner thinks it likely that 1 *Clement* is dependent upon James, considering the extent of thematic and lexical parallels.

on to God. For Wachob, the case of 2:5 is also a rhetorical example which recalls the faith of Jesus in 2:1. Thus, according to Wachob, 2:5 is "the language of Jesus .... reformulated into a statement about God, and it is marked by, subsumed under, and intimately connected to Jesus' faith ... The implication in Jas 2:5 is that Jesus" faith is thoroughly consonant with God's words and deeds towards the poor."[100] Secondly, the use of the saying makes a significant claim for the author of the letter, who, in Wachob's view, is claiming to be James the Just. Thus the lack of attribution to Jesus serves to buttress the authority and moral calibre of James the Just.[101]

James 4:4, however, appears in the context of other quotations (4:5), and there are no references to the faith of Jesus in the vicinity. In this case, there is no indication that James is interested in evoking the faith of Jesus.[102] While the audience may have recognized 4:4 as something which Jesus taught, it may also have appreciated the manner in which James has recast the saying. We have already introduced the idea of *aemulatio* within ancient rhetoric, and I would suggest that 4:4 is another example of James paraphrasing a previous teaching of Jesus. Richard Bauckham's work on James is very helpful here.[103] Bauckham has located precedent for the re-expression of a sage's words in Jewish texts in the writings of Ben Sira, who sometimes "repeats the thoughts of Proverbs but deliberately refrains from repeating the words ... [likewise] James creates an aphorism of his own, indebted to but no mere reproduction of the words of Jesus."[104] Bauckham demonstrates this practice throughout James with regard to the teachings of Jesus and comments that in the case of Jas 4:4, there are no direct word correspondences to Matt 6:24/Luke 16:13 but that "we can easily imagine inspiration from the latter."[105]

Bauckham does not think it important whether or not the audience recognized the source teaching as Jesus'. I would disagree, for one of the reasons why *aemulatio* is effective is because the hearers recognize the original maxim and thus appreciate how the second speaker rephrases it and presents it as his own. In doing so, the author has, as

---

[100] Wachob, *The Voice of Jesus*, 150.

[101] Wachob, *The Voice of Jesus*, 151.

[102] And as indicated in Chapter 3, I do not think "Jesus Christ" is original to Jas 2:1.

[103] Richard Bauckham, *James. Wisdom of James, Disciple of Jesus the Sage* (New Testament Readings; London and New York: Routledge, 1999).

[104] Bauckham, *James*, 91.

[105] Richard Bauckham, "James and Jesus," in *The Brother of Jesus. James the Just and His Mission* (ed. Bruce Chilton and Jacob Neusner; Louisville, London: Westminster John Knox, 2001) 120.

Kloppenborg illustrates, both "aligned himself or herself with the ethos of the original speaker" and rephrased the saying such that "the audience will appreciate the artistry of paraphrase and application of the old maxim to the new rhetorical situation."[106]

Given that, as I have argued, James is drawing upon the tradition of friendship in a variety of ways throughout his letter, I think that he deliberately paraphrases this saying of Jesus in the language of friendship because it coheres well with other portions of the letter. His audience will recognize that this verse finds its predecessor in the teachings of Jesus, and thus it qualifies as a maxim not only because it is a general statement, but it is wisdom drawn from Jesus and familiar to the audience. However, the audience will appreciate how James has crafted Jesus' saying to suit the context of his letter, which, as we have seen, has already introduced the character of God as friend and benefactor (the latter will be elaborated below with references to God's χάρις in Jas 4:6). It would not make sense to switch suddenly from describing the relationship between human and divine as one of friendship to one of master and servant, as Q 16:13 does. Moreover, one could see how James could associate the reference to "mammon" in the Q saying to things "of the world," the coveting of which leads to wars and fighting. James, who has a negative view of the "world" (see Jas 1:27) sees it in opposition to God just as mammon is in opposition to God, and thus substitutes "world" for mammon.

James is a deeply theocentric text; God and the human relationship to God are at the very heart of the letter. Friendship language, as we have discussed, functions as a powerful rhetorical tool to persuade the audience to James's point of view. By rephrasing one of Jesus' teachings in language that is consistent with the rest of the letter, Jas 4:4 functions as a forceful proof for the exhortation to abandon the ways of the world, fraught with envy, pride and the pursuit of wealth, and to receive and live out God's wisdom.

c. Citation (Authority): James 4:5-6

James 4:6 appeals to scripture as an ancient testimony in support of the overall argument. A citation from an ancient source establishes the truth of the nature of the overall statement.[107] The persuasive power of the quotation can be very great "because of the universal validity of the

---

[106] Kloppenborg, "The Reception of Jesus Traditions," 141.
[107] *Rhet. Her.*4.3.6.

wisdom and its unquestionable independence of the parties."[108] The citation here is from Prov 3:34.

First, however, what are we to make of Jas 4:5, a verse fraught with lexical difficulties? For example, to what is the author referring when he mentions scripture (γραφή)? The phrase beginning with πρὸς φθόνον does not appear anywhere in scripture, and despite the fact that early Christians had access to texts which were not included in the canon, when James does quote scripture he always cites the Septuagint.[109] Is it the case, therefore, that James is citing a particular idea from scripture, for the notion of a jealous God who requires complete fidelity from Israel is not uncommon in biblical texts? However, God is never described as "longing enviously" (πρὸς φθόνον ἐπιποθεῖ), rather, φθόνος is only applied to the human being or human emotion, which can be envious,[110] and ἐπιποθέω is applied to the human longing for God and not vice versa.[111] This leads Johnson, following Laws and Adamson to some extent, to conclude that "it is not God who should be taken as the subject, but the *pneuma* within humans."[112] For Johnson, the "scripture" reference is to v. 6, which contains a citation from Prov 3:34.[113] Laws does not accept such a position, as it means that Prov 3:34 would receive a double introduction; rather, she suggests that the mention of scripture is not a reference to a single text, but to a general scriptural idea, found most often in the Psalms, that "the desire of the human spirit is, according to scripture, for God and the things of God."[114]

She thus understands Jas 4:5 as two rhetorical questions: "Does scripture mean nothing? Is this (according to scripture) the way the human spirit's longing is directed, by envy?"[115] The answer obviously requires

---

[108] Heinrich Lausberg, *Handbook of Literary Rhetoric. A Foundation for Literary Study* (trans. Matthew T. Bliss, Annemiek Jansen, & David E. Orton; ed. David E. Orton & R. Dean Anderson; Leiden, Boston, Cologne: Brill, 1998) 203. Quintilian (5.11.37) discusses this type of testimony, "which is rendered all the more impressive by the fact that it was not given to suit special cases, but was the utterance or action of minds swayed neither by prejudice or influence, simply because it seemed the most honourable or honest thing to say or do."

[109] Laws, *The Epistle of James*, 177.

[110] See Laws (*The Epistle of James*, 177) who refers to LXX Wis 2:24; 6:23; 1 Macc 8:16; 3 Macc 6:7.

[111] Johnson (*The Letter of James*, 281) cites LXX Ps 41:2; 119:20, 131, 174.

[112] Johnson, *The Letter of James*, 282. See also Laws, *The Epistle of James*, 178; James B. Adamson, *James. The Man and His Message* (Grand Rapids: Eerdmans, 1989) 332.

[113] Johnson, *The Letter of James*, 280.

[114] Laws, *The Epistle of James*, 179.

[115] Laws, *The Epistle of James*, 178. Johnson (*The Letter of James*, 282) concurs with this reading.

a negative response, for according to scripture (the Psalms) the human spirit longs for God and all the things of God. Such an interpretation of the verse is not absolutely convincing, as Laws admits, but it explains the use of πρὸς φθόνον ἐπιποθεῖ and the intriguing reference to "scripture."

James 4:6 contains an obvious reference to scripture which "is not arbitrary, but in fact grounds James's argument."[116] The citation from LXX Prov 3:34 is almost exact except for an exchange of θεός for κύριος. This citation offers proof of why one should live a good life "in the meekness of wisdom" and not live according to selfish ambition for "God opposes the proud, but gives grace to the humble." God does not approve of an envious or selfish life but of a humble one; the ancient texts *say so*. God's actions are completely different from the human spirit, which can be envious. God gives a "greater" (μείζονα) gift, a notion which is comparable to Jas 1:5 in which God gives ἁπλῶς. The context of Prov 3:34, which deals with God's wisdom, walking in peace, not envying, caring for the poor, and the exaltation of the wise, fits well with the association of ideas in Jas 3:13–4:10.[117] The citation from Prov 3:34 within its context, with which the audience was likely familiar, thus forms a consummation and proof of the argument as a whole.

4. Concluding Exhortations: James 4:7-10

The closing of a pattern of elaboration often included some exhortation,[118] efforts to influence the emotions of the hearers, and an attempt to summarize or refresh the audience's memory of the overall theme.[119] The conclusion could appeal to the audience's feelings for a decision or judgment.[120]

Johnson terms Jas 4:7-10 a call to conversion from a life of envy and friendship with the world, to a life of total reliance and trust in God. This is really a call to repentance, as repentance language figures prominently in this section.[121] Although James's language is strong, it is assumed that his audience does want to be loyal to and trusting of God.

---

[116] Johnson, *The Letter of James*, 283.

[117] Johnson, *The Letter of James*, 283.

[118] Hermogenes (*Progymnasmata* line 60), for example, writes that at the conclusion of an elaboration, "you are to add an exhortation to the effect that it is necessary to heed the one who has spoken or acted." Translation by Hock and O'Neil, *The Chreia in Ancient Rhetoric*, 177.

[119] Lausberg, *Handbook of Literary Rhetoric*, 204.

[120] Mack and Robbins, *Patterns of Persuasion*, 55.

[121] Johnson, *The Letter of James*, 289.

The first verse includes the word οὖν ("therefore") which indicates that now that the author has set forth his argument and proofs, the recipients of his message must make a decision as to what they will do. James appeals to them to "submit" (ὑποτάγητε) to God (4:7) and to "resist" (ἀντίστητε) the devil, who, as the letter writer assures optimistically, will "flee" from you if you do.[122] He exhorts the readers to cleanse their hands, to purify their hearts and calls them δίψυχοι which they are as long as they remain enemies of God and rely upon their own selfish ambitions. He demands them to be wretched, and to weep and mourn, somewhat reminiscent of Matt 5:4, but unlike the prophets who use this language to describe what will happen to idolatrous people, the author does not threaten his readers or hearers with outside disaster; rather the author wants the audience to bring such tribulation upon themselves in "an act of conversion."[123] In order to be friends of God, they must undergo a dramatic reversal from following their own desires to heeding and manifesting the wisdom of God, and such a reversal requires repentance. Although the language of testing and trials is not used explicitly here, the notion that the audience must go through perhaps a painful conversion conforms to James's emphasis upon testing and trials as necessary constituents of the journey to perfection. If one desires friendship with God, one must endure trials, a theme consistent in Jas 1, 2, and 4.

Finally, the last verse functions as a nice *inclusio* to the entire section as again, it emphasizes the humility required in order to form a relationship with God. "Be humbled" says 4:10, recalling the initial reference to meekness (πραΰτης) in 3:13 and the citation of Prov 3:34 in Jas 4:6 ("God gives grace to the humble [ταπεινοῖς]"). The audience is reminded of the type of behaviour that God demands, an appeal is made to make a decision, and a promise that God will respond ("the Lord will exalt you") is made.[124]

This section would have been persuasive, for despite the fact that the audience must undergo repentance in order to become friends with God, the possibility of such a friendship is truly that, a possibility. There is optimism here that the hearers can change and an assurance that God is reliable. The exhortations to cleanse the hands and purify the heart (Jas 4:8) would have been effective rhetorically for such direc-

---

[122] Only James and *Herm. Man.* 12.4, 7; 12.5, 2 contain this idea of evil fleeing from the person.

[123] Johnson, *The Letter of James*, 285.

[124] This final phrase bears striking resemblance to Luke 18:14; Matt 18:4; 23:12. See Hartin, *James and the Q Sayings of Jesus*, 142.

tions associate living from "below," heeding the devil and ignoring God's wisdom with impurity.[125] If one is a friend of the world and enemy of God, one is also impure. This language may have been used in order to make a last effort to persuade the people of the undesirability of friendship with the world.

Within the letter of James, 3:13–4:10 forms a discrete literary unit, which conforms to the ancient rhetorical technique of the elaboration of a theme. The focus of the unit is adherence to the wisdom of God, in humility, as opposed to engaging in strife and satisfying ambitions. This theme is particularly emphasized by the use of a maxim in 4:4, which emphatically restates the theme but in the language of friendship with the world versus friendship with God. If this is a refashioning of a Jesus saying, it would have been particularly compelling for it restates something which the audience presumably already accepts, and it asserts that the will of Jesus and God are the same. The notion of friendship with God is therefore particularly important in forming a persuasive argument as to why the audience should resist their desires, resist the devil and draw near to God.

B. Friendship, Patronage and Benefaction in James 3:13–4:10
1. Author to Hearers/Listeners

In a variety of ways, the voice in Jas 3:13–4:10 speaks more harshly to the audience than in other sections of the letter. Although references to the recipients as "my brothers" (ἀδελφοί μου) appear three times in Jas 3:1-12 (3:1, 10 and 12) and 4:11 includes ἀδελφοί, the term does not occur in the unit itself. The fact that 3:1-12 contains three mentions of ἀδελφοί μου may be an indication that the author is readying the audience for a heavy onslaught of criticism while the appearance of ἀδελφοί in 4:11 is an attempt to remind them that despite the previous tough talk in 3:13–4:10, they should not forget that the author is indeed their "brother."

Thurén has observed that James speaks "frankly and directly" and "dares to approach [the audience] in a direct, even unkind, manner,"[126] and nowhere do we see this frankness more clearly than in Jas 3:13–4:10. James continues to use the second person address throughout the entire section and he asks the audience rhetorical questions about who is wise among them (3:13) and what causes them to fight (4:1) then proceeds to answer the questions with challenges and exhortation. This

---

[125] For more on pollution and purity in James, see Elliott, "The Epistle of James in Rhetorical and Social-Scientific Perspective."
[126] Thurén, "Risky Rhetoric," 283.

reasoning through question and answer is effective rhetorically because it holds the hearers' attention: whenever a question is asked, the audience anticipates a response.[127] However, James is especially tough throughout these verses and may be treading on thin ice. The bluntness of the counsel almost stings; and includes prophetic denunciations of the audience, such as the declaration that those who covet and fight are adulterous (4:1). As we have seen, ancient writers on παρρησία were well aware that there could be a fine line between constructive criticism and out-and-out ridicule and belittlement. Frank speech could be harsh provided it was for constructive purposes. Plutarch says that

> the true frankness such as a friend displays applies itself to errors that are being committed; the pain which it causes is salutary and benignant, and, like honey, it causes the sore places to smart and cleanses them too ... (*Adul. amic.* 59D).

The friend is the counsel and advocate[128] and bears the responsibility "to be frank with us, and indeed to blame us when our conduct is bad,"[129] and this is precisely what James is doing. I would argue that although the author sounds very angry in this section, the aim is not to mortify the audience, but to encourage them to change and behave properly, such that they can be called friends of God. Although he directly chastises the audience for their behaviour on all sorts of fronts, he provides an argument for why what they are doing is bad, and offers clear guidance as to what they should do to improve their behaviour. Unlike his proclamations about the rich in Jas 1:9–11 and 5:1–6, who apparently have no option to repent and avoid an apocalyptic doom, James's audience are provided clear guidance as to what they must do in order to cleanse and purify themselves such that God will exalt them (4:10).

James 3:13–4:10 also maintains the authority of the speaker. Not only does he appeal to the audience directly and strongly, in 4:4 he rephrases a teaching of Jesus to suit his own context. As stated earlier, this verse would make significant claims for the speaker, for it indicates that the speaker's views and Jesus' views are the same. Thus, the speaker would appear as one who "like Jesus, spoke and taught the wisdom of God."[130] By recasting a saying of Jesus, the speaker has increased his moral credibility with his audience. If his listeners or readers value the teachings of Jesus, they would presumably not question the

---

[127] *Rhet. Her.* 4.16.24.
[128] Plutarch, *Adul. amic.* 61D.
[129] Plutarch, *Adul. amic.* 66A.
[130] Wachob, *The Voice of Jesus*, 151.

authority of this author, for he demonstrates that his wisdom is in line with that of Jesus. Moreover, they will appreciate the artistry with which he has rephrased this teaching such that it is consistent with his overall emphasis upon God as a friend and benefactor.

2. Attributes of Community Members

This portion of the letter is focused upon criticism and exhortation to the audience to resist the ways "of the world," especially envy, which leads to fighting and destruction. The vices to come under attack in particular are ζῆλος (Jas 3:14, 15; 4:2), ἐριθεία (3:14, 16) and φθόνος (4:5), with Jas 4:5 challenging the notion that the human spirit should be governed by envy (φθόνος). Envy was considered to be inimical to friendship.[131] Plutarch, for instance, claimed that true friends do not possess envy (φθόνος) nor emulation (ζῆλος) but withstand one another's accomplishments with moderation and without vexation (*Adul. amic.* 54C). For Aristotle, these two competitive emotions are experienced with others who are similar, in particular, with friends.[132] Good virtues are worthy of emulation, but Aristotle does not approve of envy within friendship.[133] Prior to the fourth century BCE, ζῆλος was understood as a neutral term and often translated as "zeal" which could be positive in that one could have zeal or passion for a particular idea or person, or cause.[134] However, and as we saw in Chapter 2, by the fourth century BCE, it came to have a negative connotation.[135] In James it is described as "bitter" (πικρος) and placed side by side with ἐριθεία, which can be translated as "selfish ambition" and in the New Testament is related to "antisocial attitudes destructive of community (Rom 2:8; Gal 5:20; Phil 1:17; 2:3)."[136] In various Greek texts ζῆλος is used interchangeably with φθόνος, an observation which leads Johnson to conclude that James also thinks of the two words as synonyms.[137] Thus ζῆλος likely refers to "envy" in James and contains none of the positive connotations it possesses in other literary contexts. This is clearly a vice which James is determined that the audience should relinquish.

---

[131] As Johnson ("James 3:13–4:10," 336) remarks: "That φθόνος opposes friendship is obvious ..."

[132] *Rhet.* 2.4.25.

[133] *Rhet.* 2.4.25. See Viano, "Competitive Emotions and *Thumos* in Aristotle's *Rhetoric*," 91.

[134] A. Stumpff, "ζῆλος," *TDNT* II (1964) 877-78.

[135] See Chapter 2, n. 116.

[136] Johnson, *The Letter of James*, 271.

[137] Johnson (*The Letter of James*, 271) lists the following sources: Plutarch, *On Brotherly Love* 14; *How to Profit by One's Enemies* 1; 9; *On Tranquility of Soul* 10; 11; Plato, *Symposium* 213D; *Laws* 679C; Epictetus, *Discourses* III, 22, 61.

The fact that envy was declared by ancient texts to be antithetical to the values of friendship coupled with James's stress on its avoidance is further evidence, to my mind, that James wants to advance the values of authentic friendship among the members of his audience in opposition to what he understands to be the values "of the world." In this section of the letter, envy and its related characteristics are aspects of living without God's wisdom from above. Envy and jealousy cause wars and fighting within the audience. Rather than sharing their wealth in common and aiding one another, as true friends should, these people are longing for one another's possessions and as a consequence, James points out quite dramatically, engaging in war and murder. This is not the behaviour of friends, for friends "wish what is good for us."[138]

James exhorts the audience to avoid other sorts of activity that were understood to be oppositional to friendship. For example, he insists that the audience should not boast or be false to the truth (3:14). Such caution about the use of speech is consistent with other sections of the letter in which James reflects upon the use of speech (3:1-12; 4:11-17) and near the end when he commands the audience not to take oaths (5:12). As discussed in an earlier chapter, speech was an important issue within discussions of friendship for friends were expected to speak honestly, and sometimes critically[139] to one another, with παρρησία.[140] Those "friendships" between patrons and clients were often lampooned because of the prevalence of insincere talk, namely flattery, that for some writers exposed the falsity of such "friendships." James does not deal directly with flattery, but there is a deep suspicion of the tongue, to the point that the tongue cannot be tamed by a human being (3:8). James claims, although it should not be so, that both blessing and cursing come from the tongue (3:10), making it somewhat comparable to the δίψυχος person, who weaves to and fro with the wind.

The primary context for such criticism of boasting and falsity in Jas 3:14 is the author's desire for the community members to get along and stop grumbling against one another as it is in other sections of the letter (4:11-12; 5:9). Strife caused by false speech is a problem that plagued many types of associations in antiquity.[141] However, James is a little atypical compared to evidence for the associations in that it prohibits the use of oaths in 5:12, a verse that recalls Jesus' instructions in

---

[138] Aristotle, *Rhet.* 2.4.8.

[139] For example, Prov 27:6 states: "Well meant are the wounds a friend inflicts, but profuse are the kisses of an enemy."

[140] See William R. Baker, "'Above All Else': Contexts of the Call for Verbal Integrity in James 5:12," *JSNT* 54 (1994) 57-71.

[141] See Verseput, "Genre and Story," 106-107.

Matt 5:33-37. The oath was quite common among associations, for it guaranteed obedience to the regulation of conduct,[142] and it was used generally within ancient society for sealing contracts and making promises.[143] Some religious groups, such as the Pythagoreans, resisted taking the oath for it was perceived to be useless and insincere.[144] Plutarch also indicates a certain mistrust of oaths, for he describes the flatterer as one who repeatedly takes oaths, in contrast to true friends who do not require such "trifles" (*Flatterer* 21). This suggests that James has in mind the ethics espoused by sincere friends as he attempts to offer concrete guidance to his listeners; guidance that would again amplify the useless nature of flattery and the system it upheld, namely patronage.[145]

Falsity, envy, boasting, and strife all manifest, for James, the behaviour of someone who is a "friend of the world" and is completely counter to "friendship with God."[146] If one is at war with one's fellow creatures, it seems for James, then one cannot be friends with God. If one has not received the wisdom "from above" with all of its virtuous characteristics (3:17) then one cannot be a peacemaker (3:18). Moreover, the second reference to the δίψυχος person appears in 4:8 as a description of "sinners" or those who need to draw near to God; those who are living according to friendship with the world and presumably living with envy and its subsequent results. James thus maintains, in this section, the image of a person who cannot be μία ψυχή with anyone else because he or she is so divided. Such a person clearly cannot be a friend of God.

It is important to return to the fact, however, that James is not content simply to criticize those who do not receive the wisdom from above, but provides a description of what comes of receiving this wis-

---

[142] For example, see *IG* V/1.1390.

[143] See W. Burkert, *Greek Religion* (trans. John Raffan; Cambridge, MA: Harvard University Press, 1985) 250. For example, Pliny's famous letter to Trajan (*Letters* 10.96 [LCL; trans. William Melmoth; London: Heinemann; New York: Putnam, 1924]) reports of Christians who "bound themselves by a solemn oath, not to any wicked deeds, but never to commit any fraud, theft or adultery ..."

[144] See Joseph Plescia, *The Oath and Perjury in Ancient Greece* (Tallahassee: Florida State University Press, 1970) 87.

[145] Similarly, Coleman (*Patronage and the Epistle of James*, 120-21) provides evidence supporting the view that oaths were often used in patron-client contracts, and concludes regarding Jas 5:12 that "James is warning against an official oath in which a client, in return for patronal benefactions, promises service for a period of time."

[146] Kloppenborg Verbin ("Patronage Avoidance," 770) writes, "'Friendship with the world' is characterized in the immediately preceding verses as filled with conflict and rivalry (4:1-2a) ... With such 'friendship' James immediately juxtaposes adherence to God, who 'gives grace to the humble' and exalts them (4:6-10)."

dom. James 3:13–4:10 contains much positive exhortation for the life of the community. Many of the things that he stresses as characteristic of this wisdom and of one who receives it are positive emotions, such as "calmness" (πραΰτή), which Aristotle describes as the quieting of anger,[147] and mercy (ἔλεος) (Jas 3:17)[148] Aristotle describes friends as those who are ready to help others; who are neither "quarrelsome nor contentious,"[149] while Plutarch associates truthfulness, love for the good, and the ability to reason with the friend, who tries "to foster the growth of what is sound and to preserve it."[150] James advocates truthfulness (3:14), gentleness, peacemaking, and being open to reason (3:17) – all positive characteristics that resonate with this image of the ideal friend. The author is deliberately drawing upon friendship and the virtuous emotions and actions associated with it in order to promote a more harmonious community life among the audience.

3. God

First, it is clear that the image of God as benefactor is maintained in this section. God is the provider from whom the audience must make requests (4:3). James chooses the citation from LXX Prov 3:34 to emphasize that God gives "grace" (χάρις) to the humble. This language of grace is, as we have seen, regularly associated with benefaction and, to some extent friendship, in the ancient world. And James has not only opted to use the Proverbs citation here, he introduces the verse with μείζονα δὲ δίδωσιν χάριν which indicates that he wants to emphasize the characterization of God as a provider of χάρις who gives generously (Jas 1:5).[151] James goes out of his way to stress this beneficence, just as he did in 1:5 when he made it clear that God gives generously and without reproach. God is completely opposite, then, to the rich patron who may provide but also drags people to court (2:6) or exploits his labourers (5:4).

This section contains another explicit reference to friendship with God, namely 4:4, albeit stated in the reverse as friendship with the world equaling enmity with God. Some authors consider this verse to be the clearest expression of the identity the letter writer wishes his audience would reflect.[152] This may be true, but in any case 4:4 clearly

[147] *Rhet.* 2.3.1
[148] See Konstan, *The Emotions of the Ancient Greeks*, chs. 3 and 10.
[149] *Rhet.* 2.4.8-12.
[150] *Adul. amic.* 61D.
[151] See Hartin, *James*, 200.
[152] As Hartin (*A Spirituality of Perfection*, 106) writes: "Among the spiritual values that James's community is encouraged to embrace is the call to maintain friendship with God.

fits, as a maxim should, with what we have encountered in James so far. James places special emphasis upon testing, and the one who withstands great tests and trials is called a friend of God, as Abraham was (2:23). The person who withstands the trials associated with forsaking "the world," as characterized by James, can also possess this friendship with God. God, moreover, is described as friends sometimes were (1:5). Unlike the person who is δίψυχος and who vacillates, the author wants his readers to focus upon their relationship with God, which should take priority over all other relationships.

Given what we have learned in earlier chapters about what it meant to be a φίλος in antiquity, the language of friendship here would have been quite powerful, for friends were expected to bear unparalleled loyalty for one another; they should be of "one soul" instead of "double-souled"; they should share all things and even die for one another if necessary. "As a friend of God, one shares the same vision, the same values God has – one trusts God fully and sees reality as God would."[153] One has absolute faith in God. This would be a demanding relationship and one that entertains no compromises, but it articulates clearly the fundamental identity that James desires for his audience. If the community members are to be friends with God, like Abraham and Rahab, they will manifest the great characteristics, through good works, which true friends are expected to have.

The opposite end of the spectrum is friendship with the world, which, if entered into, effectively makes one an "enemy" of God. The world (κόσμος) is not portrayed positively throughout this letter: in Jas 1:27, religion is defined as keeping oneself "unstained from the world"; in 2:5, the author asks if God has not "chosen those who are poor in the world to be rich in faith to be heirs of the kingdom which he has chosen to those who love him?" thereby contrasting the "world" with the "kingdom"; 3:6 describes the tongue as a "world of injustice ... staining the whole body"; and finally in 4:4, as we see, the world is diametrically opposed to God. To be friends with the world would mean that one embraces worldly values, values which do not come from God. As the writer says, the embrace of such ideas would lead to enmity with God, for one can only be a friend of God if one is entirely devoted and places nothing in the way of that relationship. There is no evidence that the author desires his audience to forsake the world and retreat to the desert or some other geographically remote location, but

---

This expresses the very identity of the community. James 4:4 is one of the central verses of the entire letter; it captures the main thrust of the letter's central argument."

[153] Hartin, *A Spirituality of Perfection*, 110.

they must not live according to the values and standards of the world, for these do not come from God and are, in effect, opposed to God.

Maxims are powerful rhetorically, for an audience has difficulty rejecting common wisdom; moreover, maxims enhance the authority of the speaker, especially if they are recognized as originating from a great teacher. The question that arises is, Why would James not simply cite the Jesus saying, "You cannot serve God and mammon," rather than change it to contrast "friendship with the world" with "enmity with God"? The best explanation is that such a rephrasing coheres smoothly with the ideas in the letter thus far. God has been introduced as a friend and benefactor in the exordium, and James wants this characterization to continue throughout the rest of the text. Moreover, James was aware of the rhetorical power of the notion of friendship with God, and such a notion was important in the overall framework of the composition as we have seen in the few sections studied so far. The idea of friendship with God could be an effective means of exposing the specious nature of "friendship" with well-to-do patrons who, unlike God, could be changeable, and are ultimately outside the plan of salvation. "Friendship" with these people equals friendship with the world, made manifest in the envy, squabbling and the resultant killing that emerges. James's audience, I have argued, would have associated this wisdom with Jesus, but James's alteration of it would have been more appropriate given the problems his audience was having, and the overall language and thought world of the letter.

Conclusion

This chapter has argued that Jas 3:13–4:10 conforms to the classical elaboration of a theme exercise, centred on the idea that true wisdom from above resides in humility and calmness in contrast to a life of envy and resultant strife. James draws upon a variety of sources to support his argument, most notably, a teaching of Jesus in 4:4 which he has transformed into a statement about friendship such that the maxim is congruent with the overall characterization of God as a friend and benefactor. This maxim is key to James's argument, and thus it is significant that he draws upon the image of God as a friend in his expression of it.

As in the previous two chapters the author maintains an authoritative *ethos* as he speaks to the audience in this section. In fact, the tone of this section is more frank than in the previous two, and borders on the harsh. Perhaps such a voice is an indicator that envy and rivalry were some of the worst problems that the author imagined (or knew) his audience to be facing, and thus he held nothing back in addressing this issue. However, not only does he exhort his listeners or readers to avoid such quarrelsome activity, which was also understood by ancient writers to be an enemy of friendship, he provides guidance as to how they can change, and become friends with God. The virtues that the author associates with living with the wisdom from above are consistent with the qualities that authors such as Aristotle and Plutarch associate with a true friend. Although James does not explicitly command the audience to live as a community of friends, many of the characteristics that he advocates, as he did in the previous two sections examined, easily fit within the descriptions of ideal friends.

Finally, this section upholds the nature of God as one who provides benefits generously and who can be a "friend" provided one is not a friend "of the world."

In 3:13–4:10 James merges the character of God's wisdom with the desired characteristics of those who received James's message. If they receive this wisdom of God from above, then they will not envy and fight one another for this wisdom is characterized by a series of virtuous features (4:17). Indeed the audience members are exhorted to submit to God, to cleanse their hands and humble themselves before God. If they do these things they will receive God's benefits, including God's wisdom, which, if manifested in a good life of works, will contribute to a harmonious community life that reflects some of the qualities of ideal friendship. Friendship with God thus enables friendship among the recipients of James's letter.

7

Conclusion

Introduction

The aim of the previous chapters was to demonstrate that the discrete meanings inherent in the language of friendship and benefaction, especially the notion of friendship with God the benefactor, had significant roles to play in the persuasive strategy of the letter of James. James consists mainly of deliberative rhetoric, however, and as such it seeks to encourage and convince its recipients to "convert" or change their behaviour in some way. Obviously, then, the argument must relate to the experiences of those who are hearing it. There must be what Lloyd Bitzer calls a "rhetorical situation," which he defines as

> a complex of persons, events, objects, and relations presenting an actual or potential exigence which can be completely or partially removed if discourse, introduced into the situation, can so constrain human decision or action, as to bring about the significant modification of the exigence ... [1]

Thus the rhetorical situation requires (1) an "exigence," or a problem that needs correction, (2) an audience, or a group of people who are capable of "being influenced by discourse and of being mediators of change,"[2] and (3) rhetorical constraints, which include the "beliefs, attitudes, documents, facts, traditions, images, interests, motives and the like"[3] used by the speaker to convince the audience of his or her argument. In other words, rhetorical discourse is not created merely to flaunt a particular cleverness or literary style, but to address concrete issues and concerns within a desired framework or perspective; it is pragmatic and responds to a specific situation. An analysis of James's

---

[1] Bitzer, "Rhetorical Situation," 6.
[2] Bitzer, "Rhetorical Situation," 8.
[3] Bitzer, "Rhetorical Situation," 8.

7. Conclusion

rhetoric, then, can aid in positing a possible scenario, or "rhetorical situation," to which this elusive letter directs itself.

It is important to be clear that the rhetorical situation is not identical to the historical situation of the recipients, although the two are not unrelated. In attempting to determine the rhetorical situation of James, we will not be reconstructing a precise set of historical circumstances, but assessing the type of "specific condition or situation which invites utterance."[4] What set of circumstances would invite the author of James to create and send such a letter and particularly, what type of situation might the language of friendship address effectively? This situation is likely connected to the general historical circumstances of the audience, but it does not focus upon the details of their exact whereabouts, time, and distinct characteristics.

As the rhetorical situation is not analogous to the historical one, it is possible to assess it even with regard to an encyclical, such as the letter of James. The lens is not upon the precise complexion of the audience, but the general ethos and set of exigencies that need to be altered. Thus the letter need not be addressed to only one community but to numerous groups that share similar problems and for which James could be an effective voice in overcoming such difficulties.

My task is not to explore every issue in the letter of James, but to examine what possible social contexts or problems the language of friendship could address effectively. Part of this problem will inevitably be the *ennui* of the audience that the speaker must defeat in order to obtain a legitimate hearing. It is my contention that given the complex relationship between friendship and patronage within the Graeco-Roman world, James is drawing upon friendship language in order to counteract the audience's surrender or potential surrender to the influence of wealthy patrons, which greatly upsets the author because it leads to the neglect of the poor. This is by no means the only problem but there is sufficient evidence within the text to support the notion that this was one aspect of the audience's situation to which the author deemed it necessary to respond. Patronage was a pervasive and successful means of social control under the Roman Empire, for it was a central mechanism for the redistribution of wealth. As such, one could generally say that patronage had a firm grasp upon many communities; a grasp from which many would have found it difficult to wrench themselves free. Moreover, this patronage system would mask itself as friendship, thereby making it more difficult to challenge. But for some writers, including the author of James, patronage, exposed for what it

---

[4] Wilhelm Wuellner, "Where is Rhetorical Criticism Taking Us?" *CBQ* 49 (1987) 455.

truly was, was in direct contrast to the attitudes and behaviours expected of true friends as they were understood in the ancient Graeco-Roman world,[5] and indeed, to the disposition and conduct that the author of James is attempting to promote.

Patronage as an Exigence

Before summarizing the evidence in support of patronage as an exigence within the rhetorical situation of the letter of James, a few general observations about the letter are required. As one reads through James, communal relations are consistently the overriding concern.[6] Whether it focuses upon proper speech (3:1-12), anger (1:19-21); treatment of the poor (1:27; 2:1-26); true wisdom (3:13-4:10), or daily experiences of the community (5:13-20), each issue relates directly or indirectly to the life of the community. Within this context of concern for community life, James does not offer us a treatise extolling the virtues of friendship nor a systematic critique of patronage, but there are sufficient indications that these forms of human interaction, both present and undoubtedly familiar to many ancients, lie behind some of the arguments within the text. The author draws upon the *topos* of ancient friendship, both from the Jewish and Graeco-Roman worlds, in order to describe God as a true friend and benefactor, a description that could operate as a foil against which the potential patrons of the community could be compared. I suggest that James does this deliberately in order to expose the instability and manipulative character of the rich, or those who James's audience believes can be their patrons. By offering the possibility of friendship with God, James may be underscoring the futility and illusory nature of "friendship" with human patrons.

Secondly, the notion of friendship with God is tied to a specific type of moral life, characterized by testing and endurance (Jas 1:2-4, 12), by aid to the poor (1:27; 2:14-17), consistency between faith and action (2:14-17), and careful control of speech (3:1-12; 4:11). Such a life is difficult and requires patience and suffering (5:10), but it is also joyful (1:2). In addition, it is a life lived according to the wisdom from above, and is opposed to a life of envy and ultimately fighting and death (3:13–4:10). In some ways, as we saw, a life according to God's wisdom is similar to the existence a true friend leads, for it focuses upon the welfare of the other. James's audience must rely upon God to pro-

---

[5] This is Troels Engberg-Pedersen's interpretation of Plutarch's urgent distinction between friendship and flattery, as discussed in Chapter 3.

[6] See Wachob, *The Voice of Jesus*, 161.

vide them with the wisdom that will lead to this life, for indeed, wisdom can make people friends of God (Wis 7:27). In contrast with such a life is the life of friendship with the world, identified by envy, seeking after gain, and fighting. Such a lifestyle is led by the rich, who exploit the poor (Jas 5:4) and live in luxury, but who will disappear (1:11).

James is contrasting two "worldviews" in this letter, consistent with Engberg-Pedersen's reading of Plutarch's *How to Tell a Flatterer from a Friend*. For Engberg-Pedersen, Plutarch's essay represents an attempt to preserve the noble idea of friendship as the "apogee" of a moral system in which trust and sincerity were central, and status issues were not the constant preoccupation. The contrary to that system is one based upon distinctions in social rank, in which patronage and flatterers thrive, and, when it adopts the language of friendship, threatens to demean and pervert the true meaning of friendship. Thus Engberg-Pedersen suggests that

> whenever Christian writers make use of concepts belonging within the nexus of friendship, flattery and frank criticism ... , they too betray a concern about the status system and a set of counter-values. To the extent, therefore, that their use of those concepts enters directly into the formulation of their own religious message (as I think it often does), that message too will be partly *about* the status system and a set of counter-values.[7]

This suggestion is especially compelling for the letter of James, for despite the fact that James's use of the language of friendship is limited, there is great concern in this letter for status distinctions and the effect of status distinctions upon the economically weak. For example, the result of the "showing partiality" example in 2:1-13 is that the poor man has been "dishonoured" (2:6) and this showing of partiality to the rich is in fact a sin (2:9). Friendship, especially friendship with God, serves to undermine those status distinctions, for in pursuing such a friendship one must abandon this scramble for status and material gain and humble oneself before the Lord (4:10).

Audience

James's letter addresses a specific rhetorical audience, that is, an audience that is capable of putting James's teachings into action and in this case, of resisting patronage and pursuing friendship with God. Whether they in reality did put these exhortations into practice is another issue.

---

[7] Engberg-Pedersen, "Plutarch to Prince Philopappus," 79.

Given the fact that patronage was a virtually universal phenomenon in the ancient Mediterranean world, as well as the evidence that the *topos* of friendship was familiar to Graeco-Roman and Hellenistic Jewish writers, these two issues within the letter do not help us when considering the whereabouts of the letter's recipients. However, the letter is addressed to "the twelve tribes in the Diaspora." Commentators have read this either as a reference to Jewish Christians living outside of Palestine,[8] who still considered themselves to be within the bounds of Judaism, or a metaphorical description of these Christians as the true Israel, heaven being their real dwelling place.[9] Some stress the eschatological dimension of the phrase,[10] while a third possibility is that the letter is addressed to both Jews and Jewish Christians.[11] This problem is difficult to solve, for early on, Christian churches, consisting of both Jews and Gentiles, came to understand themselves as the "new Israel" with heaven being their true home.[12]

However, even though some groups had broken off from Judaism at an early date but retained the language of the Diaspora and "new Israel," there are other clues in the letter that support a literal reading of "twelve tribes in the Diaspora." Abraham is referred to as "our father" (Jas 2:21), a phrase which Joseph Mayor thinks must be taken literally "unless reasons can be shown to the contrary."[13] Other references that underline the Jewish character of this letter include the mention of the "Lord of the Sabaoth" (5:4), "synagogue" (2:2) as the term for a place of meeting, "Gehenna" (3:6), and the examples of Rahab (2:25), Job (5:11), the prophets (5:10) and Elijah (5:17). Would an audience that included Gentiles have understood these references easily, with no explanation? Although the precise relationship between James and Paul is disputed, James can take for granted his audience's respect for the

---

[8] Franz Mussner, *Der Jakobusbrief* (5th ed.; HTKNT 13, 1; Freiburg, Basel and Vienna: Herder & Herder, 1987) 2-23.

[9] For example, Ropes, *A Critical and Exegetical Commentary*, 124-25; Dibelius, *James*, 67; F. Hauck, *Die Briefe des Jakobus, Petrus, Judas, und Johannes* (4th ed.; NTD 10; Göttingen: Vandenhoeck & Ruprecht, 1949) 6; F. Vouga, *L'Épitre de Saint Jacques* (CNT 13; Geneva: Labor et Fides, 1984) 37.

[10] See Matt Jackson-McCabe, "A Letter to the Twelve Tribes in the Diaspora: Wisdom and 'Apocalyptic' Eschatology in the Letter of James," *SBLSP* 35 (1996) 504-17.

[11] This possibility has been revived by Allison ("The Fiction of James and its *Sitz im Leben*," 529-70), who points out that many early commentators on James understood James's audience to consist of this combination of Jews and Jewish Christians.

[12] For example, see Gal 6:16. 1 Peter is generally considered to be a late first century or early second century letter, but it does use the language of dispersion (1 Pet 1:1), although most scholars agree that its audience was largely Gentile.

[13] Mayor, *The Epistle of St. James*, cxlii.

Torah (2:8-13) and, unlike Paul, exhibits no worries or concerns about issues that might arise in a Jewish-Gentile audience. There are no references to a Gentile presence or set of concerns.

A literal interpretation of the prescript is further strengthened by the fact that the letter claims to have been composed by James (Jas 1:1). Most authors conclude that the only James that this could be is James the Just, the brother of the Lord (Gal 1:19) and a pillar of the church (Gal 2:9). James, of course, was an apostle and leader in the Jerusalem church, and was martyred by stoning prior to the Jewish War.[14] Whether or not the text was actually written by James is not the question here, but it is important to notice that the author claims to be James, and thus it must have been written to people who would have held this person in high regard. Furthermore, this letter bears similarities to other Jewish encyclicals that were written to Diaspora Jews, such as the *Letter of Jeremiah*, 2 Maccabees 1:1-9; 1:10-2:18 and *2 Baruch* 78-86.[15] Together, these factors provide strong support for a literal interpretation of the prescript. Whether the audience consisted of both Jewish Christians and Jews is beyond the scope of this study as is their exact whereabouts, but suffice it to say, their rootedness within Hellenistic Judaism can be taken for granted throughout the letter. The temptation to hook up with wealthy outsiders would be as real for such groups as it would be for Gentile audiences throughout the Roman Empire. Moreover, I think it likely that the audience was in an urban setting, given the fact that they must at least be familiar with figures who could afford fine clothes and gold rings (Jas 2:2), and the reference things such as a "crown" in 1:12 and "court" in 2:6.

Rhetorical Constraints

James, as we have seen, employs various methods in persuading the audience to resist friendship with the world. In so doing, the author hopes that the listeners will resist the pressures to succumb to forming alliances with wealthy patrons. At the very beginning, the author claims to be James the Just, a claim which would have immediately

---

[14] For a collection of the texts describing James's martyrdom, see R.A. Lipsius, *Die apokryphen Apostelgeschichten und Apostellegenden* II.2 (Braunschweig: G. Westermann, 1884) 238-57. For a discussion of the reasons why James may have been put to death in Jerusalem by Jews, see Richard Bauckham, "For What Offence was James Put to Death?" *James the Just and Christian Origins* (ed. Bruce Chilton & Craig Evans; NovTSup 98; Leiden, Boston, Cologne: E.J. Brill, 1999) 199-232.

[15] See Niebuhr, "Der Jakobusbrief," 420-43; Verseput, "Wisdom, 4Q185, and James," 702-703; Verseput, "Genre and Story," 101.

endowed the writer with an authoritative *ethos*, necessary at the beginning of a letter. This letter prescript thus serves one of the purposes of the exordium – to establish the authority of the speaker - even though it is not part of the exordium proper. Throughout the letter, this *ethos* of authority is maintained, however, by the use of frank speech and the use of imperatives, maxims, and assertions about the nature of God and human existence. An orator who lacked authority would not dare make such statements if the audience had little respect for him or her.

The letter of James is not cold and austere, however, but exemplifies *pathos* in expressing true concern and sympathy for the listeners' plight, affirming eschatological rewards, and offering constructive advice for communal relations. James addresses the recipients as "brothers" and "beloved brothers," and perhaps most importantly, the author presents a portrait of a God who is reliable and "simple."

I have argued that the *topos* of friendship is presented in at least three sections of James (1:2-18; 2:14-26; 3:13–4:10), a considerable portion of the letter, and that the opposite of friendship, namely patronage, is implicitly undermined when James offers criticisms of speech and wealth. It is of note that the most numerous allusions to friendship appear in the exordium, a unit of the letter that functions to introduce some of its basic themes, and to establish an *ethos* and *pathos*. This observation suggests to me that the language of friendship was important to this author for rhetorical purposes.

Even without the appearance of the *topos* in the exordium, given the old and rich traditions of this ideal in both Graeco-Roman and Jewish contexts, the appeal to friendship would have been compelling. James uses it to debunk the "friendships" that were forming with patrons, for by describing what a friend (and a benefactor) truly was, the audience would soon see that these patrons did not correspond very well. James even restates a saying of Jesus, but in friendship terms, so as to provide further authoritative proof of the validity of his advice.

These are only a few of the rhetorical constraints used in the letter of James, but they provide further evidence that this document was designed to persuade an audience to take a particular course of action. In part, such actions required a resistance to patronage, and a pursuit of friendship, both with God and with other members of the community. Both types of friendship were inseparable from "works." And whether "works" include feeding the hungry or restraining the tongue, the audience is called to live them out in the letter of James.

Conclusion

The letter of James draws upon both Jewish and Hellenistic tradition to argue for resistance to patronage and care for the poor. It does so drawing upon the *topos* of friendship in a variety of ways. This *topos*, however, came from a reasonably elitist tradition of literature in the Graeco-Roman world. Although the author does not advocate an egalitarian ethos in the communities he writes to, he does invoke friendship, and benefaction, in manners that would serve the interests of the more vulnerable in the audience. He advocates assistance or benefaction from the economically better off in the audience to those who are poor, and he offers little hope, if any, to elite and wealthy outsiders. The latter aspect of the letter has caused James to be a problematic text at various moments in the history of its reception, while James's advocacy for the poor has held appeal.[16]

We do not know how James was received by the original audience that listened to or read this letter.[17] Were some offended? Did the letter simply sound strange or alien in the way that it combined direct exhortation to depend upon God and assist the needy with denunciation of the rich, while elevating values and characteristics that only those of superior social status could reflect upon, argue about and attempt to manifest? Could we say that James is attempting to "democratize" values and ideas that had previously been limited to the upper echelons of society? Continued study of the social world of ancient Judaism and Christianity, combined with analysis of the rhetoric that sought to persuade them to act in specific ways, may enable us to come closer to answering some of these questions.

---

[16] For some examples of how James's criticism of wealth has been received, see Batten, "Ideological Strategies in James," 6-7.

[17] The earliest documented citation of James is Origen (185-254 CE), while in the Western church, the oldest extant reference is in the writings of Hilary of Poitiers, sometime between 356 and 360 CE.

Bibliography

Aasgaard, Reidar, *'My Beloved Brothers and Sisters!' Christian Siblingship in Paul*, Early Christianity in Context; London and New York: T & T Clark, 2004
Adamson, James B., *James: The Man and His Message*, Grand Rapids: Eerdmans, 1989
——, *The Epistle of James*, The New International Commentary on the New Testament; Grand Rapids: Eerdmans, 1976
Adkins, Arthur W.H., *Merit and Responsibility: A Study in Greek Values*, Oxford: Clarendon, 1960
——, "Friendship and Self-Sufficiency in Homer and Aristotle," *CQ* 13 (1963): 30-45
Aeschylus, *Prometheus Bound*, trans. Herbert Weir Smythe; LCL; London: Heinemann; Cambridge, MA: Harvard University Press, 1922
Aglen, A.S., "Friend," in *Dictionary of the Bible*, ed. James Hastings, 68; Edinburgh: T & T Clark, 1903
Allison, Dale C., "The Fiction of James and its Sitz im Leben," *RB* 118 (2001): 529-70
Ambrose of Milan, *Omnia Quae Extant Opera* 7, ed. D.A.B. Caillau; Collectio 22, Ecclesiae Patrum; Paris: Apud Parent Desbarres, 1839
Amphoux, C.-B., "L'emploi du coordonnant dans l'épître de Jacques," *Bib* 63 (1982): 90-101
——, "Études structurales: langue de l'épître de Jacques," *RHPR* 53 (1973): 7-45
Anderson, G., *Studies in Lucian's Comic Fiction*, Mnemosyne Suppl.; Leiden: Brill, 1976
Annas, Julia, *The Morality of Happiness*, Oxford and New York: Oxford University Press, 1993
——, "Plato and Aristotle on Friendship and Altruism," *Mind* 86.344 (1977): 532-54
Aristotle, *Eudemian Ethics*, trans. H. Rackham; LCL; London: Heinemann; Cambridge, MA: Harvard University Press, 1935
——, *Nicomachean Ethics*, trans. H. Rackham; LCL; London: Heinemann; Cambridge, MA: Harvard University Press, 1934
——, *Rhetoric*, trans. John Harvey Freese; LCL; London, Cambridge, MA: Harvard University Press, 1926
Arzt-Grabner, Peter, "'Brothers' and 'Sisters' in Documentary Papyri and in Early Christianity," *RivB* 50 (2002): 185-204
Asensio, Victor Morla, "Poverty and Wealth: Ben Sira's View of Possessions," in *Der Einzelne und seine Gemeinschaft bei Ben Sira*, ed. Renate Egger-Wenzel and Ingrid Krammer; BZAW 270; Berlin and New York: de Gruyter, 1998, 151-78
Asmis, Elizabeth, "The Stoics on Women," in *Feminism and Ancient Philosophy*, ed. Julie K. Ward; New York & London: Routledge, 1996, 86-92
Augustine, *Letters*, trans. James Houston Baxter; LCL; London: Heinemann: Cambridge, MA: Harvard University Press, 1930
Aune, David E. *The New Testament in Its Literary Environment*, LEC, 8; Philadelphia: Westminster, 1987

Baasland, Ernst, "Literarische Form, Thematik und geschichtliche Einordnung des Jakobusbriefes," *ANRW* 2.25.5 (1988): 3646-84
Bailey, Cyril, *Epicurus. The Extant Remains*, Oxford: Clarendon, 1926
Baillet, Maurice, "Les manuscrits de la Grotte 7 de Qumrân et le Nouveau Testament," *Bib* 54 (1973): 340-50
——, "Les manuscrits de la Grotte 7 de Qumrân et le Nouveau Testament," *Bib* 53 (1972): 508-16
Baker, William R., *Personal Speech-Ethics: A Study of the Epistle of James Against Its Background*, WUNT 2/68; Tübingen: J.C.B. Mohr (Paul Siebeck), 1995
——, "'Above All Else': Contexts of the Call for Verbal Integrity in James 5:12," *JSNT* 54 (1994): 57-71
Balch, David L., "Political Friendship in the Historian Dionysius of Halicarnassus, *Roman Antiquities*," in *Greco-Roman Perspectives on Friendship*, ed. John T. Fitzgerald; SBLRBS 34; Atlanta: Scholars, 1997, 123-44
Barrett, C.K., *The Gospel According to St. John*, London: SPCK, 1955
Bartelink, G.J.M., "Quelques observations sur παρρησία dans la littérature paléochrétienne," in *Graecitas et Latinitas Christianorum Primaeva*, Supplementa 3; Nijmegen: Dekker & Van de Vegt, 1970, 7-57
Barton, Stephen and G.H.R. Horsley, "A Hellenistic Cult Group and the New Testament Churches," *JAC* 24 (1981): 7-41
Basil of Caesarea. *Letters*, trans. Roy J. Defferrari; LCL; London: Heinemann; New York: Putnam; Cambridge, MA: Harvard University Press, 1926-34
Batten, Alicia, "The Degraded Poor and the Greedy Rich: Exploring the Language of Poverty and Wealth in the Letter of James," in *The Social Sciences and Biblical Translation*, ed. Dietmar Neufeld; Symposium Series 41; Atlanta: Society of Biblical Literature; Leiden: Brill, 2008, 65-77
——, "Ideological Strategies in James," in *Reading James with New Eyes. Methodological Reassessments of the Letter of James*, ed. Robert L. Webb and John S. Kloppenborg; LNTS 342; London: T & T Clark, 2007, 6-26
——, "The Moral World of Greco-Roman Associations," *SR* 36 (2007): 133-49
——, "God in the Letter of James: Patron or Benefactor?" *NTS* 50 (2004): 257-72
——, "Unworldly Friendship: The 'Epistle of Straw' Reconsidered," diss. University of St. Michael's College, Toronto, 2000
——, "An Asceticism of Resistance in James," in *Asceticism and the New Testament*, ed. Leif E. Vaage and Vincent L. Wimbush; New York: Routledge, 1999, 355-70
Bauckham, Richard, "James and Jesus," in *The Brother of Jesus. James the Just and His Mission*, ed. Bruce Chilton and Jacob Neusner; Louisville and London: Westminster John Knox, 2001, 100-37
——, *James. Wisdom of James, Disciple of Jesus the Sage*, New Testament Readings; London and New York: Routledge, 1999
——, "For What Offence Was James Put to Death?" in *James the Just and Christian Origins*, ed. Bruce Chilton and Craig Evans; NovTSup 98; Leiden, Boston, Cologne: E.J. Brill, 1999
Beasley-Murray, George R., *The General Epistles: James, 1 Peter, Jude, 2 Peter*, Bible Guides, 21; London: Lutterworth; New York: Abingdon, 1965
Belser, Johannes E., "Die Vulgata und der griechische Text im Jakobusbrief," *TQ* 90 (1908): 329-39
Benson, John, "Making Friends: Aristotle's Doctrine of the Friend as Another Self," in *Polis and Politics: Essays in Greek Moral and Political Philosophy*, ed. Andros Loizou and Harry Lesser; Aldershot, UK: Avebury, 1990, 50-68
Ben-Ze'ev, Aaron, "Aristotle on Emotions towards the Fortune of Others," in *Envy, Spite and Jealousy. The Rivalrous Emotions in Ancient Greece*, ed. David Konstan and N.

Keith Rutter; Edinburgh Leventis Studies, 2; Edinburgh: Edinburgh University Press, 2003, 99-122

Bernardi, Jean, ed. and trans., *Grégoire de Nazianze, Discours 42-43*; Sources Chrétiennes; Paris: Éditions du Cerf, 1992

Berry, Ken L., "The Function of Friendship Language in Philippians 4:10-20," in *Friendship, Flattery and Frankness of Speech: Studies of Friendship in the New Testament World*, ed. John T. Fitzgerald; NovTSup 82; Leiden, New York, Cologne: E.J. Brill, 1996, 107-24

Betz, Hans Dieter, *Galatians*, Hermeneia; Philadelphia: Fortress, 1979

———, ed., *Plutarch's Ethical Writings and Early Christian Literature*, Studia ad Corpus Hellenisticum Novi Testamenti; Leiden: E.J. Brill, 1978

Beyschlag, Willibald, *Der Brief des Jacobus*, 6th ed., Kritisch-exegetischer Kommentar über das Neue Testament, 15; Göttingen: Vandenhoeck & Ruprecht, 1897

Bitzer, Lloyd, "The Rhetorical Situation," *Philosophy and Rhetoric* 1 (1968): 1-14

Blackman, Edwin C., *The Epistle of James: Introduction and Commentary*, Torch Bible Commentaries; London: SCM Press, 1957

Blackman, Philip, trans., *Mishanayoth-Nezikin*, New York: Judaica Press, 1963

Blondel, J.-L., "Le fondement théologique de la parénèse dans l'épître de Jacques," *RTP* 29 (1979): 141-52

Blum, Lawrence A., *Friendship, Altruism, and Morality*, London: Routledge & Kegan Paul, 1980

Blundell, Mary W., *Helping Friends and Harming Enemies: A Study in Sophocles and Greek Ethics*, Cambridge: Cambridge University Press, 1989

Bohnenblust, Gottfried, *Beiträge zum Topos ΠΕΡΙ ΦΙΛΙΑΣ*, diss. Bern; Berlin: Gustav Schade [Otto Francke], 1935

Boissevain, Jeremy, *Friends of Friends: Networks, Manipulations and Coalitions*, Oxford: Basil Blackwell, 1974

Bottini, Giovanni C., "Sentenze di Pseudo-Focilide alla luce della lettera di Giacomo," *Studium Biblicum Franciscanum Liber Annuus* 36 (1986): 171-81

———, "Correzione fraterna e salvezza in Giacomo 5, 19-20," *Studium Biblicum Franciscanum Liber Annuus* 35 (1985): 131-62

Bowerstock, G.W., *Augustus and the Greek World*, Oxford: Oxford University Press, 1965

Boyle, Marjorie O'Rourke, "The Stoic Paradox of James 2.10," *NTS* 31 (1985): 611-17

Brinckmann, W., *Der Begriff der Freundschaft in Senecas Briefen*, diss. Cologne; Cologne: Gouder & Hansen, 1963

Brock, Ann Graham, "The Significance of φιλέω and φίλος in the Tradition of Jesus Sayings and in the Early Christian Communities," *HTR* 90 (1997): 393-409

Brownlee, William Hugh, *The Dead Sea Manual of Discipline*, BASORSup 10-12; New Haven: American Schools of Oriental Research, 1951

Brueggemann, Walter, *Theology of the Old Testament. Testimony, Dispute, Advocacy.* Minneapolis: Fortress, 1997

Brunt, P.A., "*Amicitia* in the Late Roman Republic," in *The Crisis of the Roman Republic: Studies in Political and Social History*, ed. R. Seager; Cambridge: Heffer, 1969, 197-218

Bryant, Joseph M., *Moral Codes and Social Structure in Ancient Greece. A Sociology of Greek Ethics from Homer to the Epicureans and Stoics*, SUNY Series in the Sociology of Culture; Albany: State University of New York, 1996

Burgess, Theodore C., "Epideictic Literature," *University of Chicago Studies in Classical Philology* 3 (1902): 89-248

Burkert, Walter, *Greek Religion*, trans. John Raffan; Cambridge, MA: Harvard University Press, 1985

Burrell, David B., C.S.C., "Friendship with God in Al-Ghazali and Aquinas," in *The Changing Face of Friendship*, ed. Leroy S. Rouner; Boston University Studies in

Philosophy and Religion, 15; Notre Dame: University of Notre Dame Press, 1994, 43-56

Burton, Joan B., *Theocritus' Urban Mimes: Mobility, Gender and Patronage*, Berkeley: University of California Press, 1995

Cairns, Douglas L., *Aidos: The Psychology and Ethics of Honour and Shame in Ancient Greek Literature*. Oxford: Clarendon, 1993

Campbell, John K., *Honour, Family, and Patronage: A Study of Institutions and Moral Values in a Greek Mountain Community*, Oxford: Oxford University Press, 1964

Cantarella, Eva, *Bisexuality in the Ancient World*, trans. Cormac Ó Cuilleanáin; New Haven and London: Yale University Press, 1992

Cantinat, Jean, *Les épîtres de saint Jacques et de saint Jude*, Sources bibliques. Paris: J. Gabalda, 1973

Cargal, Timothy Boyd; *Restoring the Diaspora: Discursive Structure and Purpose in the Epistle of James*; SBLDS 144. Atlanta: Scholars, 1993

Carnes, Jeffrey S., "With Friends Like These: Understanding the Mythic Background of Homer's Phaiakians," *Ramus* 93 (1993): 103-15

Carney, T.F., *The Shape of the Past: Models and Antiquity*. Lawrence, KS: Coronado, 1975

Carruth, Shawn, "Strategies of Authority. A Rhetorical Study of the Character of the Speaker in Q 6:20-49," in *Conflict and Invention. Literary, Rhetorical, and Social Studies on the Sayings Gospel Q*, ed. John S. Kloppenborg; Valley Forge, PA: Trinity, 1995, 98-115

Cassidy, Eoin, "The Recovery of the Classical Ideal of Friendship in Augustine's Portrayal of *Caritas*," ed. Thomas Finan and Vincent Twomey, in *The Relationship between Neoplatonism and Christianity*; Dublin: Four Courts, 1992, 127-40

Chadwick, H., "Justification by Faith and Hospitality," *Studia Patristica* 4 (1961): 281-85

Chaine, Joseph, *L'Epître de Saint Jacques*, Paris: Gabalda, 1927

Chariton, *Callirhoe*, trans. G.P. Goold; LCL; London and Cambridge, MA: Harvard University Press University Press, 1995

Charlesworth, James H., ed., *The Old Testament Pseudepigrapha*, II, Garden City: Doubleday, 1985

———, ed., *The Old Testament Pseudepigrapha*, I, Garden City: Doubleday, 1983

Cicero, *De Inventione*, trans. H.M. Hubbell; LCL; London: Heinemann; Cambridge, MA: Harvard University Press, 1949

———, *Laelius*, trans. William Armistead Falconer; LCL; London and Cambridge, MA: Harvard University Press, 1923

Clark, Elizabeth A., *Jerome, Chrysostom, and Friends: Essays and Translations*, New York: Edwin Mellen, 1979

Clement of Alexandria, *The Rich Man's Salvation*, trans. G.W. Butterworth; LCL. London: Heinemann; Cambridge, MA: Harvard University Press, 1968

Coleman, Thomas M., "Patronage and the Epistle of James: A New Social Setting for the Epistle of James," M.Th. diss.; University of Aberdeen, 1996

Cooper, John, "Political Animals and Civic Friendship," in *Friendship: A Philosophical Reader*, ed. N.K. Badhwar; Ithaca: Cornell University Press, 1993, 303-26

———, "Political Animals and Civic Friendship," in *Aristoteles' "Politik"*, ed. Günther Patzig; Göttingen: Vandenhoeck & Ruprecht, 1990, 220-41

———, "Aristotle on Friendship," in *Essays on Aristotle's Ethics*, ed. A.O. Rorty; Berkeley: University of California Press, 1980, 301-40

———, "Aristotle on the Forms of Friendship," *Review of Metaphysics* 30 (1977): 619-48

Corley, Jeremy, *Ben Sira's Teaching on Friendship*. BJS 316. Atlanta: Scholars, 2002

Craig, Christopher P. "The *Accusator* as *Amicus*: An Original Roman Tactic of Ethical Argumentation," *TAPA* 111 (1981): 31-37

Crook, Zeba A., "Reflections on Culture and Social-Scientific Models," *JBL* 124 (2005): 515-20

—, *Reconceptualising Conversion. Patronage, Loyalty, and Conversion in the Religions of the Ancient Mediterranean*, BZNW 130; Berlin, New York: de Gruyter, 2004

Curchin, Leonard A., "Social Relations in Central Spain: Patrons, Freedman and Slaves in the Life of a Roman Provincial Hinterland," *Ancient Society* 18 (1987): 75-87

Daniélou, Jean, *Théologie du Judéo-Christianisme*, Bibliothèque de Théologie; Histoire des Doctrines Chrétiennes avant Nicée; Paris: Desclée, 1957

Danker, Frederick W., "Benefactor," *AB* I (1992): 669-71

—, *Benefactor: Epigraphic Study of a Graeco-Roman and New Testament Semantic Field*, St. Louis: Clayton, 1982

Davids, Peter H., "Palestinian Traditions in the Epistle of James," in *James the Just and Christian Origins*, ed. Bruce Chilton and Craig A. Evans; NovTSup 98; Leiden, Boston, Cologne: E.J. Brill, 1999, 33-57

—, *James*, New International Biblical Commentary; rev. ed., Peabody: Hendrickson, 1989

—, "The Epistle of James in Modern Discussion," *ANRW* 2.25.5 (1988): 3621-45

—, "James and Jesus," in *Gospel Perspectives V. The Jesus Tradition Outside the Gospels*, ed. David Wenham; Sheffield: JSOT, 1985, 63-84

—, *James*, Harper & Row: San Francisco, 1983.

—, *The Epistle of James: A Commentary on the Greek Text*, The New International Greek Testament Commentary; Grand Rapids: Eerdmans, 1982

—, "Tradition and Citation in the Epistle of James," in *Scripture, Tradition, and Interpretation: Essays Presented to Everett F. Harrison*, ed. W. Ward Gasque and William Sanford La Sor; Grand Rapids: Eerdmans, 1978, 113-26

Davies, John K., "Cultural, Social and Economic Features of the Hellenistic World," *CAH* 8 (1984): 257-320.

—, *Wealth and the Power of Wealth in Classical Athens*, Salem, NH: Ayer, 1984

de Jonge, M., ed., *The Testaments of the Twelve Patriarchs. A Critical Edition of the Greek Text*, PVTG; Leiden: Brill, 1978

De Ste Croix, Geoffrey E.M., *The Class Struggle in the Ancient Greek World from the Archaic Age to the Arab Conquests*, Ithaca, NY: Cornell University Press, 1982

De Witt, Norman, "Organization and Procedure in Epicurean Groups," *CP* 31 (1936): 205-11

Deissmann, Adolf, *Light from the Ancient East*, trans. Lionel R.M. Strachan; New York: George H. Doran; repr., Peabdody, MA: Hendrickson, 1927, 1995

Demetrius, *On Style*, trans. W. Rhys Roberts; LCL; London: Heinemann; Cambridge, MA: Harvard University Press, 1927

Deppe, Dean B., *The Sayings of Jesus in the Epistle of James*, diss. Amsterdam; Chelsea, MI: Bookcrafters, 1989

Deutsch, Eliot, "On Creative Friendship," in *The Changing Face of Friendship*, ed. Leroy S. Rouner; Boston University Studies in Philosophy and Religion, 15; Notre Dame: University of Notre Dame Press, 1994, 15-28

DeVogel, C.J., *Pythagoras and Early Pythagoreanism*, Assen: Van Gorcum, 1966

Dibelius, Martin, *Der Brief des Jakobus*, ed. Heinrich Greeven; Kritisch-exegetischer Kommentar über das Neue Testament (MeyerK); Göttingen: Vandenhoeck & Ruprecht, 1964 (10th ed., 1959)

—, *James: A Commentary on the Epistle of James*, rev. Heinrich Greeven; trans. Michael A. Williams; Hermeneia. Philadelphia: Fortress, 1976

Diels, H. *Philodemus Über die Götter: Drittes Buch, 1. Griechischer Text*, Abhandlungen der königlich preussischen Akademie der Wissenschaften; Berlin: Verlag der Königlichen Akademie der Wissenschaften, 1917

Dihle, Albert, "ψυχικός," *TDNT* IX (1974): 661

Diogenes Laertius, *Lives of Eminent Philosophers*, LCL; London: Heinemann; New York: Putnam, 1925

Dionysius of Halicarnassus, *Roman Antiquities*, trans. E. Cary; LCL; Cambridge, MA: Harvard University Press, 1937-50
Dirlmeier, F., "ΘΕΛΦΙΛΙΑ–ΦΙΛΟΘΕΙΑ," *Philologus* 90 (1935): 57-77, 176-93
——, Φιλός *und* φιλία *im vorhellenistischen Griechentum*, Ph.D. diss., Munich: Druck der Salesianischen Offizin, 1931
Dixon, Suzanne, "The Meaning of Gift and Debt in the Roman Elite," *Echos du Monde Classique / Classical Views* 37 (1993): 451-64
——, "The Sentimental Ideal of the Roman Family," *Marriage, Divorce, and Children in Ancient Rome*, ed. Beryl Rawson; Canberra and Oxford: Humanities Research Centre; Clarendon, 1991, 99-113
Donfried, Karl P. and Peter Richardson, eds., *Judaism and Christianity in First-Century Rome*, Grand Rapids, MI, Cambridge, UK: Eerdmans, 1998
Donlan, Walter, "Pistos Philos Hetairos" *Theognis of Megara: Poetry and Polis*, ed. Thomas J. Figueira and Gregory Nagy; Baltimore and London: Johns Hopkins University Press, 1985
——, *The Aristocratic Ideal in Ancient Greece: Attitudes of Superiority from Homer to the End of the Fifth Century B.C.*, Lawrence, KS: Coronado, 1980
Donner, H., "Der 'Freund' des Königs," *ZAW* n.s. 32 (1961): 269-77
Dover, K.J., *Greek Popular Morality in the Time of Plato and Aristotle*, Oxford: Basil Blackwell, 1974
Downing, F. Gerald, *Cynics and Christian Origins*, Edinburgh: T&T Clark, 1992
——, *Christ and the Cynics: Jesus and Other Radical Preachers in First-Century Tradition*, JSOT Manuals, 4; Sheffield: JSOT Press, 1988
Drummond, Andrew, "Early Roman Clientes," in *Patronage in Ancient Society*, ed. Andrew Wallace-Hadrill; Leicester-Nottingham Studies in Ancient Society, 1; London and New York: Routledge, 1989, 89-116
Dugas, L., *L'Amitié Antique*, 2nd ed., Paris: Librairie Félix Alcan, 1914
Dunn, James D.G.., "Echoes of Intra-Jewish Polemic in Paul's Letter to the Galatians," *JBL* 112 (1993): 459-77
Duthoy, Robert, "Le profil social des patrons municipaux en Italie sous le haut-empire," *AncSoc* 15-17 (1984-86): 121-54
Dziob, Anne-Marie, "Aristotelian Friendship: Self-Love and Moral Rivalry," *Review of Metaphysics* 46 (1993): 781-801
Ebner, Martin, *Leidenslisten und Apostelbrief: Untersuchungen zu Form, Motivik und Funktion der Peristasenkataloge bei Paulus*, FB; Würzburg: Echter Verlag, 1991
Edlund, E.M.I., "Invisible Bonds: Clients and Patrons through the Eyes of Polybius," *Klio* 59 (1977): 129-36
Eilers, Claude, *Roman Patrons of the Greek Cities*, Oxford Classical Monographs; Oxford: Oxford University Press, 2002
Eisenstadt, S.N., "Friendship and the Structure of Trust and Solidarity in Society," in *The Compact: Selected Dimensions of Friendship*, ed. E. Leyton; Newfoundland Social and Economic Papers, 3; St. Johns: Memorial University of Newfoundland, 1974, 138-45
Eisenstadt, S.N., and L. Roniger, *Patrons, Clients and Friends. Interpersonal Relations and the Structure of Trust in Society*, Cambridge and New York: Cambridge University Press, 1984
Elliott, John H., "The Epistle of James in Rhetorical and Social Scientific Perspective: Holiness-Wholeness and Patterns of Replication," *BTB* 23 (1993): 71-81
——, "Patronage and Clientism in Early Christian Society: A Short Reading Guide," *Foundations and Facets Forum* 3.4 (1987): 39-48
Engberg-Pedersen, Troels, "Plutarch to Prince Philopappus on How to Tell a Flatterer from a Friend," in *Friendship, Flattery and Frankness of Speech: Studies of Friendship in*

the New Testament World, ed. John T. Fitzgerald; NovTSup 82; Leiden, New York, Cologne: E.J. Brill, 1996, 61-79

Epictetus, *Discourses*, trans. W.A. Oldfather; LCL; London: Heinemann; Cambridge, MA: Harvard University Press, 1967

Erskine, Andrew, "The Roman as Common Benefactors," *Historia* 43 (1994): 70-87

Esler, Philip F., ed., *Modelling Early Christianity: Social Scientific Studies of the New Testament in Its Context*, London and New York: Routledge, 1995

Euripides, *Orestes*, ed. Arthur S. Way; LCL; London: Heinemann; Cambridge, MA: Harvard University Press, 1912

Evans, Katherine G. "Friendship in the Greek Documentary Papyri and Inscriptions: A Survey," in *Greco-Roman Perspectives on Friendship*, ed. John T. Fitzgerald; SBLRBS 34; Atlanta: Scholars, 1997, 181-202

Exler, F.X.J., *The Form of the Ancient Greek Letter: A Study in Greek Epistolography*, Washington: Catholic University of America, 1923

Farrington, B., "Lucretius and Manilus on Friendship," *Hermathena* 83 (1954): 10-16

Fee, Gordon D., "Pneuma and Eschatology in 2 Thessalonians 2:1-2: A Proposal About 'testing the Prophets' and the Purpose of 2 Thessalonians," in *To Tell the Mystery*, ed. T. Schmidt; JSNTSup 100; Sheffield: JSOT, 1994, 196-215

Felder, Cain H., "Partiality and God's Law: An Exegesis of James 2:1-13," *JRT* 39 (1982-83): 51-69

Felix Minucius, *Octavius*, trans. W.C.A. Kerr based on the unfinished version by Gerald H. Rendall; LCL; London: Heinemann; Cambridge, MA: Harvard University Press, 1960

Fensham, F. Charles, "Widow, Orphan and the Poor in Ancient Near East Legal and Wisdom Literature," *JNES* 21 (1962): 129-39

Ferrary, Jean-Louis, "The Hellenistic World and Roman Political Patronage," in *Hellenistic Constructs: Essays in Culture, History and Historiography*, ed. P. Cartledge, P. Garnsey and E.S. Gruen; Hellenistic Culture and Society 26; Berkeley: University of California Press, 1997, 105-119

Fichtner, Johannes, "πλησίον in the LXX and the Neighbour in the OT," *TDNT* VI (1968): 312-14

Finley, M.I., *The Ancient Economy*, rev. ed., Berkeley: University of California Press, 1985

Fiore, Benjamin, "Friendship in the Exhortation of Romans 15:14-33," *Proceedings of the EGL and MWBS* 7 (1987): 95-103

——, *The Function of Personal Example in the Socratic and in the Pastoral Epistles*, AnBib 105; Rome: Biblical Institute Press, 1986

Fisher, N.R.E., *Hybris: A Study of the Values of Honour and Shame in Ancient Greece*, Warminster: Aris & Phillips, 1992

Fiske, Adele M., *Friends and Friendship in the Monastic Tradition*, Cuernavaca, Mexico: Centro Intercultural de Documentacion, 1970

Fitzgerald, John T., "Friendship in the Greek World Prior to Aristotle," in *Greco-Roman Perspectives on Friendship*, ed. John T. Fitzgerald; SBLRBS 34; Atlanta: Scholars Press, 1997, 13-34

——, ed., *Greco-Roman Perspectives on Friendship*, SBLRBS 34; Atlanta: Scholars Press, 1997

——, "Philippians in Light of Some Ancient Discussions of Friendship," in *Friendship, Flattery and Frankness of Speech: Essays on Friendship in the New Testament World*, ed. John T. Fitzgerald; NovTSup 82. Leiden, New York, Cologne: E.J. Brill, 1996, 141-60

——, ed., *Friendship, Flattery, and Frankness of Speech. Studies on Friendship in the New Testament World*, NovTSup 82. Leiden, New York, Cologne: E.J. Brill, 1996

Fortenbaugh, W.W.P.M. Huby, R.W. Sharples and D. Gutas, eds., *Theophrastus of Eresus: Sources for His Life, Writings, Thought and Influence*, vol. II, PhilAnt 54.2; Leiden: E.J. Brill, 1992
Fraisse, Jean-Claude, *Philia: La notion d'amitié dans la philosophie antique. Essai sur un problème perdu et retrouvé*, Paris: Librairie Philosophique J. Vrin, 1974
Francis, F.O., "The Form and Function of the Opening and Closing Paragraphs of James and 1 John," *ZNW* 61 (1970): 110-26
Francis, James A., *Subversive Virtue. Asceticism and Authority in the Second Century Pagan World*, University Park, PA: Pennsylvania State University Press, 1995
Frankemölle, Hubert, *Der Brief des Jakobus Kapital 1*, ÖTKNT, 17/1; Gütersloh and Würzburg: Gütersloher Verlagshaus and Echter Verlag, 1994
——, *Der Brief des Jakobus Kapitel 2-5*, ÖTKNT 17/2; Gütersloh and Würzburg: Gütersloher Verlagshaus and Echter Verlag, 1994
——, "Zum Thema des Jakobusbriefes im Kontext der Rezeption von Sir 2:1-18 and 15:11-20," *Biblische Notizen* 48 (1989): 21-49
Fredrickson, David E., "Παρρησία in the Pauline Epistles," in *Friendship, Flattery and Frankness of Speech: Studies on Friendship in the New Testament World*, ed. John T. Fitzgerald; NovTSup 82; Leiden, New York, Cologne: E.J. Brill, 1996, 163-83
Frischer, B.D., *The Sculpted Word: Epicureanism and Philosophical Recruitment in Ancient Greece*, Berkeley: University of California Press, 1982
Fuks, A., *Social Conflict in Ancient Greece*, Jerusalem, Leiden: E.J. Brill, 1984
Gaertringen, F. Hiller, et al., eds., *Inscriptiones graecae, consilio et auctoritate Acadaemiae Litterarum Borussicae editae*, 14 vols.; Berlin: de Gruyter, 1873–
Gallant, Thomas, *Risk and Survival in Ancient Greece: Reconstructing the Rural Economy*, Cambridge: Polity, 1991
——, "Crisis and Response: Risk Buffering Behavior in Hellenistic Greek Communities," *Journal of Interdisciplinary History* 19 (1989): 393-413
Gallay, Paul, ed. and trans., *Saint Grégoire de Nazianze. Lettres*, 2 vols.; Paris: Les Belles Lettres, 1964
Gammie, John G., "Paraenetic Literature: Toward the Morphology of a Secondary Genre," *Semeia* 50 (1990): 41-77
García Martínez, Florentino, "The Heavenly Tablets in the Book of Jubilees," in *Studies in the Book of Jubilees*, ed. Matthias Albani, Jörg Frey, and Armin Lange; Tübingen: Mohr–Siebeck, 1997, 243-60
——, ed., *The Dead Sea Scrolls Translated. The Qumran Texts in English*, trans. Wilfred G.E. Watson; 2nd ed., Leiden, New York, Cologne: E. J. Brill; Grand Rapids: Eerdmans, 1996
García Martínez, Florentino and Eibert J.C. Tichelaar, trans., *The Dead Sea Scrolls Study Edition*, I, London, New York, Cologne: Brill, 1997
Garnsey, Peter, *Famine and Food Supply in the Graeco-Roman World. Responses to Risk and Crisis*, Cambridge: Cambridge University Press, 1988
——, ed., *Non-Slave Labour in the Graeco-Roman World*, Cambridge: Cambridge Philological Society, 1980
Garnsey, Peter and Greg Woolf, "Patronage of the Rural Poor in the Roman World," in *Patronage in Ancient Society*, ed. Andrew Wallace-Hadrill; Leicester-Nottingham Studies in Ancient Society, 1; London and New York: Routledge, 1989, 153-70
Garnsey, Peter and Richard Saller, *The Roman Empire. Economy, Society and Culture*, London: Duckworth, 1987
Garrett, Susan R., "Beloved Physician of the Soul? Luke as Advocate for Ascetic Practice," in *Asceticism and the New Testament*, ed. Leif E. Vaage and Vincent L. Wimbush; New York: Routledge, 1999, 71-95
Gellner, E., and J. Waterbury, eds., *Patrons and Clients in Mediterranean Societies*, London: Duckworth, 1977

Geyser, A.S., "The Letter of James and the Social Conditions of His Addressees," *Neot* 9 (1975): 25-33

Gill, Christopher, "Is Rivalry a Virtue or a Vice?" in *Envy, Spite, Jealousy. The Competitive Emotions in Ancient Greece*, ed. David Konstan and N. Keith Rutter; Edinburgh Leventis Studies, 2; Edinburgh: Edinburgh University Press, 2003, 29-52

——, "Peace of Mind and Being Yourself: Panaetius to Plutarch," *ANRW* 2.36.7 (1994): 599-640

Ginzberg, Louis, *The Legends of the Jews*, V, Philadelphia: Jewish Publication Society of America, 1929

Glad, Clarence E., "Frank Speech, Flattery, and Friendship in Philodemus," in *Friendship, Flattery and Frankness of Speech: Studies on Friendship in the New Testament World*, ed. John T. Fitzgerald; NovTSup 82; Leiden, New York, Cologne: E.J. Brill, 1996, 21-59

——, *Paul and Philodemus: Adapatability in Epicurean and Early Christian Psychagogy*, NovTSup 81; Leiden, New York, Cologne: E.J. Brill, 1995

Gold, Barbara K., *Literary Patronage in Greece and Rome*, Chapel Hill, London: University of North Carolina Press, 1987

Goldhill, Simon, *Reading Greek Tragedy*, Cambridge: Cambridge University Press, 1986

Gowan, Donald E., "Wisdom and Endurance in James," *HBT* 15 (1993): 145-53

Green, Peter, *Alexander to Actium. The Historical Evolution of the Hellenistic Age*, Berkeley, Los Angeles: University of California Press, 1990

Gruen, Erich S., *The Hellenistic World and the Coming of Rome*, Berkeley: University of California Press, 1984

Grünzweig, F., *Der Brief des Jakobus*, Studienbibel; Wuppertal: Rolf Brockhaus, 1973

Habel, Norman, "Only the Jackal is My Friend: On Friends and Redeemers in Job," *Int.* 31 (1977): 227-36

Haenchen, E., *John 2. A Commentary on the Gospel of John Chapters 7-21*, trans. Robert W. Funk; Hermeneia; Philadelphia: Fortress, 1984

Hagner, D.A., *The Use of the Old and New Testaments in Clement of Rome*, NovTSup 34; Leiden: Brill, 1973

Halperin, David M., *One Hundred Years of Homosexuality*, New York, London: Routledge, 1990

Halstead, Paul, and J. O'Shea, "A Friend in Need is a Friend Indeed: Social Storage and the Origins of Social Ranking," in *Ranking, Resources and Exchange. Aspects of the Archaeology of Early European Society*, ed. C. Renfre and S. Shennan; Cambridge: Cambridge University Press, 1982, 92-99

Hands, A.R., *Charities and Social Aid in Greece and Rome*, London: Thames & Hudson, 1968

Hansen, M.H. *The Athenian Democracy in the Age of Demosthenes: Structure, Principles and Ideology*, trans. J.A. Crook; Oxford: Oxford University Press, 1991

Hanson, Anthony T., "Seminar Report on 'The Use of the Old Testament in the Epistle of James'," *NTS* 25 (1979): 526-27

——, "Rahab the Harlot in Early Christian Theology," *JSNT* 1 (1978): 53-60

Hanson, K.C., "Greco-Roman Studies and the Social-Scientific Study of the Bible: A Classified Periodical Bibliography," *Forum* 9 (1-2) (1993): 63-119

Hanson, K.C. and Douglas E. Oakman, *Palestine in the Time of Jesus. Social Structures and Social Conflicts*, Minneapolis: Fortress, 1998

Harding, Phillip, ed. and trans., *From the End of the Peloponnesian War to the Battle of Ipsus: Translated Documents*, Cambridge: Cambridge University Press, 1985

Harland, Philip A., "Familial Dimensions of Group Identity: 'Brothers' ('Αδελφοί) in Associations of the Greek East," *JBL* (2005) 491-513

——, *Associations, Synagogues, and Congregations. Claiming a Place in Ancient Mediterranean Society*, Minneapolis: Fortress, 2003

Harrington, Daniel J., "Sage Advice about Friendship," *TBT* 32 (1994): 79-83
Harrison, James R., *Paul's Language of Grace in its Graeco-Roman Context*, WUNT 172; Tübingen: Mohr-Siebeck, 2003
——, "Benefaction Ideology and Christian Responsibility for Widows," *NewDocs* 8 (1997): 106-16
Hartin, Patrick J., *James*, Sacra Pagina 14; Collegeville: Liturgical Press, 2003
——, *A Spirituality of Perfection. Faith in Action in the Letter of James*, Collegeville: Liturgical Press, 1999
——, "Called to Be Perfect Through Suffering (James 1,2-4). The Concept of Perfection in the Epistle of James and the Sermon on the Mount," *Bib* 77 (1996): 477-92
——, *James and the "Q" Sayings of Jesus*, JSNTSup 47; Sheffield: Sheffield Academic Press, 1991
——, "James and the Q Sermon on the Mount/Plain," in *Society of Biblical Literature 1989 Seminar Papers*, ed. David J. Lull; SBLSP 47. Atlanta: Scholars, 1989, 440-57
Hauck, F. and S. Schulz, "πραΰς, πραΰτης," *TDNT* VI (1968): 645-51
Hauck, Friedrich. *Die Briefe des Jakobus, Petrus, Judas und Johannes*, 4th ed., NTD; Göttingen: Vandenhoeck & Ruprecht, 1949
——, "Die Freundschaft bei den Griechen und im Neuen Testament," in *Festgabe Für Theodor Zahn*; Leipzig: Deichert, 1928, 211-28
——, *Der Brief des Jakobus*, Kommentar zum Neuen Testament, 16; Leipzig: Deichert, 1926
Hawkins, O.S., *James*. Neptune, NJ: Loizeaux, 1992
Heath, Malcolm, *The Poetics of Greek Tragedy*, London: Duckworth, 1987
Henry, A.S., *Honours and Privileges in Athenian Decrees*, Subsidia epigraphica 10; Hildesheim, Zürich, New York: G. Olms, 1983
Herman, G., *Ritualised Friendship and the Greek City*, Cambridge and New York: Cambridge University Press, 1987
——, "The 'Friends' of the Early Hellenistic Rulers: Servants or Officials?" *Talanta* 12/13 (1980/1): 103-49
Hesiod, *Works and Days*, trans. M.L. West; Oxford: Oxford University Press, 1988
Hijmans, B.L., ΑΣΚΕΣΙΣ: *Notes on Epictetus' Educational System*, Assen: Van Gorcum, 1959
Hock, Ronald F., "An Extraordinary Friend in Chariton's *Callirhoe*: The Importance of Friendship in the Greek Romances," in *Greco-Roman Perspectives on Friendship*, ed. John T. Fitzgerald; SBLRBS 34; Atlanta: Scholars, 1997, 145-62
——, *The Chreia in Ancient Rhetoric. Volume I. The Progymnasmata*, SBLTT, 27; Atlanta: Scholars, 1986
Hollander, H.W. and M. de Jonge, *The Testaments of the Twelve Patriarchs*, SVTP 8. Leiden: E.J. Brill, 1985
Hollenbach, Paul, "Defining Rich and Poor Using Social Sciences," *SBLSP* 26 (1987): 50-63
Hooker, James, "Homeric φίλος," *Glotta* 65 (1987): 44-65
Hoppe, Rudolf, *Jakobusbrief*. Stuttgarter kleiner Kommentar. Neues Testament, n.s. 15; Stuttgart: Katholisches Bibelwerk, 1989
Hopwood, Keith, "Bandits, Elites and Rural Order," in *Patronage in Ancient Society*, ed. Andrew Wallace-Hadrill; Leicester-Nottingham Studies in Ancient Society, 1; London and New York: Routledge, 1989, 171-88
Horace, *Epistles*, trans. H. Rushton Fairclough; LCL; London: Heinemann; Cambridge, MA: Harvard University Press, 1942
Horden, Peregrine and Nicholas Purcell, *The Corrupting Sea. A Study of Mediterranean History*, Oxford: Blackwell, 2000
Horsfall, Nicholas, *Poets and Patron: Maecenas, Horace and Georgics, Once More*, North Ryde, 1981

Hort, F.J.A., ed., *The Epistle of St. James, the Greek Text: With Introduction, Commentary as Far as Chapter IV, Verse 7*, London: Macmillan, 1909

Hughes, F.W. *Early Christian Rhetoric and 2 Thessalonians*, JSNTSup 30; Sheffield: Sheffield Academic Press, 1989

Hunter, R.L., "Horace on Friendship and Free Speech (Epistles 1.18 and Satires 1.4)," *Hermes* 113 (1985): 480-90

Hutter, Horst, *Politics as Friendship: The Origins of Classical Notions of Politics in the Theory and Practice of Friendship*, Waterloo, Ontario: Wilfrid Laurier University Press, 1978

Iamblichus, *On the Pythagorean Life*, trans. Gillian Clark; Liverpool: Liverpool University Press, 1989

Ingenkamp, H.G., *Plutarchs Schriften über die Heilung der Seele*, Hypomnemata, 34; Göttingen: Vandenhoeck & Ruprecht, 1971

Inwood, B., *Ethics and Human Action in Early Stoicism*, Oxford: Clarendon, 1985

Irwin, William H., "Fear of God, the Analogy of Friendship and Ben Sira's Theodicy," *Bib* 76 (1995): 551-59

Isocrates, *De Pace*, trans. George Norlin; LCL; London: Heinemann; New York: Putnam, 1929

Jackson-McCabe, Matt, *Logos and Law in the Letter of James. The Law of Nature, the Law of Moses, and the Law of Freedom*, NovTSup 100; Leiden, Boston, Cologne: Brill, 2001

———, "A Letter to the Twelve Tribes in the Diaspora: Wisdom and 'Apocalyptic' Eschatology in the Letter of James," *SBLSP* 35 (1996): 504-17

Jacobs, Irving, "The Midrashic Background for James II, 21-3," *NTS* 22 (1975-76): 457-64

Jeffers, James S., "The Influence of the Roman Family and Social Structures on Early Christianity in Rome," in *Society of Biblical Literature 1988 Seminar Papers*, ed. David J. Lull; Atlanta: Scholars, 1988, 370-84

———, "Jewish and Christian Families in First-Century Rome," in *Judaism and Christianity in First Century Rome*, ed. Karl P. Donfried and Peter Richardson; Grand Rapids, MI, Cambridge, UK: Eerdmans, 1998, 128-50

Johnson, Luke Timothy, *The Letter of James: A New Translation with Introduction and Commentary*, Anchor Bible, 37A; Garden City, NY: Doubleday, 1995

———, "The Social World of James: Literary Analysis and Historical Reconstruction," in *The Social World of the First Christians: Essays in Honor of Wayne A. Meeks*, ed. L. Michael White and O. Larry Yarbrough; Minneapolis: Fortress, 1995, 178-97

———, "Taciturnity and True Religion (James 1:26-27)," in *Greeks, Romans and Christians: Essays in Honor of Abraham J. Malherbe*, ed. D.L. Balch, E. Ferguson, and W.A. Meeks; Minneapolis: Fortress, 1990, 329-39

———, "The Mirror of Remembrance (James 1:22-25)," *CBQ* 501 (1988): 632-45

———, "Friendship with the World/Friendship with God: A Study of Discipleship in James," in *Discipleship in the New Testament*, ed. Fernando F. Segovia; Philadelphia: Fortress, 1985, 166-83

———, "James 3:13–4:10 and the *Topos* ΠΕΡΙ ΦΘΟΝΟΥ," *NovT* 25 (1983): 327-47

———, "The Use of Leviticus 19 in the Letter of James," *JBL* 101 (1982): 391-401

Joly, Robert, *Le Vocabulaire chrétien de l'amour est-il original? Φιλεῖν et 'Αγαπᾶν dans le grec antique*, Brussels: Presses Universitaires, 1968

Jones, C.P., *Plutarch and Rome*, Oxford: Clarendon, 1971

Joubert, Stephan, "One Form of Social Exchange or Two? 'Euergetism,' Patronage and Second Testament Studies," *BTB* 31 (2001): 17-25.

———, *Paul as Benefactor: Reciprocity, Strategy and Theological Reflection in Paul's Collection*, WUNT 124; Tübingen: Mohr Siebeck, 2000

Judge, E.A., "Paul as a Radical Critic of Society," *Interchange* 16 (1974): 191-203

Juvenal, *Satires*, trans. G.G. Ramsay; LCL; London: Heinemann; Cambridge, MA: Harvard University Press, 1950

Kennedy, George, ed., trans., *Progymnasmata. Greek Textbooks of Prose Composition and Rhetoric*, Writings from the Greco-Roman World 10. Atlanta: Society of Biblical Literature, 2003
——, *A New History of Classical Rhetoric*, Princeton: Princeton University Press, 1994
——, *New Testament Interpretation Through Rhetorical Criticism* Chapel Hill and London: University of North Carolina Press, 1984
Kennedy, H.A.A., "The Hellenistic Atmosphere of the Epistle of James," *Exp* 2, 8th ser. (1911): 37-52
Kenny, Anthony, *Aristotle on the Perfect Life*, Oxford: Clarendon, 1992
——, *The Aristotelian Ethics: A Study of the Relationship between the Eudemian and Nicomachean Ethics of Aristotle.* Oxford: Clarendon, 1978
Kistemaker, S.J., *Exposition of the Epistle of James and the Epistles of John*, New Testament Commentary; Grand Rapids: Baker Book House, 1986
Klassen, William, "Παρρησία in the Johannine Corpus," in *Friendship, Flattery and Frankness of Speech: Studies on Friendship in the New Testament*, ed. John T. Fitzgerald; NovTSup 82; Leiden, New York, Cologne: E.J. Brill, 1996, 227-54
Klauck, Hans-Josef, "Kirche als Freundesgemeinschaft? Auf Spurensuche im Neuen Testament," *MTZ* 42 (1991): 1-14
——, "Brotherly Love in Plutarch and in 4 Maccabees," in *Greeks, Romans, and Christians: Essays in Honor of Abraham J. Malherbe*, ed. D.L. Balch, E. Ferguson, and W.A. Meeks; Minneapolis: Fortress, 1990, 144-56
Klein, Martin, *Ein vollkommenes Werk. Volkommenheit, Gesetz, und Gericht als theologische Themen des Jakobusbriefes*, BWANT 139; Stuttgart: Kohlhammer, 1995
Klijn, A.F.J., "Jewish Christianity in Egypt," in *The Roots of Egyptian Christianity*, ed. Birger A. Pearson and James E. Goehring; Studies in Antiquity and Christianity. Philadelphia: Fortress Press, 1986, 161-75
Kloppenborg Verbin, John S., "Patronage Avoidance in James," *Hervormde Teologiese Studies* 55 (1999): 755-94
Kloppenborg, John S., "The Emulation of the Jesus Tradition in the Letter of James," in *Reading James with New Eyes. Methodological Reassessments of the Letter of James*, ed. Robert L. Webb and John S. Kloppenborg; LNTS 342; London: T & T Clark, 2007, 121-50
——, "The Reception of Jesus Traditions in James," in *The Catholic Epistles and the Tradition*, ed. J. Schlosser; BETL 176; Leuven: Peeters, 2004, 136-40
——, "Status und Wohtätigkeit bei Paulus und Jakobus," in *Von Jesus Zum Christus. Christologische Studien. Festgabe für Paul Hoffmann zum 65. Geburtstag*, ed. Rudolf Hoppe and Ulrich Busse; BZNW 93; Berlin, New York: Walter de Gruyter, 1998, 127-54
——, "Status and Conflict Resolution in Early Christian Groups" (paper delivered at the Toronto School of Theology Biblical Department Seminar, September, 1995)
——, "The Transformation of Moral Exhortation in *Didache* 1-5," in *The Didache in Context. Essays on Its Text, History and Transmission*, ed. Clayton N. Jefford; NovTSup 77; Leiden, New York, Cologne: E.J. Brill, 1995, 88-109
Koester, Helmut, *Ancient Christian Gospels. Their History and Development*, London: SCM Press; Philadelphia: Trinity Press, 1992
——, *Synoptische Überlieferung bei den apostolischen Vätern*, TU 65; Berlin: Akademie, 1957
Konstan, David, *The Emotions of the Ancient Greeks. Studies on Aristotle and Classical Literature*, Toronto, Buffalo, London: University of Toronto Press, 2006
——, "How to Praise a Friend. St. Gregory of Nazianzus's Funeral Oration for St. Basil the Great," in *Greek Biography and Panegyric in Late Antiquity*, ed. Tomas Hägg and Philip Rousseau; Transformation of the Classical Heritage 31; Berkeley and Los Angeles: University of California Press, 2000, 160-79

—, "Reciprocity and Friendship," in *Reciprocity in Ancient Greece*, ed. Norman Postlethwaite and Richard Seaford Christopher Gill; Oxford: Oxford University Press, 1998, 279-301
—, *Friendship in the Classical World*. Cambridge: Cambridge University Press, 1997
—, "Friendship, Frankness and Flattery," in *Friendship, Flattery, and Frankness of Speech: Studies on Friendship in the New Testament World*, ed. John T. Fitzgerald; NovTSup 82; Leiden, New York, Cologne: E.J. Brill, 1996, 7-19
—, "Friendship from Epicurus to Philodemus," in *L'Epicureismo Greco e Romano*, ed. M. Giannantoni and M. Gigante; Naples: Bibliopolis, 1996, 387-96
—, "Greek Friendship," *AJP* 117 (1996): 71-94
—, "Problems in the History of Christian Friendship," *Journal of Early Christian Studies* 4 (1996): 87-113
—, "Friendship and the State: The Context of Cicero's *De Amicitia*," *Hyperboreus* 1.2 (1994/95): 1-16
—, "Patrons and Friends," *Classical Philology* 90 (1995): 328-42
—, *Sexual Symmetry: Love in the Ancient Novel and Related Genres*, Princeton: Princeton University Press, 1994
—, "*Philia* in Euripides' Electra," *Philologus* 129 (1985): 176-85
—, *Some Aspects of Epicurean Psychology*, Philosophia Antiqua, 25; Leiden: E.J.Brill, 1973
Kraabel, Alf T., "Judaism in Western Asia Minor under the Roman Empire, with a Preliminary Study of the Jewish Community at Sardis, Lydia," diss., Harvard Divinity School, 1968
Krammer, Ingrid, "Scham im Zusammenhang mit Freundschaft," in *Freundschaft be Ben Sira*, ed. Friedrich V. Reiterer; BZAW 244; Berlin, New York: Walter de Gruyter, 1996, 171-201
Kraut, Richard, "Two Conceptions of Happiness," *The Philosophical Review* 88 (1979): 167-97
Kugelman, Richard, *James & Jude*, New Testament Message, 19; Wilmington, DE: Michael Glazier, 1980
LaFleur, Richard, "*Amicitia* and the Unity of Juvenal's First Book," *ICS* 4 (1979): 158-77
Lake, Kirsopp, trans., *The Apostolic Fathers*, 2 vols.; LCL; London: Heinemann; Cambridge, MA: Harvard University Press, 1912-13
La Piana, George, "Foreign Groups in Rome during the First Century of the Empire," *HTR* 20 (1927): 183-403
Lane, William L. "Social Perspectives on Roman Christianity During the Formative Years from Nero to Nerva: Romans, Hebrews, *1 Clement*," in *Judaism and Christianity in First Century Rome*, ed. Karl P. Donfried and Peter Richardson, 196-244. Grand Rapids, Mich., Cambridge, UK: Eerdmans, 1998
Lausberg, Heinrich, *Handbook of Literary Rhetoric. A Foundation for Literary Study*, trans. Annemiek Jansen, Matthew T. Bliss, David E. Orton; ed. R. Dean Anderson and David E. Orton; Leiden, Boston, Cologne: Brill, 1998
Laws, Sophie, "The Doctrinal Basis for Ethics in James," *SE* 7 (1982): 299-305
—, *A Commentary on the Epistle of James*, Black's New Testament Commentaries; London: Adam & Charles Black, 1980
Leaman, Oliver, ed., *Friendship East and West: Philosophical Perspectives*, Richmond, UK: Curzon, 1996
Leconte, René, *Les épîtres catholiques des saint Jacques, saint Jude et saint Pierre*, La Sainte Bible de Jérusalem; Paris: Éditions du Cerf, 1953
Lendon, J.E., *Empire of Honour. The Art of Government in the Roman World*, Oxford: Oxford University Press, 1997
Lesses, Glenn, "Austere Friends: The Stoics and Friendship," *Apeiron* 26 (1993): 57-75
Lipsius, R.A., *Die Apokryphen Apostelgeschichten und Apostellegenden* II.2, Braunschweig: G. Westerman, 1884

Llewellyn, S.R., "The Prescript of James," *NovT* 39 (1997): 385-93
Long, A.A. *Hellenistic Philosophy: Stoics, Epicureans, Sceptics,* 2nd ed., Berkeley and Los Angeles: University of California Press, 1986
Lucian, *Nigrinus,* trans. A.M. Harmon; LCL; London: Heinemann; Cambridge, MA: Harvard University Press, 1979
——, *Toxaris,* trans. A.M. Harmon; LCL; London: Heinemann; Cambridge, MA: Harvard University Press, 1936
MacCoull, Leslie S.B., "Patronage and the Social Order in Coptic Egypt," in *Egitto e storia antica dall'ellenismo all'età araba: Bilancio di un confronto: Atti del Colloquio,* ed. L. Criscuolo; Bologna: CLUEB, 1989, 497-502
MacIntyre, Alisdair, *After Virtue. A Study in Moral Theory,* 2nd ed., Notre Dame: University of Notre Dame Press, 1984
Mack, Burton L., *Rhetoric and the New Testament,* Guides to Biblical Scholarship, Minneapolis: Fortress, 1990
Mack, Burton L. and Edward O'Neil, "The Chreia Discussion of Hermogenes of Tarsus," in *The Chreia in Ancient Rhetoric. Volume 1. The Progymnasmata,* SBLTT, 27; Atlanta: Scholars, 1986, 155-71
MacMullen, Ramsay, "Personal Power in the Roman Empire," *AJPh* 107 (1986): 512-24
Maier, Harry O., *The Social Setting of the Ministry as Reflected in the Writings of Hermas, Clement and Ignatius,* Canadian Corporation for Studies in Religion, Dissertations SR 1; Waterloo: Wilfrid Laurier University Press, 1991
Malherbe, Abraham J., "Paul's Self Sufficiency (Philippians 4:11)," in *Friendship, Flattery, and Frankness of Speech: Studies on Friendship in the New Testament World,* ed. John T. Fitzgerald; NovTSup 82; Leiden, New York, Cologne: E.J. Brill, 1996, 125-39
——, "Hellenistic Moralists and the New Testament," *ANRW* 2.26.7 (1992): 267-333
——, *Paul and the Popular Philosophers,* Minneapolis: Fortress, 1989
——, *Ancient Epistolary Theorists,* SBLSBS 19; Atlanta: Scholars, 1988
——, *Paul and the Thessalonians: The Philosophical Tradition of Pastoral Care,* Philadelphia: Fortress, 1987
——, *Moral Exhortation, A Greco-Roman Sourcebook,* Library of Early Christianity, 4; Philadelphia: The Westminster Press, 1986
Malina, Bruce, "Patron and Client," *Forum* 4 (1988): 2-32
——, "Wealth and Poverty in the New Testament and Its World," *Int* 41 (1986): 354-67
——, *The New Testament World: Insights from Cultural Anthropology,* Louisville: John Knox, 1981
Marchal, Joseph A., *Hierarchy, Unity and Imitation: A Feminist Rhetorical Analysis of Power Dynamics in Paul's Letter to the Philippians,* Academica Biblica 24; Atlanta: Society of Biblical Literature, 2006
Marcus, Joel, "The Evil Inclination in the Epistle of James," *CBQ* 44 (1982): 606-21
Marrou, Henri-Irénée, *A History of Education in Antiquity,* trans. George Lamb; Madison: University of Wisconsin Press, 1982
Marrow, Stanley B., "*Parrhēsia* and the NT," *CBQ* 44 (1982): 431-46
Marshall, Peter, *Enmity at Corinth: Social Conventions in Paul's Relations with the Corinthians,* WUNT 2.23. Tübingen: J.C.B. Mohr [Paul Siebeck], 1987
Martin, Ralph P., *James,* WBC 48; Waco, TX: Word, 1988
Martin, Raymond A., and John H. Elliott, *James. I Peter. II Peter,* Augsburg Commentary on the New Testament; Minneapolis: Augsburg, 1982
Masseibieau, L., "L'épître de Jacques: est-elle l'œuvre d'un chrétien?" *RHR* 31-32 (1895): 249-83
Massyngbaerde Ford, J., *Redeemer-Friend and Mother: Salvation in Antiquity and in the Gospel of John,* Minneapolis: Fortress, 1997

May, James M., "The Rhetoric of Advocacy and Patron-Client Identification: Variations on a Theme," *AJPh* 102 (1981): 308-15
Maynard-Reid, Pedrito U., *Poverty and Wealth in James*, Maryknoll: Orbis, 1987
Mayor, Joseph B., *The Epistle of St. James: The Greek Text with Introduction, Notes and Comments*, 3rd ed., London: Macmillan, 1910
McCready, Wayne, "Friendship and Religious Self-Definition" (paper presented at the Canadian Society of Biblical Studies, Ottawa, 1998)
McCue, James, "Bishops, Presbyters, and Priests in Ignatius of Antioch," *TS* 28 (1967): 828-34
McGuire, Brian Patrick, *Friendship and Community. The Monastic Experience 350-1250*, Cisterican Studies; Kalamazoo: Cistercian Publications, 1988
McKerlie, Dennis, "Friendship, Self-Love, and Concern for Others in Aristotle's Ethics," *Ancient Philosophy* 11 (1991): 85-100
McNamara, Marie Aquinas, *Friends and Friendship in Saint Augustine*, Staten Island, NY: Alba House, 1964
Meagher, Robert E., "Reflections on Ancient Friendship," *Parabola* 1 (1976): 66-75
Meeks, Wayne A., *The First Urban Christians. The Social World of the Apostle Paul*, New Haven and London: Yale University Press, 1983
Meikle, Scott, "Aristotle and the Political Economy of the Polis," *JHS* 79 (1979): 57-73
Melhuus, Marit, "Shame to Honour, a Shame to Suffer," *Ethnos* 55 (1990): 5-25
Merritt, H. Wayne, *In Word and Deed. Moral Integrity in Paul*, Emory Studies in Early Christianity, 1; New York, San Francisco, Bern, Baltimore, Frankfurt am Main, Berlin, Vienna, Paris: Peter Lang, 1993
Middendorp, Theophil, *Die Stellung Jesu Ben Siras zwischen Judentum und Hellenismus*, Leiden: E.J. Brill, 1973
Millard, A.R., "Abraham," *ABD* I (1992): 35-41
Miller, Stuart, *Men and Friendship*, Los Angeles: Jeremy P. Tarcher, 1983
Millett, Paul, *Lending and Borrowing in Ancient Athens*. Cambridge: Cambridge University Press, 1991
———, "Patronage and Its Avoidance in Classical Athens," in *Patronage in Ancient Society*, ed. Andrew Wallace-Hadrill; Leicester-Nottingham Studies in Ancient Society, 1; London and New York: Routledge, 1989, 15-48
Minear, Paul S., "Yes and No: The Demand for Honesty in the Early Church," *NovT* 13 (1971): 1-13
Mitchell, Alan C., "'Greet the Friends by Name': New Testament Evidence for the Greco-Roman *Topos* on Friendship," in *Greco-Roman Perspectives on Friendship*, ed. John T. Fitzgerald; SBLRBS 34. Atlanta: Scholars, 1997, 225-62
———, "Holding on to Confidence: Παρρησία in Hebrews," in *Friendship, Flattery and Frankness of Speech: Studies on Friendship in the New Testament*, ed. John T. Fitzgerald; NovTSup 82; Leiden, New York, Cologne: E.J. Brill, 1996, 203-26
———, "Looking to the Interests of Others: Friendship and Justice in the New Testament Communities," in *Let Justice Roll Down Like Waters: Jesuit Education and Faith That Does Justice*, ed. W. O'Brien; Washington, DC: Georgetown University Press, 1993, 101-27
———, "The Social Function of Friendship in Acts 2:44-47 and 4:32-37," *JBL* 111 (1992): 255-72
Mitchell, Lynette G. and P.J. Rhodes, "Friends and Enemies in Athenian Politics," *Greece and Rome* 63 (1996): 11-30
Mitsis, P., *Epicurus' Ethical Theory: The Pleasures of Invulnerability*, Ithaca: Cornell University Press, 1988
Moffatt, James, "An Approach to Ignatius," *HTR* 29 (1936): 1-38
Moles, John, "'Honestius Quam Ambitiosius'? An Exploration of the Cynic's Attitude to Moral Corruption in His Fellow Men," *JHS* 103 (1983): 103-23

Moltmann, Jürgen, "Open Friendship: Aristotelian and Christian Concepts of Friendship," in *The Changing Face of Friendship*, ed. Leroy S. Rouner; Boston University Studies in Philosophy and Religion, 15; Notre Dame: University of Notre Dame Press, 1994, 29-42

Momigliano, Arnaldo, "Freedom of Speech in Antiquity," in *Dictionary of the History of Ideas: Studies of Selected Pivotal Ideas*, vol. II, ed. P.P. Wiener; New York: Charles Scribner's Sons, 1973-74, 252-63.

Moo, Douglas J., *The Letter of James*, PNTC; Grand Rapids: Eerdmans, 2000

———, *The Letter of James: An Introduction and Commentary*, The Tyndale New Testament Commentaries; Leicester, Manchester: Inter-Varsity Press, Eerdmans, 1966

Moore, James R., "Computer Analysis and the Pauline Corpus," *BSac* 130 (1973): 41-49

Moxnes, Halvor, *The Economy of the Kingdom. Social Conflict and Economic Relations in Luke's Gospel*, OBT; Philadelphia: Fortress, 1988

Mussner, Franz, "Die ethische Motivation im Jakobusbrief," in *Neues Testament und Ethik: Für Rudolf Schnackenburg*, ed. Helmut Merklein; Freiburg and Vienna: Herder, 1989, 416-23

———, *Der Jakobusbrief*, 5th ed., HTKNT 13/1; Freiburg, Basel, Vienna: Herder, 1987

———, *Der Jakobusbrief: Auslegung*, 4th ed., HTKNT 13/1; Freiburg im Breisgau, Basel, Vienna: Herder, 1981

———, "'Direkte' und 'indirekte' Christologie im Jakobusbrief," *Catholica* 24 (1970): 111-17

Neyrey, Jerome H., "God, Benefactor and Patron: The Major Cultural Model for Interpreting the Deity in Greco-Roman Antiquity," *JSNT* 27 (2005): 465-92

Nicols, John, "Pliny and the Patronage of Communities," *Hermes* 108 (1980): 365-85

Niebuhr, Karl-Wilhelm, "Der Jakobusbrief im Licht frühjüdischer Diasporabriefe," *NTS* 44 (1998): 420-23

Nock, Arthur Darby, "*Soter* and *Euergetes*," in *Essays on Religion and the Ancient World*, vol. II, ed. Zeph Stewart; Cambridge, MA: Harvard University Press, 1972, 720-35

Nussbaum, Martha C., *Therapy of Desire*. Princeton: Princeton University Press, 1994

———, *The Fragility of Goodness: Luck and Ethics in Greek Tragedy and Philosophy*, Cambridge: Cambridge University Press, 1986

O'Connor, D.K., "Two Ideals of Friendship," *History of Philosophy Quarterly* 7 (1990): 109-22

———, "The Invulnerable Pleasures of Epicurean Friendship," *GRBS* 30 (1989): 165-86

O'Neil, Edward, "Plutarch on Friendship," in *Greco-Roman Perspectives on Friendship*, ed. John T. Fitzgerald; SBLRBS 34; Atlanta: Scholars, 1997, 105-22

Orwell, George, "Reflections on Gandhi," in *The Penguin Essays of George Orwell*, London: Penguin, 1984, 465-72

Osborne, Robin, "Social and Economic Implications of the Leasing of Land and Property in Classical and Hellenistic Greece," *Chiron* 18 (1988): 279-323

Osiek, Carolyn, *The Shepherd of Hermas*, Hermeneia; Minneapolis: Fortress, 1999

Painter, John, *Just James. The Brother of Jesus in History and Tradition*, Studies on Personalities of the New Testament; Minneapolis: Fortress, 1999

Pakaluk, Michael, "Political Friendship," in *The Changing Face of Friendship*, ed. Leroy S. Rouner; Boston University Studies in Philosophy and Religion, 15; Notre Dame: University of Notre Dame Press, 1994, 197-213

———, ed. *Other Selves: Philosophers on Friendship*, Indianapolis/Cambridge: Hakkert, 1991

Pardee, Dennis, *Handbook of Ancient Hebrew Letters*, SBLSBS, 15; Chico: Scholars, 1982

Patterson, Stephen J., "Who Are the 'Poor in the World' in James?" (paper delivered at the Society of Biblical Literature Annual Meeting, Boston, MA, 1999)

———, *The Gospel of Thomas and Jesus*, FFRS; Sonoma, CA: Polebridge, 1993

Peachin, Michael, ed., *Aspects of Friendship in the Graeco-Roman World. Proceedings of a Conference Held at the Seminar für Alte Geschichte, Heidelberg, on 10-11 June, 2000*,

Journal of Roman Archaeology Supplementary Series 43; Portsmouth, RI: Journal of Roman Archaeology, 2001
Pearson, Birger A., "Earliest Christianity in Egypt: Some Observations," in *The Roots of Egyptian Christianity*, ed. Birger A. Pearson and James E. Goehring; Studies in Antiquity and Christianity; Philadelphia: Fortress, 1986, 132-59
Pearson, Birger A., and James E. Goehring, eds., *The Roots of Egyptian Christianity*, Studies in Antiquity and Christianity; Philadelphia: Fortress, 1986
Penner, Todd C., "The Epistle of James in Current Research," *CurBS* 7 (1999) 257-308
——, *The Epistle of James and Eschatology*, JSNTSup 121; Sheffield: JSOT Press, 1996
Perdue, Leo G., "The Death of the Sage and Moral Exhortation: From Ancient Near Eastern Instructions to Graeco-Roman Paraenesis," *Semeia* 50 (1990): 81-109
——, "Liminality as a Social Setting for Wisdom Instructions," *ZAW* 93 (1981): 114-26
——, "Paraenesis and the Epistle of James," *ZNW* 72 (1981): 241-56
Perelman, C. and L. Olbrechts-Tyteca, *The New Rhetoric. A Treatise on Argumentation*, trans. John Wilkinson and Purcell Weaver; Notre Dame, London: University of Notre Dame Press, 1969
Perkins, Pheme, "Christology, Friendship and Status: The Rhetoric of Philippians," in *Society of Biblical Literature Seminar Papers*, ed. Kent Harold Richards; SBLSP 26; Atlanta: Scholars, 1987, 509-20
Pervo, Richard I., "With Lucian: Who Needs Friends? Friendship in the *Toxaris*," in *Greco-Roman Perspectives on Friendship*, ed. John T. Fitzgerald; SBLRBS, 34; Atlanta: Scholars, 1997, 163-80
Peters, F.E., *Greek Philosophical Terms. A Historical Lexicon*, New York and London, 1967
Peterson, D., *Hebrews and Perfection: An Examination of the Concept of Perfection in the 'Epistle to the Hebrews'*, SNTSMS 47; Cambridge: Cambridge University Press, 1982
Peterson, Erik, "Zur Bedeutungsgeschichte von Παρρησία," in *R. Seeberg Festschrift*, I, ed. W. Koepp; Leipzig: D.W. Scholl, 1929, 283-97
——, "Der Gottesfreund: Beiträge zur Geschichte eines religiösen Terminus," *ZKG* 42, n.s. 5 (1923): 161-202
Philo, *Works*, trans. F.H. Colson and G.H. Whitaker; LCL; London: Heinemann; Cambridge, MA: Harvard University Press, 1929-50
Philodemus, Περὶ Παρρησίας, ed. Alexander Olivieri; Leipzig: Teubner, 1914
Pinches, Charles, "Pagan Virtue and Christian Prudence," *Journal of Religious Ethics* 23 (1995): 93-115
Pizzolato, Luigi, *L'idea di amicizia nel mondo antico classico e cristiano*, Turin: Einaudi, 1993
Plato, *Lysis*, trans. W.R.M. Lamb; LCL; London: Heinemann; New York: Putnam, 1930
Plescia, Joseph, *The Oath and Perjury in Ancient Greece*, Tallahassee: Florida State University Press, 1970
Pliny, *Letters II*, trans. William Melmoth; rev. W.M.L. Hutchinson; LCL; London: Heinemann; New York: Putnam, 1924
Plutarch, *Against Colotes*, trans. Benedict Einarson and Phillip H. De Lacy; LCL; London: Heinemann; Cambridge, MA: Harvard University Press, 1967
——, *How to Tell a Flatterer from a Friend*, trans. Frank Cole Babbitt; LCL; London: Heinemann; Cambridge, MA: Harvard University Press, 1986
——, *On Having Many Friends*, trans. Frank Cole Babbit; LCL; London, Cambridge, MA: Harvard University Press, 1928
Polanyi, Karl, *Primitive, Archaic and Modern Economy: Essays of Karl Polanyi*, ed. G. Dalton; Garden City, NY: Doubleday, 1968
Polanyi, Karl, Conrad M. Arensberg and Harry W. Pearson, eds., *Trade and Market in Early Empires: Economies in History and Theory*, Glencoe, IL: Free Press, 1957
Polybius, *The Histories*, LCL; London: Heinemann; Cambridge, MA: Harvard University Press, 1968

Pope, Marvin H., *Job. A New Translation with Introduction and Commentary*, AB, 15; New York: Doubleday, 1965
Popkes, Wiard, *Der Brief des Jakobus*, THKNT 14; Leipzig: Evangelische Verlagsanstalt, 2001
Porphyry, *Life of Pythagoras*, trans. Edouard des Places; Collection des universités de France; Paris: Les Belles Lettres, 1982
Porter, Stanley E., "The Theoretical Justification for Application of Rhetorical Categories to Pauline Epistolary Literature," in *Rhetoric and the New Testament. Essays from the 1992 Heidelberg Conference*, ed. Stanley E. Porter and Thomas H. Olbricht; JSNTSup 90; Sheffield: JSOT Press, 1993, 100-22
———, "Is *dipsuchos* (James 1,8; 4,8) a 'Christian' Word?" *Bib* 71 (1991): 469-98
Pouchet, Robert, *Basile le Grand et son univers d'amis d'après sa correspondance. Une stratégie de communion*, Studia Ephemeridis – Augustinianum, 36; Rome: Insti–tutum Patristicum Augustinianum, 1992
Powell, J.G.F., *Cicero: Laelius, On Friendship and the Dream of Scipio*, Warminster: Aris and Phillips, 1990
Powell, Jonathan, "Friendship and Its Problems in Greek and Roman Thought," in *Ethics and Rhetoric*, ed. Harry Hine, Christopher Pelling and Doreen Innes; Oxford: Clarendon, 1995, 31-45
Price, Anthony, *Love and Friendship in Plato and Aristotle*, Oxford: Clarendon, 1989
Pseudo-Aristotle, *Rhetoric to Alexander*, trans. H. Rackham; LCL; London: Heine–mann; Cambridge, MA: Harvard University Press, 1957
Pseudo-Cicero, *Rhetorica ad Herennium*; LCL; London, Cambridge, MA: Harvard University Press, 1954
Quintilian, *Institutio Oratoria*, trans. H.E. Butler; LCL; London: Heinemann; Cambridge, MA: Harvard University Press, 1960
Rabbow, P., *Seelenführung: Methodik der Exerzitien in der Antike*, Munich: Kösel, 1954
Ramage, Edwin S., "Juvenal, *Satire* 12: On Friendship True and False," *ICS* 3 (1978): 221-37
Rawson, Beryl, *The Politics of Friendship: Pompey and Cicero*, Sources in Ancient History; Sydney: Sydney University Press, 1978
Reed, Jeffrey T., *A Discourse Analysis of Philippians. Method and Rhetoric in the Debate over Literary Integrity*, JSNTSup 136; Sheffield: Sheffield Academic Press, 1997
Reese, James, "The Exegete as Sage: Hearing the Message of James," *BTB* 12 (1982): 82-85
Reicke, Bo I., *The Epistles of James, Peter and Jude*, AB 37; Garden City, NY: Doubleday, 1964
Reinhardt, Karl, *Sophocles*, trans. H. Harvey and D. Harvey; New York: Barnes and Noble, 1979
Reiterer, Friedrich V., "Gelungene Freundschaft als tragende Säule einer Gesellschaft," in *Freundschaft be Ben Sira*, ed. Friedrich Reiterer; BZAW 244; Berlin, New York: Walter de Gruyter, 1996, 133-69
———, ed., *Freundschaft bei Ben Sira*, BZAW 244. Berlin, New York: Walter de Gruyter, 1996
Rendall, Gerald Henry, *The Epistle of St. James and Judaic Christianity*, Cambridge: Cambridge University Press, 1927
Rengstorf, Karl Heinrich, *A Complete Concordance to Flavius Josephus*, IV, Leiden: Brill, 1983
Rese, Martin, "Das Gebot der Bruderliebe in den Johannesbriefen," *TZ* 41 (1985): 44-58
Reumann, John, "Philippians, Especially Chapter 4, as a 'Letter of Friendship': Observations on a Checkered History of Scholarship," in *Friendship, Flattery and Frankness of*

Speech: Studies on Friendship in the New Testament World, ed. John T. Fitzgerald; NovTSup 82; Leiden, New York, Cologne: Brill, 1996, 83-106

Rich, John, "Patronage and International Relations in the Roman Republic," in *Patronage in Ancient Society*, ed. Andrew Wallace-Hadrill; Leicester-Nottingham Studies in Ancient Society, 1; London and New York: Routledge, 1989, 117-36

Ringe, Sharon H., *Wisdom's Friends. Community and Christology in the Fourth Gospel*, Louisville: Westminster John Knox, 1999

Rist, John M., "Epicurus on Friendship," *CPh* 75 (1980): 121-29

Robbins, Vernon K., *Exploring the Texture of Texts. A Guide to Socio-Rhetorical Interpretation*, Valley Forge: Trinity Press International, 1996

——, "Making Christian Culture in the Epistle of James," *Scriptura* 59 (1996) 341-51

——, *The Tapestry of Early Christian Discourse. Rhetoric, Society and Ideology*, London and New York: Routledge, 1996

Robbins, Vernon K. and Burton L. Mack, *Patterns of Persuasion in the Gospels*, Sonoma: Polebridge, 1989

Robinson, David, "Homeric φίλος: Love of Life and Limbs, and Friendship with One's θυμός," in *Owls to Athens: Essays on Classical Scholarship Presented to Sir Kenneth Dover*, ed. E.M. Craik; Oxford: Clarendon, 1990, 97-108

Ropes, James Hardy, *A Critical and Exegetical Commentary on the Epistle of St. James*, ICC; New York: Charles Scribner's Sons, 1916

Ruckstuhl, Eugen, *Jakobusbrief, 1-3 Johannesbrief*, Die Neue Echter Bibel. Würzburg: Echter, 1985

Ruiz-Montero, C., "Chariton von Aphrodisias: Ein Überblick," *ANRW* 2.34.2 (1994): 1006-54

Sahlins, Marshall, *Stone Age Economics*, Chicago: Aldine-Atherton, 1972

Saller, Richard P., "Patronage and Friendship in Early Imperial Rome: Drawing the Distinction," in *Patronage in Ancient Society*, ed. Andrew Wallace-Hadrill; Leicester-Nottingham Studies in Ancient Society, 1; London and New York: Routledge, 1989, 49-62

——, *Personal Patronage under the Early Empire*, Cambridge: Cambridge University Press, 1982

Sampley, J. Paul, "Paul's Frank Speech with the Galatians and the Corinthians," in *Philodemus and the New Testament World*, ed. John T. Fitzgerald, Dirk Obbrink and Glenn S. Holland; NovTSup 111; Leiden, Boston: Brill, 2004, 295-322

Sanders, Jack T., *Ben Sira and Demotic Wisdom*, SBLMS 28; Chico, CA: Scholars, 1983

Sandnes, Karl Olav, *A New Family. Conversion and Ecclesiology in the Early Church with Cross-Cultural Comparisons*, Studies in the Intercultural History of Christianity; Bern: Peter Lang, 1994

Sasse, Hermann, "ἐπίγειος," *TDNT* I (1964): 680-81

Schaff, Philip, ed., *The Nicene and Post-Nicene Fathers*, trans. W.R.W. Stephens and T.P. Brandram; 1st series; New York: Christian Literature Company, 1889

Schlatter, Adolf, *Der Brief des Jakobus*, Stuttgart: Calwer, 1932

Schmidt, Steffen W., James C. Scott, Carl Landé, and Laura Guasti, eds., *Friends, Followers, and Factions: A Reader in Political Clientelism*, Berkeley: University of California Press, 1977

Schollmeier, Paul, *Other Selves – Aristotle on Personal and Political Friendship*, Albany: State University of New York Press, 1994

Schrage, Wolfgang, and Horst Robert Balz, *Die 'Katholischen' Briefe: die Briefe des Jakobus, Petrus, Johannes und Judas*, 11th ed., NTD 10; Göttingen: Vandenhoeck & Ruprecht, 1973

Schroeder, Frederic M., "Friendship in Aristotle and Some Peripatetic Philosophers," in *Greco-Roman Perspectives on Friendship*, ed. John T. Fitzgerald; SBLRBS, 34; Atlanta: Scholars, 1997, 35-57

Schwartz, Seth, "Josephus in Galilee: Rural Patronage and Social Breakdown," in *Josephus and the History of the Graeco-Roman Period. Essays in Memory of Morton Smith*, ed. Fausto Parente and Joseph Sievers; SPB 41; Leiden, New York, Cologne: Brill, 1994, 290-306

Scott, James C., *Weapons of the Weak. Everday Forms of Peasant Resistance*, New Haven and London: Yale University Press, 1985

Scroggs, Robin, "The Earliest Christian Communities as Sectarian Movement," in *Christianity and Judaism and Other Greco-Roman Cults*, II, ed. Jacob Neusner; Leiden: E.J. Brill, 1975, 1-23

Scully, S.E., "Philia and Charis in Euripidean Tragedy," Ph.D. diss., University of Toronto, 1973

Seesemann, Heinrich, "πεῖραμ, πειράω, πειράζω, πειρασμός, ἀπείραστος, ἐκπειράζω," *TDNT* VI (1968): 23-36

Seitz, O.J.F., "The Two Spirits in Man: An Essay in Biblical Exegesis," *NTS* 6 (1959): 92-95

——, "Antecedents and Signification of the Term ΔΙΨΥΧΟΣ," *JBL* 63 (1944): 211-19

——, "The Relation of the Shepherd of Hermas to the Epistle of James," *JBL* 63 (1944): 131-40

Seneca, *De Beneficiis*, trans. John W. Basore; LCL; London: Heinemann; Cambridge, MA: Harvard University Press, 1935

Sevenster, J.N., *Paul and Seneca*. NovTSup 4; Leiden: E.J. Brill, 1961

Silver, Allan, "Friendship in Commerical Society: Eighteenth-Century Social Theory and Modern Sociology," *American Journal of Sociology* 95 (1990): 1474-504

——, "Friendship and Trust as Moral Ideals: An Historical Approach," *European Journal of Sociology* 30 (1989): 274-97

Simon, Louis, *Une éthique de la sagesse: Commentaire de l'épître de Jacques*, Geneva: Labor et Fides, 1961

Sinos, Dale S., *Achilles, Patroklos and the Meaning of φίλος*, Innsbrucker Beiträge zur Sprachwissenschaft; Innsbruck: Institut für Sprachwissenschaft der Universität Innsbruck, 1980

Skehan, Patrick W., and Alexander Di Lella, *The Wisdom of Ben Sira: A New Translation with Notes*, AB 39; New York: Doubleday, 1987

Sloan, Ian B., "Ezekiel and the Covenant of Friendship," *BTB* 22 (1992): 149-54

Sloyan, Gerald S., and Reginald H. Fuller, *Hebrews, James, 1 and 2 Peter, Jude, Revelation*, Proclamation Commentaries; Philadelphia: Fortress, 1977

Smit, D.J., "'Show No Partiality ...' (James 2:1-13)," *JTSA* 71 (1990): 59-68

Smith, John E., "Two Perspectives on Friendship: Aristotle and Nietzsche," in *The Changing Face of Friendship*, ed. Leroy S. Rouner; Boston University Studies in Philosophy and Religion, 15; Notre Dame: University of Notre Dame Press, 1994, 57-73

Sophocles, *Antigone*, trans. F. Storr; LCL; London: Heinemann; Cambridge, MA: Harvard University Press, 1912

Sperber, Daniel, "Patronage in Amoraic Palestine (220-400): Causes and Effects," *JESHO* 14 (1971): 227-52

Spitaler, Peter, "Διακρίνεσθαι in Mt. 21:21, Mk. 11:23, Acts 10:20, Rom. 4:20, 14:23, Jas 1:6, and Jude 22 – the 'Semantic Shift' That Went Unnoticed by Patristic Authors," *NovT* 49 (2007): 1-39

Spitta, F., *Zur Geschichte und Literatur des Urchristentums*, II: *Der Brief des Jakobus*, Göttingen: Vandenhoeck & Ruprecht, 1896

Stählin, G., "φίλος, φιλή, φιλία," *TDNT* IX (1974): 146-71

Stegemann, Wolfgang and Ekkehard Stegemann, *The Jesus Movement: A Social History of Its First Century*, trans. O.C. Dean, Jr.; Minneapolis: Fortress, 1999

Stein, Howard F., "Note on Patron-Client Theory," *Ethos* 12 (1984): 30-36

Steinmetz, F.-A., *Die Freundschaftslehre des Panaitius: Nach einer Analyse von Ciceros "Laelius de amicitia"*, Wiesbaden: F. Sterner, 1967
Sterling, Gregory E., "The Bond of Humanity: Friendship in Philo of Alexandria," in *Greco-Roman Perspectives on Friendship*, ed. John T. Fitzgerald; SBLRBS, 34; Atlanta: Scholars, 1997, 203-23
Stern-Gillet, Suzanne, *Aristotle's Philosophy of Friendship*, Albany: State University of New York Press, 1995
Stevenson, T.R., "Social and Psychological Interpretations of Graeco-Roman Religion: Some Thoughts on the Ideal Benefactor," *Antichthon* 30 (1996): 1-18
——, "The Ideal Benefactor and the Father Analogy in Greek and Roman Thought," *CQ* 42 (1992): 421-36
Stewart, Charles, "Honour and Sanctity: Two Levels of Ideology in Greece," *Social Anthropology* 2 (1994): 205-28
Stone, Michael E., ed., *Testament of Abraham*, SBLTT Pseudepigrapha Series, 2; Missoula: SBL, 1972
Stowers, Stanley K., "Friends and Enemies in the Politics of Heaven: Reading Theology in Philippians," in *Pauline Theology*, vol. I, ed. J.M. Bassler; Minneapolis: Fortress, 1991, 105-21
——, "The Diatribe," in *Greco-Roman Literature and the New Testament*, ed. David Aune; SBLSBS 21; Atlanta: Scholars, 1988, 71-83
——, *Letter Writing in Greco-Roman Antiquity*, LEC 5; Philadelphia: Westminster, 1987
Strecker, Georg, Udo Schnelle, and Gerald Seelig, eds., *Neuer Wettstein. Texte zum Neuen Testament aus Griechentum und Hellenismus*, II. *Texte zur Briefliteratur und zur Johannesapokalypse*, Berlin, New York: Walter de Gruyter, 1996
Stumpff, A. "ζῆλος," *TDNT* II (1964): 877-78
Swetnam, James, "On the Literary Genre of the Epistle to the Hebrews," *NovT* 11 (1969): 261-69
Syme, Ronald, *The Roman Revolution*, Oxford: Oxford University Press, 1939
Tamez, Elsa, *The Scandalous Message of James: Faith without Works is Dead*, New York: Crossroad, 1990
Taylor, Mark E., "Recent Scholarship on the Structure of James," *CurBS* 3.1 (2004) 86-115
Taylor, Charles, *Sources of the Self. The Making of Modern Identity*, Cambridge, MA: Harvard University Press, 1989
Thom, Johan C., "'Harmonius Equality': The *Topos* of Friendship in Neopythagorean Writings," in *Greco-Roman Perspectives on Friendship*, ed. John T. Fitzgerald; SBLRBS 34; Atlanta: Scholars, 1997, 77-103
Thraede, Klaus, *Grundzüge griechisch-römischer Brieftopik*, Munich: C.H. Beck, 1970
Thurén, Lauri, "Risky Rhetoric in James?" *NovT* 37 (1995): 262-84
Tinnefeld, F., "'Freundschaft' in den Briefen des Michael Psellos. Theorie und Wirklichkeit," *JOEByz* 22 (1973): 151-68
Touloumakos, J., "Zum römischen Gemeindepatronat im griechischen Osten," *Hermes* 116 (1988): 304-24
Tracy, Theodore, "Perfect Friendship in Aristotle's *Nicomachean Ethics*," *ICS* 4 (1979): 65-75
Treu, K., "Freundschaft," *RAC* 8 (1972): 418-34
Trilling, Lionel, *Sincerity and Authenticity*, Cambridge, MA: Harvard University Press, 1972
Tsuji, Manabu, *Glaube zwischen Vollkommenheit und Verweltlichung: Eine Untersuchung zur literarischen Gestalt und zur inhaltlichen Kohärenz des Jakobusbriefes*, WUNT 2/93; Tübingen: J.C.B. Mohr (Siebeck), 1997

Vaage, Leif E., "Cuídate la boca: La palabra indicada, una subjetividad alternativa y la formación social de los primeros Cristianos según Santiago 3,1–4,17," *RIBLA* 31 (1998): 110-21
Van Dam, Raymond, "Emperor, Bishops, and Friends in Later Antique Cappadocia," *JTS* n.s. 37 (1986): 53-76
van de Sandt, Huub, "James 4,1-4 in Light of the Jewish Two Ways Tradition 3,1-6," *Biblica* 88 (2007): 38-63
van der Horst, P.W., *The Sentences of Pseudo-Phocylides: With Introduction and Commentary*, SVTP 4; Leiden: E.J. Brill, 1978
van der Westhuizen, J.D.N., "Stylistic Techniques and Their Function in James 2:11-26," *Neot* 25 (1991): 89-108
van Selms, A., "The Origin of the Title 'The King's Friend'" *JNES* 16 (1957): 18-23
van Unnik, W.C., "The Semitic Background of ΠΑΡΡΗΣΙΑ in the New Testament," in *Sparsa Collecta: The Collected Essays of W.C. van Unnik*, NovTSup 29-31; Leiden: E.J. Brill, 1973-83, II, 289-306
——, "The Christian's Freedom of Speech in the New Testament," *BJRL* 44 (1962): 466-88
Verboven, Koenraad, *The Economy of Friends. Economic Aspects of Amiticia and Patronage in the Late Republic*, Collection Latomus 269; Brussels: Latomus, 2002
Verseput, Donald J., "Genre and Story: The Community Setting of the Epistle of James," *CBQ* 62 (2000): 96-110
——, "Wisdom, 4Q185, and the Epistle of James," *JBL* 117 (1998): 691-707
Vetschera, Rudolf, *Zur griechischen Paränese*, Smichow/Prague: Rohliček & Sievers, 1911-12
Vhymeister, Nancy J., "The Rich Man in James 2: Does Ancient Patronage Illumine the Text?" *AUSS* 33 (1995): 265-83
Via, Dan O., "The Right Strawy Epistle Reconsidered: A Study in Biblical Ethics and Hermeneutic," *HR* 49 (1969): 253-67
Viano, Christina, "Competitive Emotions and *Thumos* in Aristotle's Rhetoric," in *Envy, Spite and Jealousy. The Competitive Emotions in Ancient Greece*, ed. David Konstan and N. Keith Rutter; Edinburgh Leventis Studies 2; Edinburgh University Press, 2003, 85-97
Vidal, Maurice, "La *Theophilia* dans la Pensée religieuse des Grecs," *RSR* 47 (1959): 161-84
Vischer, Lukas, "Das Problem der Freundschaft bei den Kirchenvätern: Basilius der Grosse, Gregor von Nazianz und Chrysostomos," *TZ* 9 (1953): 186-200
Vouga, F., *L'Epître de Saint Jacques*, Commentaire du Nouveau Testament, 13a; Geneva: Labor et Fides, 1984
Wachob, Wesley Hiram, "The Epistle of James and the Book of Psalms: A Socio-Rhetorical Perspective of Intertexture, Culture and Ideology in Religious Discourse," in *Fabrics of Discourse. Essays in Honor of Vernon K. Robbins*, ed. David B. Gowler, L. Gregory Bloomquist and Duane F. Watson; Harrisburg, London, New York: Trinity Press, 2003, 264-80
——, *The Voice of Jesus in the Social Rhetoric of James*, SNTSMS 106; Cambridge: Cambridge University Press, 2000
Wadell, P.J., *Friends of God: Virtues and Gifts in Aquinas*, American University Studies 76; New York: Peter Lang, 1991
Walbank, Frank., "Monarchies and Monarchic Ideas," in *Cambridge Ancient History* 7.1; Cambridge: Cambridge University Press, 1984, 62-100
Walker, A.D.M., "Aristotle's Account of Friendship in the *Nicomachean Ethics*," *Phronesis* 24 (1979): 180-96
Wall, Robert, *Community of the Wise: The Letter of James*, New Testament in Context. Valley Forge, PA: Trinity Press International 1998

Wallace-Hadrill, Andrew, "Patronage in Roman Society: From Republic to Empire," in *Patronage in Ancient Society*, ed. Andrew Wallace-Hadrill; Leicester-Nottingham Studies in Ancient Society, 1; London and New York: Routledge, 1989, 63-88
——, ed., *Patronage in Ancient Society*, Leicester-Nottingham Studies in Ancient Society, 1; London and New York: Routledge, 1989
Ward, Julie K., "Aristotle on *Philia*: The Beginning of a Feminist Ideal of Friendship?" in *Feminism and Ancient Philosophy*, ed. Julie K. Ward; New York & London: Routledge, 1996, 155-71
——, "Focal Reference in Aristotle's Account of *Philia*: *Eudemian Ethics* VII 2," *Apeiron* 28 (1995): 183-205
Ward, R.B., "Abraham Traditions in Early Christianity," in *Studies in the Testament of Abraham*, ed. George W.E. Nickelsburg; SBLSCS 6; Missoula: Scholars, 1976, 173-84
——, "Partiality in the Assembly: James 2, 2-4," *HTR* 62 (1969): 87-97
——, "The Works of Abraham: James 2, 14-26," *HTR* 61 (1968): 283-90
——, "The Communal Concern of the Epistle of James," Ph.D. diss.. Harvard University, 1966
Watson, Duane F., "A Reassessment of the Rhetoric of the Epistle of James and Its Implications for Christian Origins," in *Reading James with New Eyes. Methodological Reassessments of the Letter of James*, ed. Robert L. Webb and John S. Kloppenborg; LNTS 342. London: T & T Clark, 2007, 99-120
——, "Rhetorical Criticism of Hebrews and the Catholic Epistles since 1978," *CR:BS* 5 (1997): 175-207
——, "James 2 in Light of Greco-Roman Schemes of Argumentation," *NTS* 39 (1993): 94-121
——, "The Rhetoric of James 3:1-12 and a Classical Pattern of Argumentation," *NovT* 35 (1993): 48-64
——, *The Rhetoric of the New Testament. A Bibliographic Survey*, Tools for Biblical Study, 8; Blandford Forum: Deo, 2006
Watson, Duane F. and Alan J. Hauser, *Rhetorical Criticism of the Bible. A Comprehensive Bibliography with Notes on History and Method*, Leiden: E.J. Brill, 1994
Wengst, Klaus, *Humility: Solidarity of the Humiliated*, trans. John Bowden; Philadelphia: Fortress, 1988
Westermann, Claus, *Isaiah 40-66. A Commentary*, trans. David M.G. Stalker; OTL 19; Philadelphia: Westminster, 1969
White, Carolinne, *Christian Friendship in the Fourth Century*, Cambridge: Cambridge University Press, 1992
White, John L., *Light from Ancient Letters*, FFNT; Philadelphia: Fortress, 1986
——, "New Testament Epistolary Literatures in the Framework of Ancient Epistolography," *ANRW* 2.25.2 (1984): 1730-56
White, L. Michael, "Morality Between Two Worlds: A Paradigm of Friendship in Philippians," in *Greeks, Romans, and Christians: Essays in Honor of Abraham J. Malherbe*, ed. D.L. Balch, E. Ferguson, and W.A. Meeks; Minneapolis: Fortress, 1990, 201-15
White, Peter, *Promised Verse: Poets in the Society of Augustan Rome*, London, Cambridge, MA: Harvard University Press, 1993
——, "*Amicitia* and the Profession of Poetry in Early Imperial Rome," *JRS* 68 (1978): 74-92
——, "The Friends of Martial, Statius, and Pliny, and the Dispersal of Patronage," *HSCP* 79 (1975): 265-300
Wiedemann, T., *Greek and Roman Slavery*, Baltimore: Johns Hopkins University Press, 1984

Wiesehöfer, J., "Die 'Freunde' und 'Wohltäter' des Grosskönigs," *Studia Iranica* 9 (1980): 7-21
Wilcken, U., Fr. Krebs and Paul Viereck, eds., *Aegyptische Urkunden aus den Königlichen Museen zu Berlin, Griechische Urkunden 1*, Berlin: Weidmann, 1895
Williams, Bernard, *Shame and Necessity*, Berkeley, Los Angeles, London: University of California Press, 1993
Wilson, John R., "Shifting and Permanent *Philia* in Thucydides," *G&R* 36 (1989): 147-51
Wilson, Walter T., *The Mysteries of Righteousness: The Literary Composition and Genre of the Sentences of Pseudo-Phocylides*, Texte und Studien zum Antiken Judentum, 4; Tübingen: J.C.B. Mohr (Paul Siebeck), 1994
Windisch, Hans, *Die katholischen Briefe*, 2nd ed., rev.; HNT 15; Tübingen: J.C.B. Mohr (Paul Siebeck), 1930
Winston, David, *The Wisdom of Solomon*, AB 43; Garden City, NY: Doubleday, 1979
Winter, S.C., "Παρρησία in Acts," in *Friendship, Flattery and Frankness of Speech: Studies on Friendship in the New Testament*, ed. John T. Fitzgerald; NovTSup 82; Leiden, New York, Cologne: Brill, 1996, 185-202
Wiseman, T.P., "*Pete Nobiles Amicos*: Poets and Patrons in Late Republican Rome," in *Literary and Artistic Patronage in Ancient Rome*, ed. Barbara Gold; Austin, TX: University of Texas Press, 1982, 28-49
Witherington III, Ben, *Friendship and Finances in Philippi: The Letter of Paul to the Philippians*, The New Testament in Context; Valley Forge, PA: Trinity Press International, 1994
Wolf, Eric R., "Kinship, Friendship, and Patron-Client Ties in Complex Societies," in *Friends, Followers and Factions: A Reader in Political Clientelism*, ed. Steffen W. Schmidt, Laura Guasti, Carl H. Landé, and James C. Scott; Berkeley: University of California Press, 1977, 167-77
——, "Kinship, Friendship and Patron-Client Relationships," in *The Social Anthropology of Complex Societies*, ed. Michael Banton; London: Tavistock, 1966, 1-22
Wolmarans, J.L.P., "The Tongue Guiding the Body: The Anthropological Presuppositions of James 3:1-12," *Neot* 26 (1992): 523-30
Wolverton, W.I., "The Double-Minded Man in the Light of Essene Psychology," *ATR* 38 (1956): 166-75
Wood, John T., *Discoveries at Ephesus, Including the Sites and Remains of the Great Temple of Diana*, Boston: James R. Osgood, 1877
Wuellner, Wilhelm H., "Where is Rhetorical Criticism Taking Us?" *CBQ* 49 (1987): 448-63
——, "Der Jakobusbrief im Licht der Rhetorik und Textpragmatik," *LB* 43 (1978): 5-66
Xenophon, *Memorabilia*, E.C. Marchant; LCL; London, Cambridge, MA: Harvard University Press, 1923
Yee, Gale A., "Ideological Criticism," in *Dictionary of Biblical Interpretation*, ed. John H. Hayes; Nashville: Abingdon, 1999, 534-37
Young, F.W., "The Relation of 1 Clement to the Epistle of James," *JBL* 67 (1948): 339-45
Zanker, Graham, *The Heart of Achilles. Characterization and Personal Ethics in the Iliad*, Ann Arbor: University of Michigan Press, 1994
Zmijewski, Josef, "Christliche 'Volkommenheit.' Erwägungen zur Theologie des Jakobusbriefes," in *Studien zum Neuen Testament und Seiner Umwelt*, ed. Albert Fuchs; ser. A, 5; Linz: A. Fuchs, 1980, 50-78
Zucker, Friedrich, *Freundschaftsbewährung in der neuen attischen Komödie: Ein Kapitel hellenistischer Ethik und Humanität*, Berlin: Akademie, 1950

Index of Modern Authors

Aasgaard, R.   47
Adkins, A.W.H.   13
Aglen, A.S.   19
Allison, D.   124
Artz-Grabner, P.   46, 47
Asensio, V.M.   131, 132
Aune, D.E.   91, 92, 93, 96

Baasland, E.   5, 92, 97, 102, 107, 122
Baker, W.   172
Batten, A.   2, 7, 68, 126, 128, 131, 138, 149, 185
Bauckham, R.   164, 183
Bengel, J.A.   97
Ben-Ze'ev, A.   133
Betz, H.D.   2, 35, 96
Bitzer, L.   128, 178
Blundell, M.W.   12, 14
Bowerstock, G.W.   77
Brock, A.G.   16, 17
Brownlee, W.H.   18
Brueggemann, W.   49
Brunt, P.   84
Burgess, T.C.   94
Burkert, W.   173

Carruth, S.   102, 103, 104
Cassidy, E.   40
Chadwick, H.   140
Clark, E.   39
Coleman, T.M.   121, 128, 173
Cooper, J.M.   24, 62
Corley, J.   16, 34
Crook, Z.A.   71, 72, 73, 76
Cummins, W.J.   23

Danker, F.W.   71, 155
Daniélou, J.   118
Davids, P.H.   93, 122, 124, 134, 146, 150, 153
Deissmann, A.   91
de Jonge, M.   34
Deppe, D.B.   161
de Ste. Croix, G.E.M.   131
De Witt, N.W.   79
Dibelius, M.   5
Dihle, A.   152
Di Lella, A.A.   32
Dirlmeier, F.   2, 19, 48
Donlan, W.   20
Dover, K.J.   155
Dugas, L.   2

Eilers, C.   77
Elliot, J.H.   5, 97, 107, 169
Engberg-Pedersen, T.   31, 81, 82, 83, 180, 181
Erskine, A.   76, 77
Exler, F.X.J.   93

Ferrary, J.-L.   78
Fichtner, J.   17
Finley, M.I.   11
Fiore, B.   2, 94, 95
Fitzgerald, J.T.   13, 14, 20, 42, 43, 44
Ford, J.M.   35, 53
Fraisse, J.-C.   2, 14, 21, 22
Francis, F.O.   4, 92, 93, 101, 102
Frankemölle, H.   5

Gallant, T.   59

Gammie, J.G. 94
Garnsey, P. 11
Garrett, S.R. 112
Gill, C. 10, 31
Ginzberg, L. 53
Glad, C.E. 80
Gold, B.K. 85
Goldhill, S. 59
Green, P. 64, 65
Gruen, E.S. 77

Habel, N. 18
Hagner, D.A. 163
Hallenbach, P. 115
Halperin, D.M. 19
Hansen, K.C. 75
Hansen, M.H. 60
Hanson, A. 140
Harland, P.A. 47, 69
Harrington, D.J. 33
Harrison, J.R. 70, 71, 72, 74
Hartin, P.J. 94, 98, 104, 106,
    107, 109, 111, 121, 122,
    123, 124, 125, 126, 132,
    133, 134, 135, 146, 149 150,
    151, 152, 153, 154, 155,
    156, 158, 161, 168, 174,
    175
Hauck, F. 2, 150, 182
Hauser, A.J. 95
Herman, G. 59, 65, 66
Hock, R.F. 26, 27
Hollander, H.W. 34
Hooker, J. 13
Horden, P. 130
Hughes, F.W. 96
Hunter, H. 60
Hutter, H. 28, 60

Irwin, W.H. 34

Jackson-McCabe, M.A. 126,
    182
Jacobs, I. 141
Johnson, L. 2, 50, 93, 105, 111,
    115, 118, 129, 134, 142,
    143, 147, 152, 153, 155,
    157, 158, 159, 160, 166,
    167, 168, 171
Joly, R. 36
Joubert, S. 76

Kennedy, G. 96, 140, 156
Klauck, H.-J. 2, 35
Klein, M. 5
Kloppenborg, J.S. 125, 126,
    154, 157, 162, 165
Kloppenborg Verbin, J.S. 2,
    119, 128, 129, 173,
Konstan, D. 2, 11, 12, 13, 14,
    16, 19, 21, 24, 25, 30, 36,
    37, 38, 39, 40, 41, 50, 51,
    52, 60, 61, 62, 64, 73, 80,
    84, 85, 86, 87, 174
Krammer, I. 33
Kraut, R. 24
Küchler, C.G. 97

LaFleur, R. 86
Lamb, W.R.M. 23
Lausberg, H. 166, 167
Laws, S. 93, 115, 124, 150, 152,
    166
Lendon, J.E. 78, 130, 131
Lesses, G. 24, 28, 29
Lipsius, R.A. 183
Llewellyn, S.R. 91, 101

MacIntyre, A. 10
Mack, B.L. 95, 98, 99, 148,
    151, 156, 167
Malherbe, A.J. 2, 5, 35, 92, 95
Malina, B.J. 10, 115, 130, 131
Marchal, J.A. 54
Marcus, J. 112
Marshall, P. 2
Martin, R.P. 104, 105, 146,
    147, 157
Martinez, F.G. 53
Massebieau, L. 124
Mayor, J.B. 103, 150, 157, 158,
    161, 163, 182
McKerlie, D. 42
Meeks, W.A. 138
Middendorp, T. 32
Millard, A.R. 49

Miller, S. 10, 12
Millet, P. 62, 75
Mitchell, A.C. 2, 36, 44, 45, 46
Mitchell, L.G. 60
Moltmann, J. 50
Momigliano, A. 80
Moo, D.J. 154
Mussner, F. 182

Neyrey, J.H. 139
Niebuhr, K.-W. 5, 92, 183
Nietzsche, F. 10

Oakman, D.E. 75
Olbrechts-Tyteca, L. 99, 100, 103, 106, 159
O'Neil, E.N. 81, 148
Orwell, G. 29

Pardee, D. 92
Patterson, S.J. 128, 139
Peachin, M. 57
Penner, T.C. 1
Perelman, C. 99, 100, 103, 106, 159
Perkins, P. 2
Peterson, E. 50, 51
Pizzolato, L. 2, 16, 54, 59, 63
Plescia, J. 173
Polanyi, K. 56
Pope, M.H. 18
Popkes, W. 90
Porter, S.E. 96, 112, 118
Powell, J. 23, 24, 26, 60
Powell, J.G.F. 31
Price, A.W. 23
Purcell, N. 130

Reed, J.T. 96
Reese, J. 5
Reiterer, F.J. 34
Rengstorf, K.H. 35, 71
Rhodes, P.J. 60
Ringe, S.H. 36
Robbins, V.K. 7, 120, 167
Robinson, D. 13
Ropes, J.H. 5, 92, 115, 146, 150, 153, 182

Sahlins, M. 56
Saller, R. 11, 75, 78, 84
Sampley, J.P. 128
Sanders, J.T. 32
Schroeder, F.M. 62
Schulz, S. 150
Schulze, J.D. 97
Scully, S.E. 15, 20, 48
Seesemann, H. 111
Seitz, O.J.F. 114
Sinos, D.S. 19
Silver, A. 12
Skehan, P.W. 32
Spitaler, P. 113, 114
Spitta, F. 124
Stählin, G. 16, 17, 18
Stegemann, E. 56, 57, 128
Stegemann, W. 56, 57, 128
Sterling, G.E. 16, 17, 52, 53
Stevenson, T.R. 70
Stowers, S.K. 2, 95, 108, 136, 137,
Stumpff, A. 171
Syme, R. 84

Taylor, C. 10
Taylor, M.E. 1, 90
Thom, J.C. 30
Thurén, L. 5, 97, 98, 102, 106, 107, 122, 146, 169
Treu, K. 17
Tsuji, M. 5
Trilling, L. 9

Ulf, C. 19

Vaage, L.E. 2
Van Dam, R. 37
van de Sandt, H. 157
van der Westhuizen, J.D.N. 98, 122
Verboven, K. 57, 76, 85
Verseput, D.J. 115, 120, 128, 138, 172, 183
Vetschera, R. 94, 95
Vhymeister, N.J. 128
Viano, C. 31, 171
Vidal, M. 48

Vouga, F. 182

Wachob, W.H. 3, 5, 6, 7, 91,
    92, 93, 94, 95, 97, 116, 124,
    125, 126, 127, 132, 147,
    148, 149, 151, 156, 161,
    165, 170, 180
Wall, R. 5, 108
Wallace-Handrill, A. 82
Wallbank, F. 66
Ward, J.K. 62
Ward, R.B. 140, 141
Watson, D.F. 5, 6, 95, 97, 98,
    101, 123, 124, 125, 126,
    134, 135, 136, 141, 145
White, C. 16, 37, 38, 39, 40
White, J.L. 4, 101
White, L.M. 3, 35
White, P. 86
Wilke, C.G. 97
Williams, B. 9
Winston, D. 49
Wuellner, W. 5, 102, 107, 122

Yee, G.A. 7

Index of Biblical and Other Ancient References

Hebrew Bible /LXX

Genesis
15: 6   141
18   140
18:16   141
18:17   49, 141
22 :1   111
22:1-19   105, 141

Exodus
32-34   49
33:11   49

Leviticus
19 :15   125
19 :18   125, 126
24 : 10-23   134

Numbers
16 :5   133

Deuteronomy
4 :29   45
4 :37   125, 133
6 :4   135
7 :7   125, 133
8 :2   111
13:7   17, 43

Joshua
2 :1-21   140

1 Samuel
10:14-15a   18
18:1   17, 42, 113

18: 3   17
20: 17   17

2 Samuel
1:26   18

Esther
5:10   17

Job
6:14   17

Psalms
41: 2   166
72:27   159
119:20   166
119:131   166
119:174   166
134:3   134

Proverbs
3:34   147, 166, 167, 168, 174
12:26   17
14:21   18, 139
16:28   17
18:24   18
19:3   105
19:6   18
19:7   18
27:6   172

Isaiah
14:1   133
40:6-8   115
49:5-6   108
57:3   159

Jeremiah
3:6-10   159
13:27   159

Ezekiel
16:38   159
23:45   159

Daniel
2:13   17
2:17   17

Hosea
3:1   159
9:1   159

Malachi
3:5   129

Tobit
4:10   133

Wisdom of Solomon
2:24   157, 166
3:5   71
3:9   71
6:23   166
7:14   119
7:23   71
7:27   49, 72, 181
7:28   49
11:5   71
16:2   71
16:11   71

Sirach
6:1   113

Index of Biblical and Other Ancient References

6:7 34, 110
6:8 110
6:14-16 33
6:17 33
6:19 160
12:8 34
12:8-9 110
12:9 34
15:11 111
19:13-14 33
19:16b 33
20:15 117
20:16 117
20:23 33
22:13-26 33
22:22 33
24: 37 129
27:16-21 33
37:2 160
41:25 117
44:20-21 141

Letter of Jeremiah 92, 183

1 Maccabees
2:52 141
8:16 166
10:25 92

2 Maccabees
1:1-9 92, 183
1:10–2:18 92, 183
6:7 166

Pseudepigrapha

1 Enoch
97 129

2 Baruch
78-86 183

Jubilees
17:6 111
19.9 53, 141

Apocalypse of Abraham
9-10 53

Testament of Abraham
15 53

Testament of Asher
3.2 112
4.1 117

Testament of Benjamin
6.7 117, 118

Testament of Issachar
117

Christian Testament

Q
6:20 125
6:20-21 104
6:20-49 102
6:22 125
6:29 125
12:58-59 125
16:13 165

Matthew
5:4 168
5:7 133
5:9 154
5:33-37 173
6:24 158, 161, 164
8:8 16
10:28 16
18:12-13 16
19:21 139

Mark
13:12 16

Luke
6:34-35 45
7:6 16
11:5 17
11:6 17
11:8 17

12:4-5 16
14:10 17
14:12 17
14:12-14 45
15:4-6 16
15:9 17
16:13 158, 161, 164
18:28 45
21:16 16
22:25-26 46
23:12 160
23:2 17

John
10:11 35
10:15 35
10:17-18 35
15:13 35

Acts
2:44 44
2:44-47 45
3:1-10 46
4:9 46
4:32 43, 44, 45, 113
4:32-37 45
4:36-37 45
5:1-11 46
10:24 17
19:31 17
20:35 45
27:3 17

Romans
2:8 171

1 Corinthians
10:20-21 152

2 Corinthians
5:1 152
6:14-7:1 124
10:1 153

Galatians
1:19 183

2:9   183
5:20 171
6:1   150
6:16 182

Ephesians
4:2   150

Philippians
1:5, 7   44
1:17 171
1:27 43, 113
2:2   43, 44
2:3   171
2:6-11   35
2:20 43
3:10 44
4:2   43
4:14-15   44
4:11 35

1 Thessalonians
5:17 93

1 Timothy
4:1   152

2 Timothy
2:25 150

Titus
3:2   150

Philemon
4-7   92
22   93

Hebrews
11:17-19   141
13:7 150

James
1:1   91, 92, 93, 101,
      120, 123, 183
1:1-4   102
1:1-27   92
1:2   93, 104, 180

1:2-4   107, 110,
        111, 120, 121,
        124, 180
1:2-18   6, 90-121,
        184
1:3   110
1:4   136
1:5   109, 116, 160,
      167, 174, 175
1:5-7   103
1:5-8   107
1:5-11   102
1:5-18   153
1:6   93
1:6-8   114
1:8   112, 114, 160
1:9-11   107, 114,
        115, 121, 170
1:10 129, 131
1:10-11   103
1:11 131, 181
1:12 102, 104, 109,
      110, 114, 118,
      120, 138, 180,
      183
1:12-18   102, 107
1:13 102, 105
1:13-15   107
1:13-18   102, 104,
        105
1:13-5:6   102
1:14-15   156
1:16 106, 109
1:16-18   107, 118
1:17 106, 109, 118
1:18 106, 109
1:19 102
1:19-21   102, 180
1:21 150
1:22-25   102, 142
1:22-27   122
1:24 93
1:25 107
1:26-27   116
1:27 142, 165, 175,
      180
2   98

2:1   123, 124, 126,
      127, 128, 132,
      134, 136, 164
2:1-13   5, 6, 98,
        122, 123-34,
        138, 140, 145,
        149, 181
2:1-26   6, 180
2:2   131, 138, 182,
      183
2:3   131
2:2-3   122, 128
2:2-4   124, 151
2:4   125, 128, 132
2:5   98, 127, 130,
      131, 132, 133,
      134, 162, 163,
      164, 175
2:5-7   125
2:6   125, 131, 132,
      134, 153, 174,
      181, 183
2:6-7   116, 128
2:7   125, 134
2:8   125, 132, 133
2:8-11   126
2:8-13   183
2:9   181
2:9-10   126
2:11 126
2:12 133
2:12-13   126
2:13 133
2:14 105, 135, 136
2:14-17   137, 180
2:14-26   6, 98, 116,
        122, 123, 132,
        134-43, 145,
        149, 184
2:15 47, 105, 106,
      136, 143
2:15-16   122, 135,
        136, 140, 141
2:15-17   138
2:16 136
2:17 135
2:18 135, 137

Index of Biblical and Other Ancient References   217

2:18-20   136
2:18-23   135
2:18-26   124
2:19   135
2:20   135, 137
2:20-25   135
2:21   105, 132, 140, 182
2:21-22   135
2:21-24   111
2:22   136, 140, 142
2:23   135, 138, 141,142, 175
2:24   135, 136, 140
2:25   132, 138, 182
2:26   135
3:1   169
3:1-2   108
3:1-12   98, 108, 145, 149, 169, 172, 180
3:1–4:12   146
3:2   107, 139
3:6   175, 182
3:8   172
3:10   169, 172
3:12   146, 169
3:13   145, 146, 153, 169
3:13-14   149, 160
3:13-17   146
3:13-18   146, 147
3:13-4:6   147
3:13-4:10   6, 98, 129, 145-77, 180, 184
3:14   150, 151, 171, 172, 174
3:15   156, 160, 171
3:15-16   147, 153
3:15-18   149, 151-56
3:16   150, 152, 155, 156, 171
3:17   147, 153, 154, 155,160, 173, 174
3:17-18   153

3:18   146, 153, 154, 155, 156, 173
4:1   146, 169, 170
4:1-3   149, 156-58
4:1-6   76, 146, 156-67
4:1-10   146, 147, 149
4:1-13   150, 159
4:2   150, 171
4:4   6, 147, 149, 158-65, 170, 174, 175, 176
4:5   164, 166, 171
4:5-6   147, 149
4:6   150, 165, 166, 167, 168
4:7   168
4:7-10   147, 149, 167-69
4:7-12   146
4:8   112, 153, 160, 168, 173
4:10   146, 168, 170, 181
4:11   146, 169, 180
4:11-12   146, 172
4:11-13   146
4:11-17   172
4:13   146
4:13-17   129
4:17   177
5:1   131
5:1-6   116, 129, 132, 170
5:4   129, 174, 181, 182
5:7-12   120
5:7-20   5
5:9   172
5:10   180, 182
5:11   182
5:12   172
5:13-20   180
5:17   182

1 Peter
2:12   150

3:2   150
3:15   150

1 John
3:16   35
5:14-17   93

Nag Hammadi Writings

Gospel of Thomas
47:2   161

Apostolic Writings

1 Clement   114, 118
4:9-5:2   157
10.1   54
10-12   140
17:2   54, 141
23:1   163
38:2   150

2 Clement   114
6:1-15   162
19:2   163

Didache
3:2   157
6:2   139

Shepherd of Hermas
8.6.4   134

Early Christian Writings

Ambrose
De officiis ministrorum
3.22.133   44
3.132   39

Barmabas
Epistle of Barnabas
114
18-20   163

Basil of Caesarea
Epistulae
56   38
83   43

Clement of Alexandria
Protrepticus
12.12.3   54

Quis dives salvetur
32   36

Stromata
2.19   54

Cyril of Alexandria
Commentarii in Lucam
848.32-33   114

Gregory of Nazianzus
Epistulae
11.2   37
31.1   44
103.1   37

Oratio in laudem Basilii
43.20   43, 113

Irenaeus
Adversus haereses
4.14.4   54
16.2   54

Jerome
Epistulae
3   39

John Chrysostom
De sacerdotio
1.1   39

Homilae in epistulam i ad Thessalonicenses
2   113

Paulinus of Nola
Epistulae
13   40
51   40

Tertullian
Adversus Judaeos
2.7   54

Theophylact
Expositio im Epistulam Sancti Jacobi
1137.23   114

Qumran

Damascus Document
3.2   54

4Q185   115

Rabbinic Writings

Mekilta
18.22   53

b. Menahot
53b   53

t. Berakot
7.13   53

Sifre Deuteronomy
352   53

Sifre Numbers
115   53

Josephus and Philo

Josephus
Antiquitates judaicae
3.65   72
5.115-116   72
5.116   53
8.50-54   92

Philo
De Abrahamo
129   134

De cherubim
122-23   72

De confusione linguarum
48   79

De fuga et inventione
29   73

De opificio mundi
24   111

De sobrietate
54-56   73
56   52, 73, 79, 141
58   73

De somniis
1.193-95   52

De vita contemplativa
13-17   44

De vita Mosis I
1.157   52

Legum allegoriae
2.19   111
2.204   111
3.77-78   72

Quis rerum divinarum
heres sit
21   52
83   42

Quod omnis probus
liber sit
85-87   44

Graeco-Roman
Writings

Aeschylus
Prometheus vinctus
223-28   20
330   20

Aristotle
Ethica eudemia
7.4.1-2   15
7.6.8-13   42, 113
7.6.10   42
7.12.1   26

Ethica nichomachea
4.3.1   70
7.6.3   25
8.1   24
8.1.4   61, 62
8.3.1   25
8.3.6   25
8.6.2   25
8.6.7   62
8.7.3-6   63
8.8.7   27
8.9.3   61
9.4.5   42
9.8.2   42
9.8.9   35, 42
9.9.1   26
9.9.3   25

Rhetorica
1.2.4   100
1.2.8-9   156
1.9.5   150
2.3.1   174
2.4.8   172

2.4.8-12   174
2.4.25   171
2.4.28   127
2.4.29   74
2.8.12   133
2.20   140
2.21   159
2.21.16   104
2.23.1   156
3.13.3   99

Pseudo-Aristotle
Rhetorica ad Alexandrum
7   158
9   158
11   159
20.1433b.30   126
29   100
37.1445b.1   127

Aulus Gellius
Noctes atticae
1.2.3.10-20   67

Chariton
De Chaerea et Callirhoe
1.5.2   26
8.8.7   27
8.8.12   27

Cicero
De inventione rhetorica
1.23   100
1.25   99
1.26   101

Laelius
18   30
20   30
21   30
38   67
61   67
62   32
63   32, 110
64   30, 66
65   32

77   67
80   43, 113
81   43
91   32
92   43, 113, 118

Pseudo-Cicero
Rhetorica ad Herrenium
1.8   100
1.9   100
1.11   100
2.18.28   125, 140, 148, 151
2.23.35   151
4.3.6   165
4.15.22   159
4.16.24   158, 170
4.17   159
4.17.24-25   158
4.17.25   158
4.43.56   149, 160

Demetrius
De elocutione
227   96

Demosthenes
In Cononem
54.7   60
54.14-20   60
54.30-40   60

Dio Chrysostom
De regno i
41   138

De regno iii
110   44, 74

Diogenes Laertius
Vitae philosophorum
6.27   52
7.118   29
7.102   29
7.102-07   28
7.124   28
7.89   27

8.10 44
10.120 27

Epicurus
Sententia Vaticana
xxiii 27
xxxix 27
lvi-lvii 27

Epictetus
Diatribai
2.7.3 35
2.17.19 51
3.22.61 171
4.3.9 51, 2

Euripides
Orestes
652 21
655-57 21, 110
804-06 21
1046 42, 113

Fronto
Ad Verus
1.6.2 78

Hermogenes
Progymnasmata
60 167

Homer
Ilias
4.360-61 41
17.411 19
17.655 19
24.44-52 19

Odyssea
3.126-29 42

Horace
Epistulae
18.1 87
18.24 87
18.44-45 87
18.73 87, 88

18.90 87
18.101 87
18.110 87

Hypereides
Euxenippus
3.7-8 60

Iamblichus
Vita pythagorae
38 70
192-94 30
229 29
234-40 29

Juvenal
Satirae
5.170-73 86

Lucian
Nigrinus
21 129

Martial
Epigrammata
10.82 78

Maximus of Tyre
Orationes
14.18 79

Minucius Felix
Octavius
1.3 44

Philodemus
De diis
1.17-18 51
1.19-20 51

De libertate dicendi
fr. 1 108
fr. 10 108
fr. 26 109
fr. 79 80

Plato
Leges
679C 171

Lysis
212A 23
214E 23
215B 23
223B 24

Symposium
213D 171

Timaeus
53D 50

Pliny
Epistulae
2.6.2 84
7.3.2 84

Plutarch
Adversus Colotem
8.111b 35, 110

De adultore et amico
51B 74
66E 109
96E 42

De amicorum multitudine
54C 31
93E 31
94B 81
96E 113
96F 30
97B 31

De amore prolis
131

De capienda ex inimicis utilitate
1 171
9 171

De fraterno amore
14   171
479D   47

De tranquillitate animi
10   171
11   171

Quomodo adulator ab
amico internoscatur
51D   66, 63
52B   82
54C   82
58B   129
59D   170
61D   170, 174
62C   82, 117
62D   82
63F   117
64B   117
66A   170
71B   81, 109
74E   137

Pseudo-Plutarch
De vita et poesi Homeri
143   51

Quintilian
Institutio Oratoria
4.1.7   100
4.1.26   101
5.11.36   126
5.11.42   104
8.5.7-8   105
9.2.7   125

Seneca
De beneficiis
1.1.10   70
1.4.3   70
1.10.5   70
3.15.4   69
4.3.3   70
4.26.1   70
7.12   74
7.31.2   70

Epistulae
94.14   84

Sophocles
Antigone
182-88   61

Theon
Progymnasmata
109   154

Theophrastus   79

Xenophon
Memorabilia
2.4.5   21
2.4.6   22
2.6.5   22
2.6.21-22   22
2.6.22-23   22
2.6.28   22
2.6.35   22

Symposium
4.47-48   50

Inscriptions

IDidyma 502
47

IG II² 457
74

IG II² 1292
131

IG II² 1297
69

IG II² 1314
131

IG V/1.1390
173

IG XI/4 1061
68

IGLAM 798
47

IIasos 116
47

IasMinLyk I 69
47

IMagnaMai 321
47

IMylasa 571-75
47

IPontBithM 57
47

IPrusaOlymp 24
47

ISmyrna 720
47

MAMA III 580
47

MAMA III 780
47

MAMA III 788
47

SEG 26.1282
69, 78

SIG 985
71

TAM V 93
47

Papyri

BGU VIII 1874
46

POxy VII 2148
46

POxy XLII 3057
46

SB V 7661
46

SB XIV 11644
46

www.ingramcontent.com/pod-product-compliance
Lightning Source LLC
Chambersburg PA
CBHW021705230426
43668CB00008B/731